A People's Dream

Dan Russell

A People's Dream: Aboriginal Self-Government in Canada

170201

UBCPress · Vancouver · Toronto

Printed in Canada on acid-free paper ∞

ISBN 0-7748-0798-9 (hardcover)
ISBN 0-7748-0799-7 (paperback)

Canadian Cataloguing in Publication Data

Russell, Dan, 1950-
  A people's dream

  Includes bibliographical references and index.
  ISBN 0-7748-0798-9 (bound)
  ISBN 0-7748-0799-7 (pbk.)

  1. Native peoples – Canada – Government relations.* 2. Native peoples – Legal status, laws, etc. – Canada.* 3. Native peoples – Canada – Politics and government.* I. Title.

E92.R87 2000	323.1'197071	C00-910651-0

This book has been published with the help of a grant from the Humanities and Social Sciences Federation of Canada, using funds provided by the Social Sciences and Humanities Research Council of Canada.

UBC Press acknowledges the financial support of the Government of Canada through the Book Publishing Industry Development Program (BPIDP) for our publishing activities.
Canadä

We also gratefully acknowledge the support of the Canada Council for the Arts for our publishing program, as well as the support of the British Columbia Arts Council.

UBC Press
University of British Columbia
2029 West Mall, Vancouver, BC V6T 1Z2
(604) 822-5959
Fax: (604) 822-6083
E-mail: info@ubcpress.ubc.ca
www.ubcpress.ubc.ca

To my parents, Leo and Theresa Russell,
whose wisdom and teachings provided me with
the heart and insights necessary to write this book

Contents

Preface

When I began to canvass ideas and problems associated with Aboriginal self-government, a title for this book quickly came to mind. It was not the one that appears on the cover. I borrowed the original title from something once said by an American president, and I adjusted the quotation, familiar to many, to fit the context of Aboriginal self-government. Although the title was somewhat clinical, I believed that it reflected the messages contained here. For a long time, it remained the ostensible title for this book.

Then, in the spring of 1998, I attended a play put on by the Young People's Theatre of Toronto, *The Jumping Mouse*, a story attributed to the Plains Cree. It recounts how a field mouse discovers the legend of the far-off mountains and dreams that her future is to be found there. She undertakes a journey to the mountains with another mouse who, lacking sufficient courage to continue, turns back before their goal is reached. But Jumping Mouse perseveres. Along the way, she is asked to contribute each of her eyes for the benefit of another. Initially, she hesitates but then believes somehow this is the right thing to do. So she obliges. Finally, after much effort to overcome her fears along the way, she reaches the mountains and discovers the content of her dream. She realizes the truth about herself and is then miraculously transformed into an eagle, gaining all the knowledge and wisdom that an eagle possesses. Upon leaving the theatre, I realized that the title of this book must be *A People's Dream: Aboriginal Self-Government in Canada*.

Like Jumping Mouse, Aboriginal people have a dream, one with many facets. It includes recognition of and respect for treaties. It involves the return of lands that were once theirs as well as the recognition of their right to use these lands in whatever ways they choose. These may include not only traditional methods of harvesting such as hunting, fishing, and trapping but also conventional methods of resource utilization such as mining, forestry, and gaming. This Aboriginal dream also envisions respect for Aboriginal nations as first peoples of this land and anticipates nation-to-nation relations with other Canadian governments. But at the centre of this dream for all Aboriginal people lies the vision of self-government. And, like Jumping Mouse, Aboriginal people realize that to attain such a goal much discipline will be required and many sacrifices must be made. However, if they continue to persevere in this quest, which began many years ago, they know with their hearts that the goal is attainable. And, as Jumping Mouse learned, the rewards will be well worth the sacrifices made along the way. It is my hope that this book will help to make such a journey for Aboriginal people just a little easier.

Acknowledgments

I am grateful to the people who supported the writing of this book, including Carol Montagnes, Caroline Francis, Terry Sullivan, Bryant Smith, Jim Zion, Bill Munson, Fran Cornett, Professor Jerry Van Spronsen, Father Bill McVey, the Ontario Native Council on Justice, Sam Deloria, Harold Robinson, Floyd Kezele, and Phil Bluehouse. And most important, to my wife Aldina and my son Jeremy, without whose consistent encouragement and love this book could never have been written.

Introduction

The purpose of this book is threefold. It seems that, at every conference, on every news program, or in every negotiation in which I have participated, non-Aboriginal people express doubts about the viability of Aboriginal self-government. Hence, the first purpose is to dispel such doubts. Chapter 2, which recounts the historical recognition of tribal "sovereignty" in the United States, does just that. In addition, that chapter and others through-out the book offer descriptions of how these tribal communities exercise their self-governing authority. In particular, specific case law examples not only provide a picture of the judicial arms of tribal governments but also illustrate the unique expressions of justice described in Chapter 6 as Aborig-inal equity.

The second purpose is to outline some of the difficulties that must be overcome if Aboriginal self-government is to be viably implemented. Chap-ters 3 and 4 examine a number of problems associated with the implemen-tation of a constitutionally recognized form of self-government. Although the issue of process may initially seem to be theoretical, it isn't for Aborig-inal people. The issues of treaties and nation-to-nation relations are very important and perhaps carry equally significant emotional commitments within the Aboriginal community. Indeed, the final report of the Royal Commission on Aboriginal Peoples recommended the use of treaty making as part of its solution to the issue of self-government. The recently agreed-to Nisga'a treaty is just such an example. Today the issues associated with this subject remain significant impediments to the adequate resolution of our aspirations for self-government.

As important as these issues have been in any discussion related to self-government, perhaps none has been as significant as that of Aboriginal col-lective rights. In particular, what should be the relationship between the Canadian Charter of Rights and Freedoms and the structures of Aboriginal governance? Many Aboriginal women's organizations have asserted the need to ensure that future forms of Aboriginal government should not be permitted to discriminate against women. Consequently, they have argued for the imposition of the Charter to prevent gender discrimination. On the other hand, many Aboriginal people and their representative organizations have claimed that the collective rights of their respective communities must be exempt from the application of the individual rights guaranteed by the Charter.

The issue, as articulated by Aboriginal women's organizations, is clear enough and must be addressed. There is nonetheless a serious question whether the entire Charter must be employed to serve this purpose. I believe that the debate about collective rights versus the Charter has gone unaddressed largely because Aboriginal leaders have not adequately articulated what their collective rights practices would be or, particularly, how the Charter could affect those customs to the detriment of Aboriginal communities. Chapters 5 through 7 not only offer specific examples of these customs but also indicate specific sections of the Charter that threaten to prohibit them. Chapter 7 offers a number of specific proposals designed to address these conflicts. The suggestion of an Aboriginal metaphorical charter of rights is an attempt both to recognize and to resolve these conflicts in a culturally sensitive fashion. There may be other institutions that would perform this same function, perhaps even better than the one I propose. For my purposes, what is important is that the conflict between collective and individual rights be recognized and discussed. I trust that my comments on the traditional ethical underpinnings of these communities will assist the non-Aboriginal reader to understand the motivation behind the Aboriginal commitment to collective rights practices.

The third purpose of this book is to express a warning. All Canadians must be wary of going about this exercise of recognizing and implementing Aboriginal self-government in the wrong way. Perhaps such a caution is obvious. If not, then the American *Duro* case illustrates the folly of permitting those without adequate understanding of Aboriginal issues to make crucial decisions. This case is explained and referred to a number of times throughout this book. However, perhaps the best example of dubious decision making is illustrated in the recommendations of the final report of the Royal Commission on Aboriginal Peoples. Chapter 8 explains how these recommendations are largely the product of academic reasoning and are almost devoid of any practical insights. The report is articulated in such a way that one wonders whether its recommendations are an expression of wilful blindness. Regardless of how one resolves these doubts, one thing is clear: the implementation of the commission's recommendations would result in the failure of Aboriginal people to achieve self-government.

The criticism in Chapter 8 focuses on Aboriginal self-government, an element of the report of the Royal Commission on Aboriginal Peoples that I believe is seriously flawed, but my criticism is not meant to suggest that the entire report is without merit. In many ways, the opinions in other areas of the report are not only very scholarly but very insightful and will guide further developments in various fields for years to come.

An undertaking such as that proposed here is faced with an immediate dilemma. How does one speak about Aboriginal issues and aspirations without falling into the trap of pan-Indianism or pan-Aboriginalism? That is, how does one convey these issues and aspirations in the general terms necessary to articulate problems of a national magnitude without also implying that all Aboriginal peoples are essentially the same? Such an assertion would simply not be true. Aboriginal peoples across this land may indeed share many historical and cultural similarities, but it would be unwise to assume that these communities reflect identical cultural values.[1]

I have decided to borrow the approach often employed by my own community. Aboriginal people often refer to the "European colonists" or "Western influences" without clearly identifying the specific national origins of these people (whether French or English). Purely for convenience, therefore, I will make similar references regarding Aboriginal peoples in Canada. Although I qualify many statements by referring to a "traditional" or "historical" approach, I trust that the reader will appreciate that within my comments, no matter how general they are, I intend to recognize multicultural diversity in the Aboriginal community.

I think that it is also worth mentioning what this book is not about. It does not address generic issues such as treaties and land claims or harvesting rights such as hunting and fishing. Nor does it resolve the question of how self-governing communities will finance their futures. These and other issues await future discussion. Although self-government is invariably associated with each of these ideas, it is a concept discrete enough to warrant independent treatment. To this end, I have made no specific distinction between the three constitutionally recognized Aboriginal peoples. Although I occasionally mention their different positions on certain matters, for the most part the issues that I elaborate bridge the differences between these peoples.

Nor does this book attempt to provide all the answers to the problems raised. I believe that viable answers must come from the people who are most affected. However, before that can occur, all Canadians must have some sense of the nature and importance of the issues. I hope that this book provides a better understanding of an Aboriginal perspective concerning this subject. Once again, to this end, I offer comments on the plausibility of certain proposals, and occasionally I point in directions that may resolve others. But the final decision must always rest with the people themselves, Aboriginal and non-Aboriginal alike.

I believe that it is appropriate that I declare my personal bias. As an Aboriginal person who has spent much of my life in both Aboriginal and non-Aboriginal Canadian communities, I favour Aboriginal self-government. I believe that the only path to the eventual resolution of the many ills that trouble my people is through the doorway of self-government. Although self-government alone will not solve all of the problems, without it the alternative methodologies, I believe, are doomed to failure. Partial commitments will never generate the required support of the people who are most affected. And it is the people themselves who must find the most appropriate answer.

Having stated my personal bias, I believe, nonetheless, that the issues have received a largely objective treatment. If it does not seem at times to be as detached as it might otherwise be, then perhaps that is the price that must be paid in order to understand these issues in an Aboriginal context. Many of the examples offered in this book would not have been so readily available to a non-Aboriginal person. In particular, case examples and traditional teachings from the United States would not have been shared by those traditional leaders and judges. In addition, the collective rights customs articulated here would have been available only to a person familiar with these communities. Thus, I hope that any sense of bias will be understood as a reasonable compromise necessitated by the effort to gain a broader understanding of these issues.

Finally, before endeavouring to understand the dream of Aboriginal self-government, it seems to be appropriate to consider this comment by Edmund Burke: "The rules best suited to promote the welfare of a community will emerge only from the experience of that community, so that more trust must be put in established social culture than in the social engineering of utilitarians who suppose they know better than history." These words resonate with truth for Aboriginal people. One can only hope that non-Aboriginal people will soon understand their value to the Aboriginal dream for self-government.

1
The Self-Government Ideal: A Recent Concept

The term "Aboriginal self-government" seems to stimulate a variety of responses. Most Aboriginal people respond to the term with fervour, often viewing it as an answer to most of the problems afflicting their communities. When the term is mentioned to politicians or bureaucrats, their eyes usually glaze over as they slowly recede back into their chairs, now somewhat less comfortable. Average Canadians also hold equally disparate views. Many, often out of some sense of fairness, enthusiastically support Aboriginal people's right to control their own destinies. Others, perhaps out of fear, simply ask if Aboriginal self-government means that they would now lose their homes. Responses to the term are truly mixed. However, if the inquiry is pursued further, many people admit that they have little real understanding of this term. Indeed, this lack of understanding should not be too surprising under the circumstances.

The term "Aboriginal self-government" is a fairly recent invention. Prior to 1980, Aboriginal people in Canada were more commonly known by the terms "Indian," "Inuit," and "Métis." Among even these three designations, there were frequent divisions. Consequently, a number of non-governmental organizations (NGOs) evolved and came to represent the varied interests of these respective peoples.[1] Within the Indian community, interests were commonly divided between those with treaties and those without treaties or between those who viewed treaties as having practical value and those who did not. The Métis were also philosophically divided, principally about whether prairie history and lifestyle were more defining characteristics than simple blood quantum. However, the acquisition of a land base has always been a binding element among these people. The Inuit, although apparently more unified in their sense of identity and aspirations, remained divided over how their lands should be dispersed and subsequently governed. The recent recognition of the Nunavut territory reflects a reconciliation of some of these differences.

This Aboriginal political landscape changed dramatically in the early 1980s. Where there had been mistrust and division both within and between Aboriginal groups, there was soon to be an issue that galvanized the interests of all Aboriginal peoples. In 1982, the federal government, with the consent of the provinces (except Quebec), asked the British Parliament to amend its authority to pass laws affecting Canada.[2] The Canada Act, 1982, included as a schedule the terms of the Canadian Constitution Act. In passing such a law, Canada was effectively repatriating control over its Constitution. The Canadian governments enacted a Constitution with terms and conditions that would forever change how Canadians perceive life in their country. Part of this constitutional change included an outline, albeit vague, for the future development of Aboriginal people in Canada. Whereas in the past Aboriginal people and their NGOs drifted without direction or common purpose, this "new Constitution" provided a clear focus for all Aboriginal people, even today.

The Constitution Act, 1982, is perhaps best known by Canadians for its newly adopted Canadian Charter of Rights and Freedoms. These rights, though not entirely new to Canadian law, are now enshrined as the supreme law of the land. Special care must now be taken by the courts in resolving conflicts whenever any government enacts a law that impinges on these guarantees.[3] However, Aboriginal people have been occupied with the inclusion of rights in other areas of the Constitution Act, in particular Section 35, which states that

1. The existing aboriginal and treaty rights of the aboriginal peoples of Canada are hereby recognized and affirmed.
2. In this Act, "aboriginal peoples of Canada" includes the Indian, Inuit and Métis peoples of Canada.
3. For greater certainty, in subsection (1) "treaty rights" includes rights that now exist by way of land claims agreements or may be so acquired.
4. Notwithstanding any other provision of this Act, the aboriginal and treaty rights referred to in subsection (1) are guaranteed equally to male and female persons.

For Aboriginal people, this section[4] of the Constitution included three important assertions. First, it recognized these three Native groups as the Aboriginal peoples of Canada.[5] Second, it asserted that they possess both inherent rights as Aboriginal people (i.e., Aboriginal rights) and, where appropriate, treaty rights.[6] These rights were also later enshrined with a guarantee that they must be exercised without regard to gender.[7] Third, a meeting of first ministers (i.e., the prime minister of Canada and the provincial premiers) must be held for the purpose of the "identification and definition" of the rights of Aboriginal peoples.[8] Although other elements of the Constitution may have an important influence on Aboriginal communities, these three principles generated the present assertions of Aboriginal self-government.

However, the three Aboriginal peoples were soon confronted with both good news and bad news almost ad infinitum. The good news was that they were recognized within the Constitution as Aboriginal peoples, but the bad news was that they had no understanding of what was intended by this new stature. Although they now had their respective Aboriginal and treaty rights recognized and entrenched, no one knew what this meant legally or practically.[9] Similarly, although the Constitution guaranteed a first ministers' conference to address Aboriginal issues, no one was ready for such a dialogue.

Many such conflicts arose shortly after the repatriation of the Constitution. Aboriginal people had been given what they had sought, at least initially. Yet few within the communities were prepared for the implications of a constitution which now recognized their rights. Conflicting thoughts abounded about what had been achieved and about which direction Aboriginal people were now headed. However, none of these concerns touched upon the issue of Aboriginal self-government. This idea, as a political position, had yet to raise its provocative head.

A Constitutional Dialogue

The single first ministers' conference required by the Constitution and intended to address Aboriginal issues evolved into three such meetings throughout the 1980s. Initially, Aboriginal people approached these meetings with optimism. Perhaps one or two non-Aboriginal parties to these conferences held similar feelings, but enthusiasm among federal and provincial participants was limited. Without a commitment to enlightened change, these meetings were doomed to failure. When the final conference ended in 1988, there was still no substantive movement by the non-Aboriginal governments on any of the proposals presented by the Aboriginal leaders. Consequently, there were no amendments to the Constitution that would in any way assist in the "identification and definition"[10] of the rights of Aboriginal people. However, if there is blame to be apportioned for the "failure" of these conferences, then there is certainly enough to be shared by all sides of the table.

Aboriginal people approached these meetings believing that televised statements and emotional lectures on their history and traditions would be enough to sway politicians to alter the age-old positions of Canadian governments. But they were not sufficient. There was seldom any coordination among the three Aboriginal parties for the development of a unified position, at least in the first two conferences. Even within separate organizations there were divisions between members about the organization's position.[11] Arguably, little was accomplished throughout the 1980s by any of the Aboriginal NGOs to engender a unified[12] and pragmatic Aboriginal proposal that could be accepted by the Canadian governments. However, equally deficient were the positions of these non-Aboriginal governments.

No federal or provincial leader placed on the table for discussion any proposal about the content or scope of either Aboriginal or treaty rights that the respective government was prepared to accept. The Aboriginal parties at least presented positions on the issues, while the Canadian governments sat back and either criticized or rejected the proposals out of hand. They failed to offer any constructive positions of their own, either as amendments to the Aboriginal positions or as original proposals.

These conferences were ultimately doomed to failure. Yet these meetings changed the focus on Aboriginal issues in this country. Although Aboriginal peoples went into the first ministers' conferences of the 1980s somewhat disorganized and unfocused, they emerged from them with a clarity and fervour not seen before in the history of Aboriginal politics. Uncommitted to any single issue shared by all Aboriginal parties before the 1980s, the Aboriginal representatives emerged from the last conference to espouse Aboriginal self-government as the preeminent issue.

Aboriginal people discussed many issues throughout the first ministers' conferences of the 1980s. However, after early failures in convincing the non-Aboriginal parties to accept the merits of their proposals,[13] many leaders came to believe that self-government was central to their concerns. Indeed, some thought it to be the key to solving the various problems in Aboriginal communities.

Self-government was viewed as a position that all Aboriginal peoples (Inuit, Métis, and First Nations alike) could share, and it did not pose the problem of conflicting claims. Assertions for the recognition of a land base, Aboriginal title, and even treaty enforcement sometimes cast one Aboriginal group against another. Some of the territorial claims overlapped and resulted in competing arguments between Aboriginal peoples.[14] However, no such competing claims stemmed from the mutual assertion of Aboriginal self-government. Section 35 recognized that Aboriginal people shared a similar, if not identical, right to the recognition and protection of Aboriginal rights. Self-government is now viewed by many Aboriginal advocates as perhaps the quintessential expression of such rights. It is thought to provide the structural basis on which to implement the many interests of these collectives. In turn, many of these concerns are viewed as the cultural expression for collective Aboriginal rights.[15]

Not to be lost in discussions of self-government within the framework of the first ministers' conferences is the impact of the Penner Report on the development of the concept of Aboriginal self-government. The *Report of the Special Committee on Indian Self-Government in Canada*,[16] commonly referred to as the Penner Report after Keith Penner, the committee's chairperson, provided an important impetus for the self-government dialogue. The report included a number of positive recommendations for self-government, including expanded jurisdictions for First Nations governments, the exclusion of provincial jurisdiction from Aboriginal lands, and a process of First Nations accountability to Aboriginal people.[17]

The Penner Report did not outline the scope of the jurisdictions that these Aboriginal governments would control; instead, the committee recommended that this question be resolved through negotiations.[18] The weakness of this approach is discussed at some length in Chapter 8. Nevertheless, the critical impact of this report brought into sharper relief not only the significance of the general topic but also some of its collateral issues. A great deal of the dialogue of the first ministers' conferences, both in front of the cameras and behind closed doors, was driven by ideas first articulated in the Penner Report.

The shift in emphasis to self-government by Aboriginal peoples has also been motivated by a practical realization. Aboriginal leaders have come to understand that many of the day-to-day problems expressed during the early first ministers' conferences cannot be resolved even if the other big-ticket issues are successfully reconciled. Should a land base be acquired,[19] Aboriginal title recognized, or treaties interpreted more equitably, most of the practical problems facing Aboriginal communities would remain.

None of these issues addresses the problems affecting Aboriginal children who receive an education that lacks sensitivity towards cultural differences and their own history. And Aboriginal communities have always been underserviced by the health care system. Neither the need for more doctors nor the establishment of health care centres in these communities would be directly affected by the resolution of these big-ticket issues. Similarly, the reconciliation of constitutional issues would not provide immediate answers to the inordinate level of incarceration of Aboriginal people in penal institutions. Nor are any of the difficulties caused by Aboriginal criminal offenders – difficulties that result in fractured communities – ameliorated by land claims or treaty rights resolution. Child welfare, including adoption and the care and protection of Aboriginal children, is another issue of great significance. Such matters touch the hearts of all Aboriginal people. Yet the problems in these areas receive no direct benefit from the resolution of the big-ticket issues.

Many other areas of civil law also remain unaddressed by these constitutional issues. When an individual dies or there is a marital breakdown, many Aboriginal communities have traditional methods of dealing with the disposition of family property. Such practices often conflict with existing provincial laws in these areas.[20] Similarly, in communities that practise a traditional "ethic" of care and duty (see Chapter 6 for elaboration), existing rules of negligence law are inconsistent with these principles. Many Aboriginal people wish to change such laws to conform to the traditional standards of a good-Samaritan ethic. These aspirations receive no assistance from the big-ticket items. Thus, not surprisingly, once Aboriginal leaders became aware that resolving the larger constitutional issues would not address the many practical problems facing their people, they began to alter their focus.

Often the leaders began to view self-government as the mechanism by which many of the practical problems facing their communities would be resolved. Aboriginal people generally believe that self-governing communities can use resources in an efficient and culturally sensitive manner when tackling endemic problems. Clearly, the approach of solving a community's problems from the outside looking in has met with little success. This has been the history of the Canadian approach whether directed by provincial governments at Métis concerns or through federal legislation such as the Indian Act. Such an approach has produced physical and social conditions shared only with Third World communities. In addition, the cultural integrity of these communities today hangs by only the thinnest of threads.

Many Aboriginal people also believe that, if a community were to achieve a significant level of self-government, then this accomplishment would reinforce all the other big-ticket constitutional items for which they have argued. The argument is that, if one accepts Aboriginal self-government as an Aboriginal right, then the perspective regarding land claims becomes clearer. Once the existence of a people is recognized, particularly at a constitutional level,[21] surely this recognition implies a land base that they must once have occupied. Attention is then drawn to the manner in which this land has been dealt with historically, not whether the land rights exist. This perspective would apply to either a Métis land base or the classical Aboriginal title claim. This thinking essentially skips a step by assuming the credibility of the actual claim. One still needs to prove its merits, but for Aboriginal people at least the foundation for the claim seems to have greater credibility.

Similarly, a more contextual understanding of treaty claims is achieved through the lens of self-government. These historical agreements would now be viewed from the perspective of negotiations between peoples or nations. Such a perspective is more mature than viewing these negotiations as having transpired between a colonial government and disorganized bands of nomads. One might anticipate that the standards governing the interpretation of these agreements might now be considered as contracts between peoples. Accordingly, viewing the terms of these agreements in such a fashion would result in a more favourable interpretation for the

Aboriginal parties than has been practised by Canadian courts to date. Perhaps more beneficial international doctrines could now be employed by Aboriginal parties in their disputes. These standards could be viewed as more supportive of the Aboriginal position.[22]

The "reinforcement strategy" is appealing to Aboriginal people who often express a holistic view of the world. However, this inferential thinking inherent in the assertion of self-government may not be as appealing to the courts. They may prefer to retain a more classical and less integrated approach to their reasoning.[23] Nonetheless, this holistic approach, which has helped to motivate the position of Aboriginal people on self-government, seems to be the most sensible one to them, even if it does not eventually produce all its desired benefits.

Surprisingly, the Aboriginal claim of the right to self-government has met with unanticipated success. To date, not a single court case[24] has recognized any Aboriginal people as possessing the right to self-government, certainly not as an Aboriginal right.[25] Nevertheless, this term is commonly used not just by Aboriginal people but also by ministers and bureaucrats at both federal and provincial levels of government. Since this concept was first introduced during the first ministers' conferences, its acceptance seems to have taken on a life of its own. The term is frequently employed and seemingly never challenged. Perhaps its truth is self-evident and therefore does not require elaborate expression. Yet someone might have requested a greater explanation of the concept. Although there are many within the Aboriginal community who could rise to such a challenge, doing so now appears to be unnecessary. Political developments seem to have moved significantly beyond this stage. Having eaten from the tree of knowledge, there will be no going back to the simple naïve beliefs of the past.[26]

The Charlottetown Accord, agreed to by both federal and provincial governments, recognized Aboriginal self-government. The federal government has since stated its policy position:

> The Government of Canada recognizes the inherent right of self-government as an existing Aboriginal right under section 35 of the Constitution Act, 1982. It recognizes, as well, that the inherent right may find expression in treaties, and in the context of the Crown's relationship with treaty First Nations. Recognition of the inherent right is based on the view that the Aboriginal peoples of Canada have the right to govern themselves in relation to matters that are internal to their communities, integral to their unique cultures, identities, traditional languages and institutions, and with respect to their special relationship to their land and their resources.[27]

Many provincial governments, though less forthcoming in official policy statements, have engaged in such discussions with Aboriginal NGOs within their respective jurisdictions. Some have even offered funding to explain local interpretations of this term. However, these early successes should not be misinterpreted.

Although the Charlottetown Accord generated a great deal of federal and provincial agreement on the entrenchment of Aboriginal self-government, this entrenchment was notional at best. Moreover, the Charlottetown package failed to overcome its own referendum hurdle. The proposed package of amendments to the Constitution was defeated in a national referendum held on 26 October 1992. Thus, no constitutionally entrenched right to self-government has ever been formally passed into law. Similarly, a federal government policy position is not legally binding. This observation should be disquieting for Aboriginal people since it is more than just a technical point.

The 1998 Supreme Court of Canada Reference held to address the question of Quebec's unilateral secession from Canada is highly insightful in this regard. On the last day of hearings, Chief Justice Antonio Lamer posed a series of questions to the lead lawyer for the attorney general of Canada. These questions dealt with the federal government's legal position regarding whether a democratic choice by the people of Quebec to leave Canada would be legally binding. The response of Yves Fortier, the lead lawyer for the federal government, is enlightening. He began by stating the position of Attorney General Allan Rock: "The Government of Canada would not remain united against the clear wish of Quebeckers, clearly expressed." Fortier then clarified this statement: "That is an expression of government policy. That is not to say ... that there is a right to secede or that Ottawa has ever conceded such a right. Ottawa, the Government of Canada, has never conceded that there is a right to secede. Quite the contrary. The Government of Canada has maintained that there is no such right."[28]

Such statements should trouble Aboriginal people. It appears that, even though Ottawa expresses a policy position on an issue, it will not also concede that this position should be maintained in law. If policy positions and legal positions may not necessarily be the same, then of what legal value is the federal policy regarding Aboriginal self-government? Most Canadians might reasonably assume that, if the federal government commits itself to an official policy, then surely it will not oppose this position in the courts. Such an assumption does not appear to be well founded. However, even if a federal government agrees to maintain in law its statement of policy, such a statement will not be binding on a provincial government. Any province may choose to challenge through the courts the assertion of Aboriginal self-government. Thus, notwithstanding the use of this term by ministers of the Crown or their bureaucrats, the agreed understanding of the Charlottetown Accord, or an official policy statement of the federal government, Aboriginal people still have no enforceable rights in law to self-government. At least not yet.[29]

Does Self-Government Have Content?

The explanation of Aboriginal self-government rising from the ashes of the first ministers' conferences may be of historical interest to some, but it does little to enlighten the initial inquiry.[30] What is intended by this term? Does it have any content, or will one be forever forced to guess at its substance? Perhaps, like an astrophysicist detecting black holes,[31] one can similarly approach the meaning of Aboriginal self-government by inference.

It is only somewhat helpful for Aboriginal people to assert that they wish to direct their lives as they see fit. To state that this undertaking will include a governing body to enact laws concerning crime, health care, education, commercial transactions, and so forth, all enforceable by Aboriginal courts, may cause one to wonder about its feasibility. Here inference may be a useful tool.

Canadian history and laws, since shortly after initial contact with European settlers, have limited the possibilities of easily exercising Aboriginal self-government in Canada. There is thus little opportunity for Canadians to draw inferences and to learn from recent examples of Aboriginal self-government in this country. However, the history of Aboriginal people and their sociopolitical development in the United States is remarkably different. Tribal governments and the underlying concept of sovereignty and nationhood have been clearly recognized in law for more than 150 years. Hence, it is there that one might look to better understand this notion of Aboriginal self-government. The situation in the United States may provide some insight into the potential for Aboriginal self-government in Canada.

But before pursuing the idea of American tribal sovereignty, it is worth noting a remarkable irony in the history of the Canadian concept of Aboriginal self-government. Current ideas associated with the expression of this right evolved directly out of the repatriation of the Canadian Constitution. Before this occurred, most Aboriginal people, if asked, would have denied that they had ever been conquered or negotiated away their right of nationhood. Even before the development of current assertions of self-government,[32] there was always an Aboriginal sense of nationhood or at least of a right to some degree of self-direction. But it is arguable that this claim would not have matured, certainly to the extent that it has currently reached, without an amended constitutional document. Of particular significance is the clearly expressed wording of Sections 25 and 35, which strongly reflect a recognition of the rights of Aboriginal people, even though the precise nature and legal scope of these rights have not yet been determined. It is equally arguable that the principal proponent of this constitutional repatriation, without whom it might never have occurred, was Prime Minister Pierre Elliott Trudeau. But he has not always basked in the glow of Aboriginal appreciation; not long ago, indeed, Trudeau was vilified by many Aboriginal people.

In 1968, Trudeau's government introduced a "white" policy paper concerning the future of Aboriginal people in Canada. Entitled "A White Paper on Indian Policy," it is referred to in Aboriginal circles simply as the "White Paper." It has always been viewed with a great deal of contempt. In essence, it proposed the abolition of the "separateness" that it claimed was created by the Indian Act. Thus, it purported to do away with the legal distinction of Indian together with the existing reserve system. It assumed that these people were simply to be integrated into the larger Canadian cultural mosaic without any of the legal entitlements that they possessed under the Indian Act. Naturally, federal responsibilities to expend millions of dollars on reserve communities each year were also to disappear. The proposal failed. The White Paper was soundly rejected in a national expression of pan-Aboriginal solidarity. Aboriginal opposition to the proposal was also supported by many outspoken non-Aboriginal leaders, interest groups, and religious organizations.

Some have since claimed that the White Paper was simply an attempt to eliminate problems associated with Aboriginal people, in much the same way as it had been undertaken by the American governments during the termination period of the 1950s. Simply put, there is no problem if there are no Indians (see Chapter 2 for a discussion of this policy). The unique sociopolitical and financial challenges associated with Aboriginal communities would no longer strain the fabric of the Canadian political system if Aboriginal people are just assimilated into the larger society. Should Aboriginal people continue to have problems with housing, education, or other social services, most of these matters would fall to the respective provincial governments to resolve. Perhaps more important, the public profile of highly volatile issues would all but disappear.[33] This fact alone would have been enough to galvanize the support of many within the federal government.

However, the motivation for the White Paper need not appear so cynical. Although the Liberal policy paper may have been proposed with the best intentions in mind for Aboriginal communities, the federal government soon learned the weakness of what can only be described charitably as a naïve understanding of Aboriginal communities, which have never wanted to either abandon their Aboriginal identity or give up their rights to occupy and steward the land. The Innu are now engaged in reclaiming authority over their lands through the creation of two territories, Nunavut and Denedah. They are fortunate that, given the geography and intemperate climate in which they reside, they constitute democratic majorities in these regions. Hence, they can achieve their goals in a largely non-confrontational and democratic manner.

Many Métis people will assert that recognition of their right to lands on which to govern themselves has always been their political priority. First Nations people who leave reserves and move to urban centres to find employment commonly state that "home" is on the reserve. Aboriginal people have for cultural, not financial, reasons always maintained the uniqueness of their culture and these communities. The federal proposal that they should henceforth forfeit their identity and be evicted from their lands was criticized nationally by both Aboriginal and non-Aboriginal people alike. The Trudeau government soon permitted its suggestions to fade away as it discreetly abandoned this position.

Recognizing today that the 1982 constitutional amendment occurred only as a direct consequence of the efforts of Prime Minister Trudeau[34] and that the present acceptance of the notion of Aboriginal self-government exists only because of this amendment, the irony is obvious. Trudeau's position in the 1960s, which proposed the assimilation of Aboriginal distinctiveness, evolved to the point of endorsing a constitutional amendment that would engender and crystallize profound beliefs in the recognition of Aboriginal self-government. Perhaps Trudeau paused to consider the errors of his position in 1968. More probably, he recognized that compromises simply had to be made if a new constitutional order was to restructure how Canadians dealt with one another, particularly in the area of civil liberties. If the civil liberties of all Canadians were to be entrenched, then the rights of Aboriginal people also had to be recognized. Surely such a compromise seemed to be reasonable. Nevertheless, one thing is certain: the political image of Pierre Elliott Trudeau has taken on an entirely new complexion, at least in the eyes of Aboriginal people – so much so that one might even detect slight grins when Aboriginal people are reminded of the proposals for a "just society."[35]

2
The American Tribal Government Experience: Lessons for Canada

If one were to drive casually through any of the over 400 Indian reservations scattered throughout the United States, one would receive a variety of impressions. One impression might be of small communities similar to many found in Canada but often spread over remarkably large areas.[1] Another impression might be how poor some communities are or perhaps how surprisingly wealthy other reservations seem to be.

On the other hand, if one chose to speed through any of these communities, his or her impressions would likely change dramatically. A police siren would quickly bring the speeding car to a halt. Typically, one would be charged with a highway traffic offence or perhaps a more serious crime. But it would not be a state trooper laying the charge, nor would it be a state law being enforced. In all probability, the officer would be a Navajo, Hopi, or Pueblo or any one of over 100 similar tribal officers. They would be local tribal members, duly deputized to lay a summons (or other type of charge) requiring one to appear before a tribal court for breach of a local law. One would have just come into contact with the sovereign authority of an American Indian government.

Indian tribal governments have existed throughout the United States for centuries and have always been self-governing. This history and the underlying legal framework are particularly relevant for Canadians with regard to understanding the possible scope of Aboriginal self-government in Canada. The American example provides not only obvious insights into the kinds of jurisdiction being sought but also clear indications that such authorities can indeed be viably exercised in tribal communities.

For my purposes here, the most significant legal events occurred in the mid-1820s through 1830s. The first court case of significance occurred in 1823. The case of *Johnson* v. *McIntosh*[2] involved tribal chiefs who wanted to sell some of their lands to non-Indians. The ability of the tribe to enact such land transfers was called into question and eventually brought before the Supreme Court of the United States. The court decided that the federal government, as a consequence of "discovery," owned the underlying legal title to all Indian lands. The tribe, however, did possess the right of occupancy on such lands. If they wished to dispose of this title, then they could do so – but only to the federal government. If the government chose to sell this land, then it was also free to do so. However, if the government had not yet purchased the right of occupancy from the tribe, then any purchase of such lands would be encumbered by the tribe's right of occupancy.[3] The court stated that "the rights of the original inhabitants were, in no instance, entirely disregarded; but were, necessarily, to a considerable extent, impaired. They were admitted to be the rightful occupants of the soil ... but their rights to complete sovereignty, as independent nations, were necessarily diminished, and the power to dispose of the soil, at their own will, to whomsoever they pleased, was denied by the original fundamental principle, that discovery gave exclusive title to those who made it."[4] Although the tribe was unsuccessful in establishing clear title to lands that they had occupied for centuries, they achieved a significant victory. This case not only established the concept of Indian title to land (however tenuous) but also recognized the ability of a tribe, as a political entity,[5] to possess such title.

The next significant case at the Supreme Court of the United States, heard nearly ten years later, elaborated upon what this declaration meant. In 1831, the first of the Cherokee Nation cases came before the court. The case of *Cherokee Nation* v. *Georgia*[6] was again based on actions taken by the State of Georgia concerning the lands of the Cherokee people and their government. Georgia, wishing to divide the lands of the Cherokee tribe into state counties, attempted to assert its own laws over these lands. In addition, the state passed criminal laws that sought to prevent the Cherokee people from exercising any self-governing authority. The tribe brought a civil action before the Supreme Court seeking to prevent Georgia from enacting such laws. However, before the court could address the legality of Georgia's actions, it had to address the issue of whether the tribe had the appropriate "standing" to initiate this legal action. That is, was the tribe a "foreign state" within the meaning of the Constitution and, therefore, entitled, as they claimed, to institute this civil action?[7] The court replied that it was not.

Although the civil action was therefore dismissed, the tribe succeeded in establishing the basis for its present unique constitutional status. Chief Justice Marshall took the opportunity to elaborate the unique constitutional character of a tribe: "So much of the argument as was intended to prove the character of the Cherokees as a state, as [a] distinct political society separated from others, capable of managing its own affairs and governing itself, has in the opinion of a majority of the judges, been completely successful."[8]

As to what type of state this tribe was, he continued:

> Though the Indians are acknowledged to have an unquestionable, and, heretofore unquestioned right to the lands they occupy, until that right shall be extinguished by a voluntary cession to our government; yet it may well be doubted, whether those tribes which reside within the acknowledged boundaries of the United States can, with strict accuracy, be denominated foreign nations. They may, more correctly, perhaps, be denominated *domestic dependent nations*. They occupy a territory to which we assert a title independent of their will, which must take effect in point of possession, when their right of possession ceases. Meanwhile, they are in a state of pupilage; their relation to the United States resembles that of *a ward to his guardian*.[9]

From these statements evolved the recognition of two principles: first, that Indian tribes were "domestic dependent nations"; and second, that these nations were in a trustlike relationship with the federal government. These two principles have not been rejected over the ensuing years, but they have evolved from this initial declaration. They have occasioned much interpretation and opinion by courts, academics, and tribal leaders. Nonetheless, Chief Justice Marshall's comments have formed the basis for the present state of "tribal sovereignty" in the United States.

As a consequence of these two cases, the respective roles of and relationships between tribal and federal authorities began to take shape. The court was silent about what role the states would play in these relationships, but that silence would not last long.

In 1832, the second of the Cherokee Nation cases came before Chief Justice Marshall's court. Once again the State of Georgia, seeking to exercise its jurisdiction over Cherokee Nation territory, enacted criminal prohibitions regarding who could live within those lands. The state convicted two missionaries who chose to live within Cherokee lands without the required permit. Mr. Worcester appealed his conviction to the Supreme Court of the United States, arguing that Georgia had no authority to require him to possess such a permit. The court agreed.

The case of *Worcester* v. *Georgia*[10] again provided Chief Justice Marshall with the opportunity to expand on the unique status of the Cherokee Nation. After articulating a history of the relationship between the tribe and the federal government, he stated that the federal government should "manifestly consider the several Indian nations as distinct political communities, having territorial boundaries, within which their authority is exclusive."[11] He also declared that "the Cherokee Nation, then, is a distinct community, occupying its own territory, with boundaries accurately described, *in which the laws of Georgia can have no force*."[12] Thus, not only did

Marshall declare that the concept of the domestic dependent nation recognized the tribe as having governmental authority within its boundaries, but he also clarified that state governments had no authority in these lands. The circle had been closed.

These three cases clearly established that tribal nations were sovereign entities,[13] domestic in character,[14] and drew their inherent authority from the people.[15] The federal government had full plenary authority over these tribes that permitted it not only to modify or diminish their authority but also, if Congress wished, to extinguish it (the termination era and Public Law 280 are described in this chapter). The states, it appeared, possessed no authority in Indian country.[16] Although the rules now seemed to be clear, perhaps no one had a full understanding of what they would mean in practice.

This picture was brought into focus dramatically with the decision in *Ex parte Crow Dog*.[17] In 1883, the chief of the Brulé Sioux, Spotted Tail, was killed by another Indian, Crow Dog. The federal government tried Crow Dog pursuant to a federal statute and convicted him for the crime of murder. He subsequently appealed the conviction to the Supreme Court.[18] He asserted that, according to the Cherokee Nation cases, absent any express federal intention to assert criminal law jurisdiction over tribal members while on the reservation or in "Indian country," it was only the tribe that possessed the jurisdiction to convict him of such an offence. The Supreme Court agreed. Congress had not given federal officials the specific authority to intervene in the affairs of this domestic nation, which had been recognized as possessing full authority over its internal affairs. *Ex parte Crow Dog* clarified that a tribe's criminal law authority included jurisdiction over cases of murder.

Reaction around the country to the court's decision was shock. However, Congress soon proposed two measures. In the same year, Congress introduced the Courts of Indian Offences, otherwise known as the CFRs (Courts of Federal Regulations). Their purpose, together with the law and order codes that they implemented, was both to "civilize" Indians and to rein in their criminal law authority. Judges were appointed by the local Indian agent, who then administered an entirely Eurocentric code of criminal laws. Not only were these laws not culturally sensitive to the community, but they also often prohibited specific local religious and cultural activities such as the Sun Dance ceremonies, the recounting of legends and myths, and even the singing of traditional songs. Astonishingly, no federal law was ever passed to legally enact these codes or to give authority to their courts.

Nonetheless, this effort proved both effective and debilitating. Many of the tribes began to rely on these CFRs for the administration of justice within their reservations. Not surprisingly, local processes of dispute resolution began to fall into disuse. As a consequence, at least within the ambit of criminal law, tribal jurisdiction began to decline across the country. Only a few tribes, such as the Navajo and some of the more traditional Hopi and Pueblo communities, retained traditional laws and dispute-resolving processes. However, another significant occurrence transpired as a direct result of the intrusion by the CFRs. Since these codes were intended to cover crimes by Indians against other Indians, they did nothing to control crimes by non-Indians against tribal members. And since local tribal courts were falling into disuse, a vacuum began to develop. Who was to protect tribal communities from the criminal activities of outsiders? This question still troubles tribal leaders (I will comment on this issue later in the chapter).

In 1885, as a direct consequence of *Ex parte Crow Dog,* Congress enacted the most significant piece of "Indian legislation" in US history, the Major Crimes Act.[19] This act recognized exclusive jurisdiction in the federal authorities over seven of the most serious criminal offences: murder, arson, burglary, rape, manslaughter, assault with intent to kill, and larceny. This number has fluctuated over the years, and today the Major Crimes Act includes thirteen crimes.[20]

The passage of this act was a direct response to the decision in *Ex parte Crow Dog* and was designed to limit[21] the criminal law jurisdiction of the tribe. However, like the CFRs, this legislation was intended to address only those situations in which the accused was an Indian.[22] When the accused was a non-Indian, the federal government continued, at least notionally, to assert its criminal law jurisdiction pursuant to the General Crimes Act.[23]

Although the Major Crimes Act dealt a significant blow to tribal sovereignty, much criminal law authority is retained by the tribes today. Many criminal activities ranging from quite minor to very serious offences remain within the jurisdiction of the tribal courts. Moreover, arguably the more significant civil law jurisdiction of the tribes remains almost wholly intact.

Criminal Law Jurisdictional Developments

Although the Major Crimes Act withdrew from tribal authority criminal law jurisdiction over seven offences, many other significant activities remained within tribal jurisdiction. Even today tribes exercise authority over the possession and sale of drugs, alcohol, prostitution, some forms of assault and fraud, firearms violations, certain kinds of sexual offences, and so forth. The scope of a tribe's jurisdiction remains broad, albeit somewhat restrained in comparison to the pre-*Crow Dog* days. Although the Major Crimes Act focused on which crimes a tribe could or could not adjudicate, the more significant case law developments since then have dealt with which individuals are subject to a tribe's criminal law jurisdiction in Indian country.[24]

The role of state authority in Indian country changed significantly in 1881. Although the Cherokee Nation cases, decided fifty years earlier, seemed decisively to indicate that state governments had no jurisdiction of any kind in Indian lands, the case of *United States* v. *McBratney*[25] opened the door to a new perspective on this relationship. The federal government prosecuted a non-Indian for the murder of another non-Indian while on a Ute reservation. McBratney, on appeal of his conviction to the Supreme Court, argued that the state authority was the more appropriate one for the case. The court, in a laboured act of reasoning, agreed.

Following on this decision, in the case of *Draper* v. *United States*[26] in 1896, the Supreme Court again had an opportunity to clarify whether *McBratney* had simply been a unique exception to the Cherokee Nation principle excluding state jurisdiction. The court clarified that it had not. In another murder case involving only non-Indians, the court reaffirmed the apparently new rule established in *McBratney*. Where only non-Indians are involved in a crime, the state has exclusive authority to adjudicate both victim and offender. This is subject, of course, to Congress not clearly legislating its paramount jurisdiction in Indian country.[27]

The *McBratney* and *Draper* decisions are significant because they opened the door to state intervention in Indian country. Correspondingly, these decisions reflected a diminishing of the sovereign authority of a tribe to control affairs in its communities. Although these cases addressed criminal law issues, the very idea of now having some ability to exercise authority in tribal communities buttressed the aspirations of the state in matters of civil law.

Following *Ex parte Crow Dog* and prior to the developments in *McBratney* and *Draper*, some tribal governments may have assumed that their domestic jurisdiction extended to criminal law authority over non-Indians. However, subsequent case law clarified that the General Crimes Act recognized the federal government as possessing this jurisdiction almost exclusively. The federal Enclaves Act,[28] also known as the General Crimes Act, was enacted in 1817. Its original intention was to ensure the prosecution of crimes by non-Indians against tribal members. It also permitted the prosecution of non-major crimes by Indians against non-Indians.

Except as otherwise expressly provided by law, the general laws of the United States as to the punishment of offences committed in any place within the sole and exclusive jurisdiction of the United States, except the District of Columbia, shall extend to the Indian country.

This section shall not extend to offences committed by one Indian against the person or property of another Indian, nor to any Indian committing any offence in the Indian country who has been punished by the local law of the tribe, or to any case where, by treaty stipulations, the exclusive jurisdiction over such offences is or may be secured to the Indian tribes respectively.[29]

Due to the *Worcester* decision, it was assumed that state governments had no authority within reservations. But a problem arose because, for the most part, state governments passed laws concerning criminal behaviour. These laws have often been similar to those found in the Canadian Criminal Code. State criminal codes typically prohibit certain activities, outline appropriate penalties for violations of the code, and articulate the criminal procedures used in the prosecution of an accused. The federal government passes few laws governing criminal activities. The dilemma presented by this division of criminal authority was that if state laws did not apply in Indian country, then this would also prohibit the application of these criminal codes. But which criminal laws would then apply to non-Indians who committed criminal offences against tribal members? If the state and not the federal government enacted criminal codes, then what criminal law was left to be enforced? It would appear that there was no federal criminal law that would apply. Would this mean that any criminal behaviour was fair game on the reservation? The General Crimes Act was intended, in part, to remedy this uncertainty, yet it did not articulate an extensive list of criminal prohibitions. The act simply stated that any federal law applied in Indian country.

It was the Assimilative Crimes Act[30] that indicated which substantive criminal laws would apply. Passed in 1825 by Congress, it supplied the necessary mechanism for bringing the activities of both Indians and non-Indians within the standards of American criminal law: "Whoever within ... [the special maritime and territorial jurisdiction of the United States] is guilty of any act or omission which, although not made punishable by an enactment of Congress, would be punishable if committed or omitted within the jurisdiction of the State, Territory, Possession, or District in which such place is situated, by the laws thereof in force at the time of such act or omission, shall be guilty of a like offence and subject to a like punishment."[31] This law ensured that, in those areas of federal jurisdiction in which Congress had not enacted criminal laws (e.g., forts and arsenals), state laws were to be adopted and applied as federal laws. Significantly, this process of adoption could now also be applied to Indian territory as well. Since the General Crimes Act stated that all federal laws applied to Indians, and since the Assimilative Crimes Act was a federal law, it was to apply to tribal communities. Thus, the criminal laws of the state in which an Indian tribe resided would now be adopted as federal criminal laws and applied in tribal communities. The trial would be held in a federal court, but the definitions of the crime and its penalty would be borrowed from state legislation.

It was anticipated that these laws would apply to both Indians and non-Indians alike. Both kinds of offenders could be brought before a federal court and the cases adjudicated accordingly. When only Indians were involved in the crime, or an Indian perpetrator was punished by a tribal court, the federal government would defer to tribal jurisdiction. It was the non-Indian perpetrator who would feel the greatest impact of this legislation.

However, the decisions in *McBratney* and *Draper* undermined these assumptions. As a result of the impacts of these cases, the federal authority could assert itself only when either the accused or the victim was an Indian. When neither party was an Indian, state criminal law jurisdiction would now apply.

Although these distinctions created apparent incongruencies, the laws on these matters remained largely consistent for years – that is, until 1978, when *Oliphant* v. *Suquamish Indian Tribe*[32] came before the Supreme Court. Many tribes were upset over the lack of federal enforcement of criminal laws against non-Indians in tribal communities. For too long, tribal members were the victims of non-Indian offenders whom the federal government failed to prosecute. Federal officials alternately claimed that they lacked the necessary resources to prosecute these offenders or that insufficient evidence precluded successful prosecution. Tribal leaders disputed these arguments. These leaders claimed that convictions of non-Indians would prove unpopular locally and jeopardize the future political aspirations of prosecuting attorneys. Offences as serious as murder went unprosecuted. Understandably, many of these communities came to believe that, if they had to rely on federal prosecutors, then they would be insufficiently protected from non-Indian offenders. Hence, the Suquamish tribe itself decided to prosecute Oliphant for an offence included under the Major Crimes Act. Acknowledging federal jurisdiction under the act, the tribe nevertheless asserted that it possessed concurrent criminal authority, which, it claimed, had simply been dormant for years. The tribe now wanted to reassert this authority in the absence of aggressive federal prosecution.

The Supreme Court was less than receptive to this argument, reasoning that the authority of a tribal government over a non-Indian in matters of criminal law was inconsistent with its status as a domestic and dependent nation. Moreover, it concluded that, since the accused could not run for political office, vote in a local election, or sit on a criminal jury panel, he or she should not be subject to the criminal laws of the tribal government.

Although the tribal prosecution was not sustained by the Supreme Court, the decision in *Oliphant* should not be viewed as a rejection of the tribe's sovereignty as established in the Cherokee Nation cases; rather, this case has been described simply as a refinement of that principle. However, whether the stone hits the vase or the vase hits the stone, either way it's bad news for the vase. In this instance, it was more than just bad news for tribal jurisdiction.

The subsequent case of *Duro* v. *Reina* proved the reasoning in *Oliphant* to be devastating. In 1990, Albert Duro brought an appeal before the Supreme

Court.[33] The accused had been convicted of unlawfully discharging a firearm on the Salt River Reservation.[34] The defendant appealed his conviction by challenging the jurisdiction of the tribal court. It appeared to most observers that this jurisdiction was secure since both victim and accused were Indians and therefore subject to the exclusive criminal law authority of the tribe. In addition, although Duro had killed a young tribal member, he had not been prosecuted for murder, an offence restricted to federal authority by the Major Crimes Act. Instead, because the federal government had once again failed to prosecute this crime, the tribe had attempted to protect itself by prosecuting Duro, if only for the misdemeanor offence of unlawfully discharging a firearm (not a Major Crimes Act offence).

However, to the surprise of most observers, Duro successfully borrowed the court's reasoning from *Oliphant.* He argued that, although indeed he was an Indian, he was not an Indian from this reservation. Thus, just as in *Oliphant,* in which the accused could not run for tribal office, vote in elections, or sit as a member of a jury, Duro should also be exempt from the criminal laws of this tribe. Astonishingly, the Supreme Court agreed.[35] *Oliphant* had provided the court with an opportunity to further diminish the jurisdiction of a tribal government simply by refining the Cherokee Nation principles.

After intense lobbying by tribal governments, Congress subsequently corrected the effects of *Duro,* once more reinstating the criminal law jurisdiction of the tribe over all Indians within its communities.[36] Nonetheless, legislative and case law alterations to the Cherokee Nation principles have evolved significantly over the years. Most developments have resulted in some erosion of tribal sovereignty. The complicated and somewhat convoluted picture of criminal law jurisdiction in tribal communities today is given in Tables 1 and 2.

Table 2.1

Major Crimes Act offences

Participants	Jurisdictional authority
Indian accused Indian victim	Federal government (Major Crimes Act)
Indian accused Non-Indian victim	Federal government (Major Crimes Act)
Non-Indian accused Indian victim	Federal government (General Crimes Act)
Non-Indian accused Non-Indian victim	State government

Table 2.2

Non-Major Crimes Act offences

Participants	Jurisdictional authority
Indian accused Indian victim	Tribal government
Indian accused Non-Indian victim	Tribal government
Non-Indian accused Indian victim	Federal government (General Crimes Act)
Non-Indian accused Non-Indian victim	State government

Most tribal governments nevertheless continue to assert shared jurisdiction in all Major Crimes Act cases.[37] They argue that, should this legislation be repealed, their authority would once again fill the void.

Civil Law Jurisdiction of a Tribe

Civil law generally includes all areas of law that are not part of criminal law. Thus, the scope of this area of law is quite broad. Moreover, although criminal law is a subject about which many people have strong views (e.g., on capital punishment, plea bargaining, or parole), it is civil law issues that affect their lives the most dramatically. Traffic laws, commercial transactions, housing contracts, and family law matters such as marriage, custody, and support affect the average Canadian far more significantly than does criminal law. Hence, this jurisdictional subject area in US tribal law is highly significant.

The Cherokee Nation cases, in particular *Worcester,* established rules that did not distinguish between the notional kinds of jurisdiction that courts enforce today. Justice Marshall's statements were seen as applicable to both criminal and civil areas of authority. Hence, a tribe's jurisdiction over civil law matters was viewed as broad and limited only by acts of Congress. State jurisdiction was prohibited unless federal authority clearly permitted it.

For years, these principles served tribal governments well. These governments asserted their civil jurisdiction to regulate both Indians and non-Indians alike while on a reservation. The tribe's authority concerning Indians was never seriously challenged,[38] and the recent case of *Iowa Mutual Insurance Company* v. *LaPlante*[39] reaffirmed tribal jurisdiction over non-Indians. The Supreme Court stated that "tribal authority over the activities of non-Indians on reservation lands is an important part of tribal sovereignty."[40] Thus, unlike criminal law activities, tribal authority over non-Indians regarding civil law matters was confirmed.

Over the years, the courts have recognized tribal jurisdiction over tribal members in all areas of civil law jurisdiction. In addition, tribal laws have been viewed as applicable to non-Indians when regulating hunting and fishing,[41] environmental activities,[42] gaming,[43] liquor licences,[44] negligence claims,[45] and health and building codes.[46] Similarly, judicial opinion has confirmed that non-Indians are subject to taxation of personal property,[47] sales tax,[48] and commercial transactions.[49] When one party in a dispute is a tribal Indian, the courts have consistently recognized the sovereign authority of a tribe to adjudicate. In addition to commercial property issues, such as those mentioned above, tribes have successfully exercised jurisdiction in cases of divorce[50] as well as adoption and child custody.[51] The Indian Child Welfare Act enunciates specific rules governing these issues.[52] These rules set out priorities and procedures for court administration of these issues even when Indian children are located off the reservation.

The civil jurisdiction of a tribe is indeed broad and is clearly applicable to both Indians and non-Indians. However, just as in the case of the criminal law jurisdiction of a tribe, the seminal findings in the Cherokee Nation cases have evolved over the years regarding civil law matters. And, once again, the integrity of a tribe's authority has been compromised as state authority has been broadened.

The general prohibition against state jurisdiction in Indian country, as established by *Worcester,* received its first significant reinterpretation in *Williams* v. *Lee.*[53] This 1959 Supreme Court case was based on a civil law suit brought in a state court by a non-Indian for the collection of a commercial debt alleged to have been incurred by an Indian couple. The purchases were made on a Navajo reservation. The court reaffirmed the holdings in *Worcester* by declaring that state courts have no civil law jurisdiction on an Indian reservation. The court restated this in a unique way. According to Justice Black for the majority,

> Over the years this Court has modified these principles in cases where *essential* tribal relations were not involved and where the rights of Indians would not be jeopardized, but the basic policy of *Worcester* has remained.
>
> ... Essentially, absent governing Acts of Congress, the question has always been whether the state action infringed on the right of reservation Indians to make their own laws and be governed by them.[54] There can be no doubt that to allow the exercise of state jurisdiction here would undermine the authority of the tribal courts over Reservation affairs and hence would infringe on the right of the Indians to govern themselves.[55]

Although the court in *Williams* v. *Lee* reaffirmed the general prohibition established in *Worcester,* it introduced a new test to replace the blanket prohibition established in the Cherokee Nation cases. This case articulated what has become known as the "infringement test." According to this standard, a state is prohibited from exercising authority where doing so would infringe on "essential" tribal interests or the ability of a tribe to govern itself. The natural questions that followed upon *Williams* were: "Are there any areas in which a state might wish to legislate regarding non-Indian activity that don't infringe on essential tribal interests? If so, would a state be able to exercise its authority in those instances?"

Although the infringement test is not as all-encompassing a prohibition as is enunciated in *Worcester,* it has nevertheless been highly effective in barring the exercise of a state's jurisdiction. *Williams* v. *Lee* has been used to reaffirm tribal authority and to exclude state jurisdiction in a long list of cases. In *Merrion* v. *Jicarilla Apache Tribe,*[56] the Supreme Court, in a case involving the tribal imposition of a tax on oil and gas profits from a non-Indian company, reaffirmed the tribe's right to "territorial management." Similarly, courts have invoked the infringement test to exclude state authority in cases of child custody,[57] taxation of an Indian's employment income,[58] the personal property of an Indian located on a reservation,[59] taxation of non-Indian businesses on a reservation,[60] regulation of hazardous waste,[61] and negligence on a reservation.[62]

However, as tribal leaders feared, the *Williams* v. *Lee* holding did permit the state to intervene in a few cases where "essential" tribal interests – notably self-government – were not affected. Thus the Supreme Court has permitted state governments to regulate some activities on a reservation, including the sale of alcohol by a non-Indian on the reservation,[63] a tax upon the sale of non-Indian property,[64] and the zoning of pockets of non-Indian land within a reservation.[65] Indeed, in a few instances, Indians were found to be subject to regulation by the state for the purpose of taxing non-Indian customers who made purchases in their stores.[66] Importantly, the infringement test appears to permit state intrusion upon tribal sovereignty almost exclusively only when non-Indians are involved.

The blanket prohibition from *Worcester* also evolved in a second direction. *Worcester* was alternatively interpreted to assert that a federal law is supreme when it conflicts with a state law regarding tribal matters. Once again states, wishing to exercise authority on an Indian reservation, argued a unique characterization of this principle. In 1965, the case of *Warren Trading Post Company* v. *Arizona Tax Commission*[67] came before the Supreme Court. In this instance, the State of Arizona sought to impose an income tax on a non-Indian business operating on the Navajo reservation. Arizona argued that, since this tax was not in conflict with any federal tax, it was not a direct violation of federal legislation. Consequently, it should not be precluded by federal law. The court did not agree with this view. However, unlike the infringement test, the analysis excluded state authority not because it infringed on tribal interests but because that particular area of law was already "occupied" by federal law. The court found that the state was "preempted" from enacting laws even if they did not conflict with existing federal legislation. General occupation of the subject area by Congress seemed to be sufficient to exclude state authority. Although in this instance Navajo tribal integrity was protected, the result of this was that the court introduced a new characterization of *Worcester:* the "preemption test."

The uncertainty created by the *Warren* case was brought into sharper focus eight years later. In *McClanahan* v. *Arizona Tax Commission*[68] the Supreme Court again defended tribal integrity but in a fashion that would open the door to further state intrusion. The State of Arizona sought to tax the income of an Indian living and working on the Navajo reservation. The court denied the state's authority but reiterated, as the basis for doing so, the preemption test of *Warren,* not the infringement test of *Williams:*

> The trend has been away from the idea of inherent Indian sovereignty as a bar to state jurisdiction and toward reliance on federal preemption ... The modern cases thus tend to avoid reliance on platonic notions of Indian sovereignty and to look instead to the applicable treaties and statutes which define the limits of state powers.
>
> The Indian sovereignty doctrine is relevant, then, not because it provides a definitive resolution of the issues in this suit, but because it provides a backdrop against which the applicable treaties and federal status must be read. It must always be remembered that the various Indian tribes were once independent and sovereign nations, and that their claim to sovereignty long predates that of our own Government.[69]

Thus, *McClanahan* seems to suggest that what is important in determining whether state law will apply is whether the law has been preempted by federal law. This is clearly a new interpretation of *Worcester* and is arguably less prohibitive than the infringement test of *Williams* v. *Lee.*

This reasoning was subsequently reiterated in *New Mexico* v. *Mescalero Apache Tribe.*[70] The court stated that "state jurisdiction is preempted by the operation of federal law if it interferes with or is incompatible with federal and tribal interests reflected in federal law, unless the state interests at stake are sufficient to justify the assertion of state authority."[71]

The extreme limits of the preemption test may have been articulated in the Supreme Court's holding in *Cotton Petroleum Corporation* v. *New Mexico.*[72] In this case, the State of New Mexico wished to impose a tax on oil and gas profits from a non-Indian company operating on the reservation. The state acknowledged that such a "double tax" could have some impact on businesses located on the reservation and thus on tribal interests, but this impact was not significant enough to invoke the infringement test criteria; rather, the court focused on the preemption test and reasoned that, although the federal government had legislated in this field, the law was neither direct enough nor comprehensive enough to exclude the state. Hence, the state was free to impose its tax. This case may now stand for the principle that, if a federal law is to preempt the operation of a state law, then it must do so in a clear, direct, and comprehensive fashion. Occupation of the field by vague assertions is not enough to deter a state from arguing the *Cotton Petroleum* interpretation of the preemption test. However, the Supreme Court may further clarify this test and rein in its extreme limits.

The preemption doctrine has not eliminated the principles of *Worcester* nor the *Williams* v. *Lee* infringement test. Courts view the preemption test as simply a further elaboration of the meaning of *Worcester,* as is the infringement test. Significantly however, both permit state intrusion upon tribal authority, which was not generally inferred from the original remarks of Justice Marshall when he prohibited state intrusion in the *Worcester* decision.

Nor has the preemption doctrine displaced the principles of *Williams* v. *Lee*. Since *McClanahan,* the Supreme Court, in the 1987 case of *Iowa Mutual Insurance Company* v. *LaPlante,*[73] once again denied the authority of state law on a reservation. The court stated that such a law interferes with a tribal government's ability to exercise self-government. The court did not mention the preemption test; instead, its reasoning centred on essential tribal interests. In the same year, the Supreme Court, in *California* v. *Cabazon Band of Mission Indians,*[74] denied state jurisdiction over bingo operations because it interfered with an exercise of tribal self-sufficiency. In the case of *Merrion* v. *Jicarilla Apache Tribe,*[75] the court reaffirmed that the ability of a tribe to tax non-Indians for activities on a reservation is entirely consistent with its status as a domestic dependent nation. In each case, the focus was not on whether a federal law occupied the field but on the implications for the tribal government with regard to protecting important tribal interests. The infringement test appears to be alive and well.

Today, notwithstanding the meandering case law in this area, the courts continue to reaffirm the broad scope of a tribe's civil law authority. A tribe may exercise its jurisdiction over all matters affecting tribal self-government. Congress can pass any legislation that it wishes in this area of law, though it has generally refrained from doing so.[76] It is widely believed that state governments must now meet two tests if they wish to exercise jurisdiction within an Indian reservation. First, the laws must not conflict with any federal laws (the preemption test); second, they must not limit the ability of a tribe to govern itself (the infringement test). Both hurdles must be overcome before a state can enforce its laws. And, for all practical purposes, the laws would only affect non-Indian interests. States have been extremely reluctant to attempt to assert authority over the activities of tribal members, perhaps with good reason. With authority comes responsibility. State governments have never rushed to offer financial assistance to tribal communities. Hence, unlike its criminal law jurisdiction, a tribal government today exercises almost unlimited civil law jurisdiction over anyone who enters its community.

Felix Cohen coined the term "residual sovereignty" to describe the kind of authority retained by American tribal governments today.[77] The term is apt, but Cohen was not suggesting that this residual expression of self-government is either ineffectual or to be endorsed. Rather, he was simply providing a perspective for considering the context and the evaluation of a tribe's inherent authority. Today the scope of this authority remains very broad.

Public Law 280 and the Termination Era

A description of tribal self-government would not be complete without comment on the period of termination and, in particular, Public Law 280. Although the events associated with these concepts had no impact on the guiding principles of tribal jurisdiction, their significance is critical if one is to appreciate the state of tribal self-government today.

The termination period began in 1953 with Congress passing House Concurrent Resolution 108.[78] This resolution began the process of terminating federal benefits and services to Indian tribes. It was believed that once such benefits and services were cancelled the tribes themselves would soon wither away. However, to help move this process along, Congress terminated the legal existence of over 100 tribal governments. On 15 August of that year, Congress enacted the only law that extends general state laws into Indian reservations. That was Public Law 280 (PL 280).[79]

This law has been viewed as an attempt by Congress to reduce federal expenditures by eliminating Indian tribes and turning over authority for these nations to state governments. Although Congress stated that its aim was to better control crime within reservations, the Supreme Court disagreed. It viewed PL 280 as an attempt to assimilate tribal communities and to renounce federal trust responsibilities for the tribes.[80]

PL 280 recognized the authority of five state governments[81] over criminal law matters in Indian country. Certain areas of civil law were also included. Initially, this authority was delegated outright, but Congress later passed legislation for the remaining states, which were given the "option"[82] to assume essentially the same jurisdiction. Thus, the integrity of tribal sovereignty was jeopardized by those "mandatory states" that had been given this authority outright and by the threat from those option states, which could choose at any time to assume a tribe's jurisdictional authority. Both situations constituted attacks on the jurisdictional authority of the tribes.

Not all option states chose to adopt both criminal and civil law authority. Although some assumed jurisdiction over criminal law, most opted only for limited control over certain civil law matters. Some states enacted criminal law control only over certain tribes[83] or certain areas of civil law, such as the environment.[84] Some states later retroceded the jurisdiction that they had assumed back to the tribes.[85] Consequently, the topography of tribal sovereignty today resembles a patchwork of jurisdictions across the United States.

The termination period is considered to have ended in 1968 with the passage of amendments to PL 280 contained in the Indian Civil Rights Act.[86] These amendments prohibited states from assuming any tribal jurisdiction without first obtaining the consent of tribal members.[87] They also authorized the retrocession of any jurisdiction already assumed by the state. Congressional enactment of the Indian Business Development Fund[88] and the Indian Financing Act,[89] both of which stimulated tribal business development, occurred in 1968. As well, the Native American Progress Act[90] and the Indian Self-Determination and Education Assistance Act[91] have been viewed as clear indications that congressional attempts to terminate tribal governments had ended.

As mentioned, neither the termination policies nor Public Law 280 had any direct effect on the principles of jurisdiction as articulated in the Cherokee Nation cases and their progeny. However, the impact on tribes that were terminated and never reinstated, as well as those whose criminal and civil jurisdiction today remains diminished, has been devastating.

Tribal Constitutions and Law and Order Codes
Before the Cherokee Nation cases, tribal communities were represented by many forms of government. These cases simply established recognition of the rights of these communities to govern themselves within a federal constitutional structure. But these tribal governments have always manifested different expressions. Leadership has sometimes been based on principles of heredity, while at other times religious customs have dictated governing structures. Today the vast majority of tribes are led by elected councils and chairpersons.

In 1934, Congress passed the Indian Reorganization Act (IRA),[92] intended to establish tribal governing structures along recognized federal and municipal forms. Over the previous fifty years, particularly since the introduction of the Major Crimes Act and the CFRs to reservation life, the traditional government structure of many tribes had fallen into disuse. The IRA introduced institutional forms of government that the tribes could adopt as their own. However, these "boilerplate" government forms presented their own problems.

The act introduced structures for the implementation of governance (e.g., tribal councils) as well as a codification of laws to be enforced. These law and order codes included rules of both criminal and civil law. Perhaps not surprisingly, all of the laws were of the kind deemed necessary to run small local municipal communities. They did not take into account the rural nature of these communities, the vast territories over which they sometimes exercised authority, or the idea that the communities were bound together as one nation or people and should be treated as such. Understandably, the IRA created divisions between peoples who had until then been united by cultural and historical bonds.

In addition, the governing structures and the law and order codes were Eurocentric. Neither was particularly sensitive to the vast cultural differences between the tribal communities and the framers of these documents, who resided far away in Washington. The federal bureaucrats made no attempt to accommodate these differences, with one exception. Some of these codes outlawed certain local customs deemed to be "barbaric" or "savage" (the Sun Dance was one such custom).

Not all communities adopted these IRA governing structures. Notably, the Navajo resisted these expressions of self-government and continued to exercise their own methods of governance. But they did so at a price. The principal incentive for the tribes to adopt the IRA forms of government was that only through these specific government structures could a tribe contract with the federal government for finances and services. Tribes that chose not to opt in were left out. Consequently, some tribes lacked the financial assistance needed for the development of their communities. Nevertheless, the Navajo and other tribes remained steadfast in their rejection of the IRA.

After the termination period ended in the 1960s, many socioeconomic programs became available to all tribes. Over the years, however, dissatisfaction with the IRA style of governance had grown. Many tribes believed that their traditional forms of government and law would serve their communities better. Thus, during the past thirty years, tribes have opted out of the IRA forms of government and their codes of behaviour. In their place, tribal governments have begun to develop institutions more culturally appropriate to their communities.

Today most tribal governments are elected by their communities. Often tribal councils have presidents or chairpersons. These community leaders enact criminal laws and a number of civil laws. Community decisions are made by a central government, by a local one, or sometimes by both. The Navajo Nation has a governing council located at Window Rock, Arizona, where decisions are made concerning its many communities, or chapters. These chapters are spread out over almost 18,000,000 square acres of land. However, each chapter has its own governing council to decide local issues.

The central government in Window Rock gives general direction and makes decisions for the Navajo Nation as a whole.

The Hopi tribe, whose reservation is located within the Arizona area of the Navajo Nation, resides on a territory spread out over 3,000,000 acres. The central tribal government has representation, based on population, from each of its nine communities. However, each "village" establishes how it will be governed locally. Some have elected councils, while others are led by religious leaders in a more traditional style of government. In these latter instances, there have been periodic disputes about whether the Hopi Tribal Council can speak on their behalf regarding certain matters.

Just next door, in the State of New Mexico, reside the Pueblo people, cultural cousins of the Hopi. The nineteen Pueblo reservations are loosely bound together by a Pueblo council. However, each reservation has its own independent government and its own unique laws. For example, the government on the Laguna reservation governs six communities and farming lands within its 412,000 acres. The Laguna tribal code authorizes the local courts to enforce Laguna tribal ordinances and traditional laws. These courts also enforce both federal and state laws when they do not conflict with local laws.[93] Appeals from the Laguna trial court are to the Laguna Court of Appeal. This court, also established pursuant to the tribal code, consists of a panel constituted by one representative from each of the six communities.[94]

The Laguna communities have highways, schools, health centres, churches, and commercial centres with an assortment of industries. The mining of uranium, carried out through leases with both tribal and non-tribal businesses, is a significant source of local income together with tribal enterprises such as an electronics plant. These communities exist in much the same manner as do small Canadian communities. They possess a cultural vigour drawn from their people, but like many other small communities they are subject to the whims of an uncertain marketplace.

However, if one were to consider simply the physical dimensions of these societies and judge them to be similar to most rural communities, then one would be greatly misled. These tribal communities are indeed different. The language most commonly spoken may be English, but an Aboriginal language is also frequently heard in these communities. Where the Native language has fallen into disuse, most communities have, over the past twenty years, invested considerable effort in reviving it. Similar efforts are under way in Aboriginal communities in Canada.

Local tribal laws may also be unfamiliar to outsiders. Some traditional Hopi villages recognize in law a grandmother's right of access to her grandchildren even while in the care of their natural parents. A grandmother's traditional teaching role vis-à-vis her grandchildren is both honoured and enforced by this unique customary law. Some matrilineal communities, such as those of the Pueblo, still use customary laws that pass all property to the wife's or mother's side of the family upon divorce or death. Other Navajo communities exercise traditions that pass property equally to all family survivors upon death, even though doing so sometimes results in the division of a small piece of land among so many survivors that the parcels are so small as to be virtually unusable. The Navajo are learning to adapt their traditional practices to accommodate better land usage. However, the strongly held values that underlie these customs mean that change occurs at a measured pace.

The value structure of these communities is often unique. (A traditional sense of values for most Aboriginal communities in North America is explored at some length in Chapter 6.) These values, expressed in laws dissimilar from the experiences of most people outside these communities, are also found in many of the community cultural festivals. These festivals, often tied to seasonal changes, are practised by most tribal communities. Not only are these practices culturally based, but many also have strong religious significance. Participation in them is generally voluntary, but in some circumstances, as in the case of the Laguna people of New Mexico, Pueblo members are required by law each year to participate in certain traditional customs (the Myadormos Ordinance is discussed in Chapter 6). They include not only practices that rehabilitate the physical structures of the Pueblo but also customs designed to reinforce the cultural and spiritual elements of this community. These customs do not typically have a coordinate expression in non-tribal communities.

Tribal educational institutions also vary dramatically from typical Eurocentric systems. Both primary and secondary schools are found in most tribal communities. The educational systems teach the usual courses in math, science, and the humanities, but they often teach something else as well, such as a tribe's unique history. Such courses would also include local myths, legends, and stories that relay the specific values and norms of the community. Perhaps the purpose of schooling in any community is to address similar goals, but these tribal teachings are often very dissimilar to those of Eurocentric educational systems. Hence, the values imparted by these lessons are similarly different from those of Eurocentric systems.

When one appreciates the many differences of a tribal community, it should not be too surprising that familiar languages, customs, and particularly value systems strongly motivate tribal members to cherish their unique expressions of self-government.

Tribal Forms of Justice

Court structures vary from tribe to tribe. Some tribes, such as the Laguna Pueblo, have both full-time and part-time judges. The appeal structure is constituted by representatives from the political arm of the government.

Council members sit as the appeals forum for all tribal court decisions at the trial level. Some have argued that such an appeal format ensures a culturally relevant resolution to the dispute. Others have argued that this format lends itself to a political bias in any decision. Both observations seem to be fair.

Some have tried to resolve the differences between these two opinions through the creation of a multiconstituted appeals forum. The Southwest Inter-Tribal Court of Appeal (SITCA) is just such a mechanism. This court is authorized to act as an appeals forum for regional tribal courts. Local tribes enter into an agreement with the SITCA to determine which kinds of dispute will be heard and which laws will govern the disposition of the appeal. The SITCA will then render decisions based on the laws and customs of the respective tribes.[95] Importantly, it has no authority to render a decision inconsistent with either source of law.[96] Hence the SITCA does not possess the authority to substitute what it may believe is a better legal principle. It is bound to work with the legal doctrines, case law, and local customs with which it has been provided. This forum is even used by tribes that have maintained more traditional court systems, notably Santa Ana and San Phillipe Pueblos. In such circumstances, advisory opinions are usually offered rather than official decisions. Although the SITCA process is a relatively new invention, some communities have their own similarly sophisticated approaches to justice.

Such is the diverse and intricate tribal court structure of the Navajo Nation. The reservation is divided into seven districts, each with its own trial-level district court. Each district court entertains both criminal and civil law actions. In addition to the district courts, these communities have access to family courts, where matters such as separation, support, and child custody are resolved. These trial-level courts make their determinations based on Navajo statutory law, customary law, local case law, and certain federal and state laws. The Navajo Supreme Court is the appeals forum for reviews of the decisions of these courts. The chief justice and two associate justices preside over all appeals.

Of considerable significance to those observing the development of tribal justice in the United States has been the evolution of the Navajo Peacemaker Court system. This unique process of dispute resolution was established on 23 April 1982. Its purpose was to act as an alternative forum for dispute resolution to the local district and family courts (the Navajo Children's Court, as it then was). These courts were generated by recognition that the adversarial context of the district courts was not as sensitive as it should be to certain cultural matters. Thus, the Peacemaker Court was created to instil a uniquely Navajo method of dispute resolution at a local government level.

The process is similar to the familiar forms of mediation but is heavily reliant on Navajo customary laws. The peacemaker is chosen from within the community by the parties[97] to the dispute. He or she may know the parties and must be familiar with Navajo customs and traditions. Within the context of the dispute, the peacemaker commonly reminds the disputants of their respective family and clan responsibilities. He or she also points out particular teachings or lessons from their common heritage. Thus, when necessary, they also play the role of teacher. Importantly, the peacemaker invites the participants to find their own resolutions to their problems within the context of Navajo culture. Unlike most mediators, a peacemaker takes an active role in the process. Proponents of the Peacemaker Court system believe that this type of consensus building is far preferable to the confrontational methods of Eurocentric courts, particularly for a culture that values the traditions of caring for and duty towards others (this issue is pursued at greater length in Chapter 6).

The Northwest Intertribal Court System (NICS) is yet another way in which tribal communities enforce their laws. This court system was established in 1979 by fifteen tribes in the State of Washington "to assist the member tribes, at their direction, in a manner which recognizes the traditions of those tribes in the development of tribal sovereignty, individual character, and courts which will provide fair, equitable, and uniform justice for all who fall within their jurisdiction."[98] To meet the terms of this mission, NICS established a circuit court structure to provide adjudicatory functions for its member tribes. Each of the member tribal nations – such as the Nooksack, Hoh, Tulalip, Sauk-Suiattle, and Swinomish – has a written constitution, and most have clearly articulated law and order codes (many of these tribes have redrafted their codes within the past twenty years). These codes enunciate local laws dealing with both criminal and civil matters, in particular family protection, juvenile justice, commercial licensing, taxation, zoning, and gaming. In addition, the codes provide for court procedures in both criminal and civil law cases, and they direct a "tribal court" or "court judge" to interpret the written law in a manner consistent with traditional practices. Not all the tribal codes clearly state these customs. The nature and content of the traditional laws are usually shared within oral customs. Hence, traditional laws and practices are only pleaded verbally by the parties at trial, with their application then decided by NICS.

The Northwest Intertribal Court System, the Southwest Inter-Tribal Court of Appeal, the Navajo traditional Peacemaker Court and district courts, as well as the Laguna Pueblo expression of trial- and appellate-level courts, reflect different forms of the same exercise. They represent a common intention by tribal communities to resolve internal problems in their own unique ways. Significantly, these courts are viewed from within as expressions of the domestic sovereign will of these tribal nations. The nature and scope of tribal jurisdictions, together with their respective constitutions and tribal codes, continue to evolve. Perhaps both the strengths and the weaknesses of these approaches will serve as models for the development of similar institutions in Canada in the years to come.

Comment

Over the years, tribal communities in the United States have reasserted a great deal of their inherent authority. Much of the criminal and civil law authority of these communities is now expressed through various forms of adjudication. These tribal communities are in large measure self-governing legislatively, administratively, and adjudicatively. However, seldom would any of them be mistaken for Utopia. Nor should they be.

These communities suffer from many of the same problems that afflict all communities in North America. Economic instability, unemployment, crime, and social decay have as serious an impact in these communities as they do in the small towns or large cities of Canada.

If one believes that, by simply recognizing Aboriginal self-government in Canada, these problems will disappear, then one need only consider the American tribal experience. Economic instability or high unemployment will not fade away simply because a local government has the power to so decree it. However, local governments may know how best to utilize resources within their communities in resolving such problems. Similarly, crime and social disruptions will not vanish just because an Aboriginal person occupies an adjudicatory position. However, US tribal courts, particularly more traditional ones such as the Navajo Peacemaker and the Pueblo courts, have illustrated that community problems are perhaps best resolved consensually rather than adversarially. American tribal communities have made great strides in undertaking the resolution of these and many other social problems, attracting health care, legal, and other professionals and initiating economic investment.

However, unlike other American communities, tribal ones still struggle to establish and maintain strong bonds with both federal and state governments. Tribal governments continue to come under attack from states wishing to exercise more control over territorial affairs, while the federal government seeks to lessen trust responsibilities to these communities. The federal-tribal trust relationship, recognized in the early Cherokee Nation cases, has obliged the federal government to expend millions of dollars on financing and social programs – an obligation from which it would like to extricate itself. In addition, some problems still exist in enforcing the decisions of tribal courts beyond reservation boundaries in state courts.[99] Similarly, states often refuse to cross-deputize tribal police officers, thus permitting criminal offenders to avoid prosecution by simply stepping over tribal boundaries. And the jurisdictional confusion over criminal law is aggravated by the failure of the federal government to adequately prosecute Major Crimes Act offenders. Few federal or state resources are expended on lands that produce little financial or political rewards. Thus, these communities are prevented by law from adequately defending themselves, while the federal government declines to properly exercise its authority. As a consequence, they can be left without adequate protection from criminal offenders.

Nonetheless, Canadians can learn from tribal experiences in the United States. They have time to avoid the mistakes and to improve the successes. Above all, Canadians should learn one lesson from the long evolution of tribal governance in the United States: it can be accomplished.

Two issues deserve comment here. The first concerns whether the developments in the United States, which clearly recognize a substantial degree of self-governing authority, achieve the level of self-direction sought by Aboriginal people in Canada. The evidence is that they do not. Aboriginal communities here would not be satisfied with a federal government that can overrule or even eliminate laws with which it does not agree. (This criticism, along with a number of other jurisdictional matters, will be considered more closely in Chapter 4.) Nevertheless, Canadian Aboriginal communities share the urge to exercise authority over broad areas of both criminal and civil law, as is currently accommodated by American constitutional law.

The second issue is that the American tribal experience does not characterize Aboriginal people in the same way as does the Canadian Constitution. Canada's fundamental law recognizes the Inuit, Métis, and Indian as three distinct Aboriginal peoples.[100] How will the separate peoples associate themselves so as to express their unique forms of self-government? Moreover, even within a group such as "Indian," how will First Nations articulate their right to self-government? Will they govern themselves based on distinctions in the Indian Act that have created over 500 reserves in this country? Is each community to be self-governing, even though many reserves now have fewer than 100 full-time residents? Or should regional governments be established based on provincial divisions or perhaps on associations premised on traditional cultural distinctions? An example of the latter would be the Six Nations peoples of Ontario and Quebec. Will a variety of communities be obliged to come together to establish a single government? If so, how?

Any attempt to resolve these questions would recognize cultural distinctions not only between Aboriginal peoples such as Inuit and Métis but also within an Aboriginal group such as First Nations. It would also recognize differences between southern and northern communities, isolated and less remotely situated communities, and rural and urban persons. These and other complementary issues will need to be engaged by Aboriginal people before they choose their political associations. In the end, Aboriginal communities themselves must decide where the authority of self-government will reside.

This belief is based on general notions of democracy as well as on current ideological approaches in international law. The right of Aboriginal peoples to both their existence and their cultural expression is pursued at some length in Chapter 6.[101]

The argument in favour of self-identification also receives support in Western political theory. When political scientists have asked why any government should have the right to impose laws or obligations on its citizens or, for that matter, why these citizens should comply, a contractual theory is often offered in reply. Political philosophers such as Thomas Hobbes, John Locke, Jean-Jacques Rousseau, and, more recently, John Rawls have all tendered a theory of "social contract" to explain their respective ideas concerning a government's balancing of personal obligations with individual rights. Social contract theory is essentially a tool of reasoning often used to justify or explain how autonomous individuals join together in a community and impose obligations on themselves through the establishment of a government while retaining certain basic freedoms. Often these rights have been characterized as fundamental or natural.[102] In general, this tradition has stated that citizens have implicitly, if not explicitly, contracted with one another to establish and bring themselves under the umbrella of some governing structure. Such a theory serves to legitimize the existence of a state and its institutions, such as concepts of justice, law making, and so forth. At the core of such legitimacy is the assertion that such states govern lawfully due to the accepted terms of this social contract. Indeed, they can claim to do so with a certain moral right. This process of "legitimization" further establishes a pedigree in which government actions and law making can be firmly entrenched.[103] In Canada, the Constitution acts reflect a modern form of social contracting. In particular, the Charter elements of the 1982 act clearly establish some of the fundamental liberties that the early social contract theorists only speculated upon.

Since it is widely accepted that this justification of state authority applies to Canadian governments, one would also expect it to apply to Aboriginal governments. Hence, what justifies treating Aboriginal people differently from other Canadians? In addition, for purely pragmatic reasons,[104] forcing a community of people to submit to a governing body not endorsed by them will ultimately lead to the disintegration of the community. For an example of how such meddling can undermine the effective governance of an Aboriginal community, one need only consider how the Indian Act has detrimentally affected the people of the Six Nations Confederacy.[105] Brian Maracle's vivid portrait of a community divided as a consequence of a government being imposed on it should give ample warning to those who would consider reiterating this mistake.

The concern that this self-identifying approach does not establish preordained rules and thus does not achieve the degree of certainty desired by some may be unfortunate. But uncertainty should not be a deterrent to accepting this position. Moreover, what is the rejoinder to a people's democratic expression of their right to choose how they will establish their governing structures? That such an approach will make it difficult for federal and provincial governments to negotiate with these communities is certainly a practical concern. But is there also some supporting objection out of principle? Perhaps in the law of contract, but surely not in democratic theory. Nor even in constitutional law, since this is the process of establishing the parameters of this very area of law. Thus, the argument against an Aboriginal people's right to determine their own structures of self-government is purely federal-provincial convenience. This is hardly a compelling argument. Since this is an exercise in nation building, a more principled and quite frankly more imaginative approach is called for.

But one must not minimize difficulties that may emanate from a self-identifying process that threatens to be unworkable. Should Aboriginal groups choose to establish themselves along Indian Act parameters, Canadian governments will be compelled to deal with over 500 self-governing communities. How would such an arrangement accommodate the effective provision of services, such as health care or housing, to these communities? How could Canadian governments reasonably be expected to negotiate jurisdictional disputes with these governments or provide block transfer payments to support these communities, as some have suggested?

It seems to be a fair assumption that, without some symmetrical way of engaging these communities, the ability of Canadian governments to accommodate their concerns about services and jurisdictions will be greatly impaired. But is the fundamental assumption realistic? Should Canadian governments be so concerned about this possibility? Probably not.

Aboriginal communities are well aware of the issue, for the Charlottetown discussions dealt specifically with it. Conferences that address the general topic of Aboriginal self-government often include a session or two about which communities are to be self-governing. The final report of the Royal Commission on Aboriginal Peoples provided its own recommendations on the matter. Unfortunately, these recommendations were unremarkable.[106] Thus, with so much discussion of the topic, Aboriginal people are likely well aware of the advantages provided by concepts such as economies of scale. Similarly, they must be given credit for understanding the disadvantages of establishing self-governing communities that create a wholly unworkable basis for interacting with Canadian governments. If this is true, then why do governments assume that, in spite of this understanding, Aboriginal people will insist on doing just that? Why would any reasonable person believe that Aboriginal communities such as First Nations will turn a blind eye to these well-known issues and insist on the recognition of more than 500 separate governing entities? Surely they know that they more than anyone else have the most to lose by taking such a position. If there is any doubt about Aboriginal people understanding the implications of this issue, then one need only consider the present state of Aboriginal politics in Canada.

For years, Aboriginal communities have joined together in a variety of organizations to harness the advantages of unified economies and political associations. There is a host of national[107] and regional[108] Aboriginal organizations that conduct research, coordinate policy, implement programs, and represent various Aboriginal communities' interests. Indeed, the recent Nisga'a Treaty recognizes the Nisga'a Lisims government as the sole government entity entitled to carry on intergovernmental relations with its federal and provincial partners. The four villages within the Nisga'a territory are authorized to govern only local functions.[109] The Nisga'a people agree that these separate communities are precluded from exercising any intergovernmental relations. Apparently, the benefits of uniting their many concerns within a single governing structure are well appreciated by the Nisga'a people.

Thus, misgivings about how Aboriginal communities will align themselves seem to be misplaced. One reason for this cynicism may simply be naïveté. A less generous interpretation would suggest that many still view Aboriginal people as unsophisticated and in need of guidance from those who think they know better. One can only hope that this latter opinion is in the minority.

For those who remain concerned about proceeding down the self-government path before this matter can be completely nailed down, consideration of how a similar dilemma has been treated elsewhere may be helpful. Cosmologists have theorized that the universe originated from a single explosion. This "big bang" theory has never been confirmed, nor has anyone adequately explained just how or why such a massive explosion took place. The failure to fully explain the origins of the universe has left humankind with a profound gap in its collective understanding of not only the cosmos but of science itself. And yet this deficiency has not prevented these same scientists from continuing to plot the stars, sending manned craft into space, and occasionally using Mars as a cosmological dartboard for unmanned spacecraft.[110] The point being, life must go on, for both science and Aboriginal self-government, notwithstanding the absence of a clear appreciation for how all the facts will play themselves out. The implications of waiting for complete certainty, which may never arrive, are just too onerous.

3
Entrenching Self-Government: The Treaty Option

The Charlottetown Accord included a proposal for the entrenchment of the right of Aboriginal self-government.[1] Ultimately, this proposal, together with all of the non-Aboriginal proposals in the accord, was subsequently rejected by the Canadian public in the referendum of 1992. However, one must be cautious about reading too much into the public's feelings about self-government just because the whole accord was rejected. This rejection was not determinative of the issue of self-government. Recently, the federal and provincial governments have undertaken discussions with Aboriginal leaders to consider the process of achieving Aboriginal self-government, albeit in a non-constitutional manner. Indeed, the federal government has also recently undertaken an initiative with the Congress of Aboriginal Peoples to discuss a number of issues affecting Aboriginal people. Principal among these issues, at least for Aboriginal people, remains the reaffirmation of the constitutional entrenchment of the right of Aboriginal self-government.[2]

Should the present discussions between the principal Aboriginal organizations and the federal and provincial governments produce a renewed commitment to entrenching Aboriginal self-government, a challenging task remains. How does one recognize this self-government authority? That is, given the intention to entrench this recognition, how can it be achieved so that Aboriginal people's interests will be adequately recognized and protected? Furthermore, how can this goal be achieved while at the same time recognizing and balancing federal and provincial concerns about preserving a workable Canadian federation?

Parties to Any Constitutional Amendment

When the subject of Aboriginal self-government is discussed, Aboriginal parties tend to focus on three issues. First, they cannot receive fair treatment within the present federal system of government. Second, they can manage their own communities better than the current governments. And third, due to the unique history of the occupation of these lands, Aboriginal people have a prior and inextinguishable right to govern themselves.[3]

Aboriginal people commonly justify the first claim by pointing to the disproportionate number of Aboriginal people in Canadian prisons. Consequently, when the issue of self-government is raised, not far behind is usually a discussion of a justice system that will be more sensitive to the circumstances of the Aboriginal community and offender. However, despite the pressing need to make the criminal justice system more sensitive to the needs of Aboriginal people, the administration of this system is only a tiny part of the day-to-day expression of Aboriginal self-government. Indeed, if criminal law authority were the only power being sought, then the scope of discussions would be far more limited, as would be the number of parties to these negotiations.

As illustrated in Chapter 2, Aboriginal communities seek the authority to determine a multitude of expressions of self-government. They include determining educational and health standards, zoning bylaws, traffic laws, rules regarding personal and commercial contracts, taxation laws, and an assortment of everyday matters that affect every community in this country. Hence, people should be disabused of the perception that Aboriginal people seek greater control of their communities only in the area of criminal justice.

Noteworthy about this (incomplete) list of jurisdictions is that, with few exceptions, these areas reside within the provincial domain. In a bilateral agreement, the federal government may be able to negotiate a recognition of Aboriginal jurisdictions, which may be found within Section 91 of the 1867 Constitution Act (these include authority regarding matters affecting unemployment insurance, banks, fisheries, copyrights, marriage, divorce, and so forth). However, the federal government has no mandate to negotiate the powers of the provincial governments found in Section 92 of the act. Even the administration of federal criminal law authority is tied to provincial responsibility for the administration of justice.[4] This has significant consequences for the constitutional revision regarding Aboriginal self-government. Clearly, any effort to extend the self-governing authority over these civil law areas will involve discussions to which the provinces must be parties.[5]

It is important to recognize, however, that provincial participation is not required because the new Aboriginal government would receive any of the provincial government's authority in these areas. Indeed, discussions to date have presumed an inherent authority as the basis for the recognition of Aboriginal self-government. Thus, the provinces would not devolve any current jurisdiction to Aboriginal governments. However, since the provinces now exercise jurisdiction over many areas that would have to be shared in the future, the provinces would have to agree with these developments.[6]

This requirement may be unpalatable for certain Aboriginal communities. Although some Métis people have had a long history of dealings with provincial governments, there has commonly been a great deal of animosity between provincial governments and First Nations. Reluctance by some First Nations to negotiate with provincial governments will have to be overcome. However, notwithstanding present legal requirements (e.g., demands in Part V of the Constitution Act, 1982), the provincial level of government should be represented in any discussions, for purely practical reasons.

It is important that one appreciate that the most commonly exercised authorities that Aboriginal governments are seeking are those similarly exercised by provincial governments. To ensure cooperative coexistence between Aboriginal governments and their anticipated principal sources of jurisdictional conflict, the provinces, the latter parties will have to attend any negotiations for self-government. Aboriginal parties will have to bear this in mind when considering what approaches to take in the negotiations.

The Treaty Option

Treaties have always been of great significance to Aboriginal people, who have viewed them as reflections of the nation-to-nation basis for the relationship between Canada's governments and Aboriginal peoples. Much case law has not only supported this historical perspective of the socio-political development of this country but also reinforced the notion of Aboriginal people as distinct Canadians. Therefore, it is not surprising that treaties have been proposed by Aboriginal people as a process for the entrenchment of the right of self-government.[7] Another significant reason for considering a treaty process is that the Royal Commission on Aboriginal Peoples proposed this tool as the chief vehicle for entrenching and implementing the terms of Aboriginal self-government. Although the RCAP recommendation and the treaty option proposal are not identical, they propose an approach that should be considered. However, there has been little discussion of the merits of this mechanism.

Much of the discussion of treaty making finds its genesis not in any particular section of the Canadian Constitution but in the Aboriginal perception of nation-to-nation bilateral relations between "peoples." Many Aboriginal people assert that their nations occupied these lands long before Europeans waded ashore centuries ago. And, despite the evolution of the present relationship with Canadian governments, these Aboriginal peoples still exist, though perhaps somewhat the worse for wear. Consequently, Aboriginal people believe that their inherent right as a people to deal with another people still exists. Thus, they have often warmed to the idea of continuing the nation-to-nation relationship through some process of bilateral agreement, in this instance a treaty.

Since the first ministers' conferences of the 1980s, the First Nations of the Prairie provinces have been strong proponents of this position. Given the intense ideological commitment of these communities to their present treaties, it is not surprising that they have proposed a treaty mechanism as the desired manner of entrenching self-government.[8]

Notionally, the argument has merit, at least among Aboriginal people; the difficulty is in finding a way to make it work. Aboriginal parties to the first ministers' conferences of the 1980s proposed the treaty option as a way of enshrining Aboriginal rights in the Constitution. However, they also argued that this treaty process should be bilateral, much as were those associated with the numbered treaties.[9] That is, the provinces should be excluded from such negotiations. It is doubtful that such a proposal will ever bear fruit.

It is broadly accepted in law that the federal government can make treaties, but possessing the authority to sign a treaty is not the same as having the authority to implement one. As once observed by Che Guevara, "It is easier to make a revolution than it is to make a revolution work." Similarly, the federal government has found to its consternation that it is easier to sign a treaty than it is to implement it.

Most people view treaties as formal binding agreements between international parties within an international forum. The federal government of Canada has always argued that it need look no further than its international status as an independent sovereign to make such treaties. The Constitution refers in Section 132 to the "Parliament and Government of Canada" as possessing all the powers necessary for the proper performance of its obligations.[10] This section has been interpreted by the Supreme Court of Canada as enabling the government of Canada to sign treaties. It has also been argued that the "peace, order, and good government" clause of the Constitution Act, 1867, enables the federal authority to make treaties. Hence, the ability of the federal government to sign treaties is not in doubt. Fulfilling the terms of a treaty, however, is a completely separate matter.

The Need for Agreement
In 1935, the government of Canada ratified three treaties that dealt with what might generally be characterized as commitments to the implementation of progressive labour law standards. Canada had adopted these conventions earlier as part of its commitment to the International Labour Organization, of which it was a member. However, when Parliament sought to enact legislation adopting these conventions, the government of Ontario argued that the essential subject matter of the treaty fell within a provincial government's jurisdiction. Consequently, Ontario claimed that Parliament could not fulfil the terms of the treaty through legislative enactments.

In 1937, the Privy Council agreed,[11] declaring that, if the subject matter falls within federal jurisdiction, then Parliament is free to enact the terms of the treaty. However, if the subject matter more properly falls within the provincial domain, then the federal authority cannot unilaterally enact such legislation, even if the federal government has already agreed to the terms of the treaty. This decision gave the federal government the unenviable task of having to bring all relevant provinces on side to pass the provincial legislation necessary to enable the terms of the treaty to be met.[12]

The implications of this decision are profound for Aboriginal peoples. The requiem often heard in many Aboriginal communities (almost exclusively First Nations) is that the historical nation-to-nation relationship exists only between Aboriginal people and the federal authority. This relationship does not include provincial governments, and the numbered treaties are commonly used as an example of this relationship. However, the labour conventions case indicates that, if a treaty-making process were adopted, and if provincial powers were the subject of negotiations, then the provincial governments must be involved in this process. Moreover, the level of involvement would likely be substantially more than that of a consultative party. In point of fact, the provinces would have to agree to the terms of any such agreement, at least if the Aboriginal governments wished to exercise jurisdiction, which presently resides within this group of government powers. Although some First Nations prefer not to negotiate with provincial governments, the relevant law indicates that a compromise is necessary, and some First Nations have been willing to consider such a compromise. Any treaty-making process must, out of legal necessity, be trilateral.

However, this scenario presents another problem for the Aboriginal proposal of the treaty option. The treaty option proposal put forth by Aboriginal parties at the first ministers' conferences was characterized by them as possessing international status. In particular, it was proposed that the treaties between peoples be enforced within the international forum. Vague references to the use of the International Court of Justice as a forum for enforcement, should one side not meet its obligations, were not uncommon. However, such propositions pose serious difficulties.

Although Canadian law views the federal government as possessing the power to engage in international treaties, no such inherent authority has been recognized in the provincial governments. They regularly enter agreements with other international states for the enforcement of custody or maintenance orders, reciprocal commercial arrangements, and so forth. But these are not treaties. They have not been recognized either domestically or internationally as such. Thus, how does a provincial government sign an internationally recognized treaty when neither Canadian nor international law recognizes its "standing" as a party to the agreement? A province might argue that, since Section 132 of the Constitution is equivocal on the treaty-making authority of the federal government, and since the Constitution is otherwise silent on the matter, the provinces must also have some degree of treaty-making authority. If this argument has support from the Supreme Court of Canada, it has not yet been expressed.[13] Consequently, it appears that the provinces have no authority under the Constitution to be full signatories to any trilateral international treaty. Similarly, international law does not recognize the authority of provincial or purely domestic governments to enforce their agreements in an international forum.

This analysis presents a disturbing proposition. Once again Aboriginal people would be subject to the threat of broken treaty promises. Should Aboriginal communities sign treaties with the federal authority (though doing so also presents problems, as will be illustrated), unless the subject matter that falls within provincial jurisdiction is implemented by the provinces, the Aboriginal parties will not be able to enforce them, certainly not by any international dispute mechanisms, as would be their preference. The inclusion of the provinces as a party to such international agreements in order to address this deficiency has no support in law. Once again, Aboriginal parties would face the prospect of being left with promises not honoured.

Aboriginal people have their own problem of "standing" in the treaty-making process. As has been stated, treaties are international agreements between internationally recognized parties – in other words, recognized sovereign states.[14] The difficulty for Aboriginal people seeking to utilize the treaty option is that no Aboriginal people in Canada possesses this internationally recognized distinction. Although they may be recognized in international law as a "people," this is not the same as being recognized as a "state" or "nation-state." Since a state alone possesses the authority to sign international treaties as a party, Aboriginal people have an obvious problem. Notwithstanding the sociopolitical merits of the nation-to-nation argument, recognition of their desired legal standing does not exist in Canadian or international law.

Consequently, this type of international treaty making as represented by the treaty option seems to be beyond the present reach of Aboriginal people. However, another type of treaty making not only avoids the problems of standing and implementation but also reflects the very process that many Aboriginal people have in mind. Although it would not provide the same status that arguably accrues to international treaties, it is significant.

The Constitution Act, 1982, included in Part II recognition of a special kind of treaty-making process. Section 35(3) states that, "For greater certainty, in subsection (1) 'treaty rights' includes rights that now exist by way of land claims agreements or may be so acquired." This subsection not only recognizes the existence of constitutionally protected treaty rights but also clearly anticipates a process for the acquisition of such rights in the future. Some kind of treaty-making process could thus be undertaken. The James Bay and Northern Quebec Agreement is a good example of the type of agreement that could justifiably fall within the ambit of this subsection.

But perhaps there is a difficulty in using this subsection to resolve self-government issues. It is arguable that the rights covered by subsection 35(3) can be realized only through a pact that also involves a transfer of land rights. The rights referred to in this subsection appear, at least on the surface, to be tied to land claims negotiations. The James Bay and Northern Quebec Agreement contains significant provisions for the disposition of land and may be a good example of the purpose anticipated by this subsection. However, if this is the case, then this vehicle is certainly not the one on which Aboriginal peoples wish to climb aboard.

It is doubtful that Aboriginal people will agree that the recognition of their inherent right of self-government will only be given in exchange for property or land rights. Aboriginal people assert that there is currently an insufficient land base to support existing populations, let alone future generations. There is no intention among Aboriginal people to bargain away more land in exchange for an inherent authority that, they argue, they already possess, despite the absence of clear recognition of the nature and scope of this authority in the Constitution.

Moreover, a land base is simply not pertinent to many matters over which Aboriginal jurisdiction is sought, matters dealing with who is to be subject to the jurisdiction of an Aboriginal court, criteria to be used in deciding local child custody decisions, or which form of Aboriginal government is to be implemented. Hence, any attempt to use subsection 35(3) as a tool to link these matters with the resolution of land claims agreements is simply inappropriate.

Thus, a plain reading of the subsection seems to limit its application to land claims processes.[15] Where issues of self-government do not involve land disposition, the subsection would simply not apply. Accordingly, self-government jurisdiction would be denied to an Aboriginal community that does not possess land with which to bargain or that simply refuses to negotiate for something that it claims to possess inherently. If it is appropriate to use subsection 35(3) only when land is part of the negotiations, then this vehicle will be rejected by many Aboriginal governments.

However, there may be even more serious problems associated with the treaty-making process as the preferred method of entrenching self-government. Although treaties may offer each Aboriginal community the opportunity to negotiate its own deal and, therefore, provide some flexibility in approach, this argument is more tenuous than it sounds.

Parties to the negotiations will not come to the table with equal bargaining positions or the same commitment to the process. An Aboriginal negotiating team will have fewer physical and financial resources than will a provincial or federal delegation. Also, if an Aboriginal community has little with which to bargain, then the result of any treaty negotiations may not be very promising for this community.

Furthermore, should a party such as a provincial government not be overly interested in accommodating the interests of the Aboriginal party, how will the Aboriginal party induce the provincial government to compromise? Even if provincial reluctance to bargain in good faith is overcome, any treaty process will produce a patchwork of varying jurisdictions of Aboriginal self-government across Canada. This is perhaps the most significant criticism of the practice of using a negotiating model (the treaty option) as the forum for establishing a community's fundamental rights.[16]

Using treaty negotiations to establish the fundamental recognition of self-government will no doubt result in a variety of formats for governance. However, this is to be expected since there are so many different cultural groups, each with its own form of both traditional and modern government, across this country. This in itself does not present any significant concern. The real problem is not that the forms of government will vary but that the essences of their respective authorities will not be the same.

In one instance, a community may be able to negotiate the recognition of a large measure of civil and criminal law jurisdiction. Meanwhile, in another part of the country, discussions may result in Aboriginal communities negotiating something more akin to the authorities of a municipal government, with little or no judicial enforcement authority over its legislative enactments. Aboriginal communities that are more resource rich or perhaps more culturally adaptive to the negotiating process may be the greatest beneficiaries. Meanwhile, smaller, perhaps more rural or traditional, communities will receive less benefit from these negotiations simply because they are either less culturally motivated, professionally prepared, or resource rich.

If the principal motivation for using a treaty-making vehicle is to recognize the inherent right of self-government, which is presumed to be found in Section 35, and to do so in a traditional and culturally respectful way, then the treaty process does not appear to provide an appropriate mechanism for Aboriginal people. If the treaty option is to be viewed as viable, it must meet at least the threshold of adequacy. This would appear to be highly unlikely.

Enforcement
The treaty option presents a further difficulty for Aboriginal people, that of enforcement. International treaties often include terms clarifying methods of enforcement. International covenants such as free-trade agreements typically include mechanisms for the resolution of disputes. These agreements

often provide for institutions such as arbitration panels that may be constituted to resolve such disputes, with their judgments binding on the parties. Failure by a party to comply with the finding of the panel would result in further sanctions in the international forum. However, if a Canadian government party fails to meet its obligations under a self-government treaty, then where would Aboriginal people go to enforce their rights?

Perhaps a Canadian court could enforce the terms of a treaty, but what if the treaty-making process itself were unduly delayed? This may occur when a Canadian government fails to negotiate expeditiously or bargains in bad faith. Where does one find a remedy for these difficulties? Moreover, which remedies are available to ensure commitment to the treaty-making process? Delaying the process is not inconsequential, and the Charlottetown Accord included terms to address this issue (as discussed in Chapter 8).

Although current international law may provide a system of redress for these issues,[17] Aboriginal communities would be without standing in international forums. This would leave only domestic courts as a potential mechanism of enforcement for treaty-related disputes. Historically, these courts have not been kind to the interests of Aboriginal parties. It would be foolish for an Aboriginal party to enter negotiations concerning its future without knowing that the negotiations would proceed expeditiously and in good faith and that the eventual agreement would be enforced. No such assurances currently exist in Canadian law.

The Canadian Constitution contains its own enforcement mechanisms. However, the question remains whether these mechanisms could resolve nation-to-nation treaty disputes. Subsection 24(1) provides a means for the enforcement of violations of the Charter of Rights: "Anyone whose rights or freedoms, as guaranteed by this Charter, have been infringed or denied may apply to a court of competent jurisdiction to obtain such remedy as the court considers appropriate and just in the circumstances."[18] Although this subsection provides a broad choice of remedies, it is doubtful that it could be used to enforce the treaty-making process anticipated by subsection 35(3). Subsection 24(1) refers specifically to "rights or freedoms, as guaranteed by this Charter," and there is no reason to believe that these "rights and freedoms" include the right to self-government, the intended object of treaty negotiations. The Aboriginal self-government and treaty sections are found outside the Canadian Charter of Rights and Freedoms, which is found in Part I of the act. This perception is reinforced by the wording of Section 25:

> The guarantee in this Charter of certain rights and freedoms shall not be construed so as to abrogate or derogate from any aboriginal, treaty or other rights or freedoms that pertain to the aboriginal peoples of Canada including

(a) any rights or freedoms that have been recognized by the Royal Proclamation of October 7, 1763; and

(b) any rights or freedoms that now exist by way of land claims agreements or may be so acquired.

It appears that this section is intended to protect treaty rights from Charter intrusions. If this interpretation is sound, then it would naturally preclude Section 24 as a treaty enforcement mechanism.

Another enforcement mechanism perhaps available to subsection 35(3) treaties is found in Section 52(1) of the Constitution Act: "The Constitution of Canada is the supreme law of Canada, and any law that is inconsistent with the provisions of the Constitution is, to the extent of the inconsistency, of no force or effect."[19] This section clearly anticipates federal and provincial legislation thought to be contrary to the Constitution. This is the entrenchment section, which serves to provide the greatest protection for those rights enshrined within the Charter. There is little disagreement that it is this section that will in future provide the Canadian courts with the greatest amount of judicial scrutiny of Canadian laws. But it is unclear how a section whose principal remedy, that of essentially nullifying legislation, would be flexible enough to address a kaleidoscope of issues presented by a treaty designed to recognize and implement Aboriginal self-government. Presumably, one would intend not to nullify legislation but to recognize and implement a jurisdiction. Clearly, the broad and flexible enforcement provision in Section 24, which permits one "to obtain such remedy as the court considers appropriate," is far superior. Unfortunately, as just illustrated, it would appear not to be available to Aboriginal parties.

There is, however, a way out of this dilemma. The Constitution could be amended to reflect the right of Aboriginal self-government through a clearly defined treaty-making mechanism. This amendment would overcome some of the legal impediments referred to earlier. However, any constitutional amendment that enables the treaty-making process to entrench Aboriginal self-government would face a series of other dilemmas. How would such a mechanism work? Would it be judicial? How would such a tribunal be constituted? Would it include Aboriginal participation? Who would be entitled to exercise or enforce the treaty process? Communities or individuals? Which remedies would be available to it? Would principles of traditional Aboriginal law be used for the interpretation of the treaties or would only Eurocentric laws be used? If there are to be Aboriginal rules of construction, then what might they be? Is there to be an appeals forum for this treaty process? Will it be domestic or international?

Even if a constitutional amendment recognized a forum for negotiating an Aboriginal self-government authority, there is a host of other problems. Thus, perhaps any effort to overcome the obvious difficulties attendant upon a constitutional revision to accommodate the treaty option out-weighs the value that might derive from that effort. A brief review of the recently negotiated Nisga'a Treaty may provide further incentive for recon-sidering the merits of the treaty option.

The Nisga'a Lessons

In early November 1998, the Nisga'a Nation of British Columbia reached an agreement with the federal government and the BC government concern-ing a land claims dispute.[20] This treaty was the product of negotiations begun more than twenty years earlier. The treaty provides the Nisga'a Nation with ownership of almost 2,000 square kilometres of land as well as approximately $500 million in cash, grants, and program funding ($165.7 million in cash). Importantly, for present purposes, this agreement also pro-vides for a degree of self-governing authority over Nisga'a people and land. The parties to this agreement intend it to be considered as a treaty within the terms of Section 35(3) of the Constitution Act, 1982.[21] As such, it will receive both the unique recognition and the protection that the section affords (the limitations imposed on Section 35 agreements are discussed in Chapter 8).

Before discussing some of the particular terms of this treaty, I should clar-ify one point. This agreement began as a land claims dispute and must be considered as a treaty that, first and foremost, addresses this issue. Clearly, most of the treaty's terms deal with land claims matters. Over the many years of negotiations, the issue of self-government for the Nisga'a Nation achieved greater prominence. In the end, the treaty included significant terms that address the subject of Nisga'a self-government. Had negotiations begun exclusively with the issue of self-government, the result might have been quite different. Some of the Nisga'a voters asked to ratify the treaty over two days of voting on 6 and 7 November 1998 expressed to the media reservations about the limitations of the self-government provisions. Nev-ertheless, it seems that these persons approved the package, if only to achieve resolution of the land claim. Similarly, the Nisga'a would likely have focused their efforts differently had the negotiations been only about self-government. This point should be kept in mind when one considers the outcome of these negotiations for self-government purposes.

The Nisga'a achieve a great deal with this treaty. It recognizes the Nisga'a Nation as a self-governing entity and establishes two levels of Nisga'a gov-ernment. The Nisga'a Lisims (central) government speaks on behalf of the Nisga'a Nation on many matters. Not only is it entitled to enact and enforce a broad set of laws over its territory, but it also provides the only avenue for intergovernmental relations with the federal and provincial gov-ernments.[22] The four Nisga'a villages also exercise government authority but at a more local level and only over their respective communities.[23]

Three urban locals, comprised of Nisga'a citizens living in urban centres,[24] also participate directly in the governing of the Nisga'a community.[25] The treaty provides these urban locals with direct input into governing decisions made in Nisga'a territory.

The treaty establishes a constitutional form of government.[26] This constitution provides for a variety of contingencies, among them the basic authority of Nisga'a governments, a process for enacting laws, the constitution of courts, the establishment of rules for conflicts of interest, and the requirements for democratically accountable governments. The treaty also requires that any subsequent amendment to this constitution will require a public referendum in which a minimum of 70 percent of the votes cast must approve of the proposed changes.[27]

The treaty also makes provisions for persons living within Nisga'a territory who are not Nisga'a citizens.[28] Importantly, it is the Nisga'a Nation that determines Nisga'a citizenship.[29] However, persons living in or conducting activities in Nisga'a territory whom Nisga'a law determines are not Nisga'a citizens are not forgotten by the treaty. The Nisga'a government is required to consult with these individuals when Nisga'a laws or institutions affect them. This could include decisions regarding education, health, or land zoning. Indeed, the Nisga'a have agreed to establish formal participation and appeal processes to accommodate non-Nisga'a persons affected by these and other matters. The Nisga'a have even gone so far as to ensure that these non-Nisga'a citizens can participate as members in Nisga'a public institutions.[30] These sections of the treaty thus attempt to balance the interests of both Nisga'a and non-Nisga'a persons occupying Nisga'a lands.

The treaty also attempts to balance the interests of the Nisga'a legislative authority with those of the federal and provincial governments. The agreement does not articulate each area of jurisdiction over which the Nisga'a governments may pass laws; it simply states that the Nisga'a can enact and exercise laws subject to this agreement and that this jurisdiction will evolve over time.[31] This may constitute a statement of limitations, but it also appears to provide for a certain flexibility and growth.

The agreement goes on to explain where the Nisga'a governments are clearly entitled to exercise their authority, and it states that, in many instances of conflict between Nisga'a law and federal or provincial law, Nisga'a law will prevail. These instances include laws concerning Aboriginal healing, child and family services, adoption, and education.[32] These are significant steps forward for the Nisga'a people. These sections of the treaty provide the Nisga'a Nation with an opportunity to exercise jurisdiction over areas for which they have long sought control. It appears that this increased jurisdiction will provide the Nisga'a people with an opportunity to have an immediate impact on matters that affect their day-to-day lives.

However, not all the terms of this treaty provide such favourable interpretations. A number of areas of jurisdiction will not yield such a broad exercise of Nisga'a authority. To begin with, the Nisga'a governments have no independent authority to raise revenue through gaming. The ability to license gaming houses (i.e., casinos) is still entirely within the competence of the government of British Columbia.[33] Although the Nisga'a are recognized as having the final say as to whether casinos and similar gaming houses can be established in their communities, the treaty does not recognize their authority to arbitrarily establish them. It will still be the provincial government that determines whether the Nisga'a can take advantage of this valuable source of community financing.

Similarly, Nisga'a governments have no criminal law authority.[34] They can only exercise jurisdiction over activities that constitute a "nuisance, trespass, danger to public health, or threat to public order, peace, or safety."[35] Moreover, even if they enact laws in these rather limited areas, unless they are consistent with federal or provincial laws of general application, they are unenforceable.[36] The treaty also stipulates that the Canadian Charter of Rights and Freedoms must apply to Nisga'a forms of government.[37] (The many problems created for Aboriginal communities by the Charter are discussed in Chapter 6.)

Similar limitations are imposed in other areas. The Nisga'a are permitted to exercise jurisdiction over industrial relations and employment standards[38] but not to the exclusion of federal or provincial jurisdiction.[39] Buildings, structures, and public works also fall within the legislative competence of Nisga'a governments; however, if a conflict arises, then federal and provincial laws prevail. The same rule applies to the solemnization of marriages,[40] the regulation of intoxicants,[41] social services,[42] and health services.[43] Even the regulation of traffic, described by the treaty as municipal,[44] may be overruled if Nisga'a laws conflict with federal or provincial laws of general application. One might characterize such terms as giving with one hand while taking back with the other, at least in instances when the Nisga'a intend to enact laws at odds with federal and provincial laws.

If one were to turn a critical eye to other areas of this package, similar blemishes reveal themselves. For example, even in regard to matters in which the Nisga'a governments exercise paramount authority over conflicting federal and provincial legislation,[45] the Nisga'a laws are often required to meet federal or provincial standards if they are to be enforced.[46] Alternatively, Nisga'a authority is simply proscribed from legislating in certain federal areas of competence.[47] Thus, even in instances when Nisga'a jurisdiction is paramount, Nisga'a latitude in enacting culturally novel laws may be quite limited.

Perhaps an example of such culturally conflicting laws would prove useful. Some of the standards imposed on the Nisga'a appear to many to be reasonable. The requirement in Section 106(a) that Nisga'a laws regarding adoption "expressly provide that the best interests of the child be paramount" seems to be a reasonable limitation. Whose interests could be more important than the child's in such matters? But this may not be the proper question or at least not the only question worth asking. Chapters 5 through 7 illustrate the unique perspective of many Aboriginal people regarding their communities. This view is much more collective or communitarian than that reflected in most Western liberal democracies. Hence, many Aboriginal communities may argue that a communitarian interest be reflected in laws regarding adoption. For example, the interests of a community may best be served by having a child remain within the community (perhaps the child's role within a clan or family would support this view). In such a case, a decision on adoption might give equal consideration to both the community's interests and the child's interests. One can imagine circumstances in which competing interests in adopting a child have great merit. In either home, a child would be expected to flourish. Candidate A may score nine out of ten regarding the best interests of the child, while candidate B, though also highly regarded, may score only eight.[48] In such circumstances, candidate A, who lives outside the community, would be approved for adopting the child and permitted to take the child away from the community.

On the other hand, if a Nisga'a law also stipulates that the interests of the community must play a determining role in adoption, then these circumstances might change dramatically. If the child were to play an important cultural role in the community (see the discussion of the role of clans in Chapter 6), then candidate B would likely be chosen as the custodial parent. The child would then stay within the community, and both would prosper.

It should not be inferred that the best interests of the community always overrule the best interests of the child. The child's interests are always critical in these circumstances. Many Aboriginal communities would simply argue that other interests should also be part of the evaluation. But the way that the Nisga'a treaty currently reads, consideration of the community's interests would be minimized or even ignored once the child's best interests are ascertained. Such an approach would prove unsatisfactory to many Aboriginal communities, perhaps even the Nisga'a. A communitarian argument would simply require that the community's interests also receive consideration.

Whether such legislative constraints are specifically stated or only implied in the treaty,[49] they nevertheless impose clear limitations on the discretion of Nisga'a governments to enact laws deemed to be culturally relevant. Perhaps this suggests why the federal and provincial governments were prepared to allow Nisga'a laws to prevail in these instances of conflict.

If the Nisga'a laws are required to meet the thresholds established by the federal and provincial governments, how much of a real conflict should be expected to arise? Perhaps more importantly, how different and creative can the Nisga'a laws ever hope to be?

It is my intention neither to analyze the implications of this entire agreement nor to suggest that the Nisga'a Treaty is a poor settlement. It must be presumed that the Nisga'a people, who have spent so many years negotiating this agreement, know what is best for their communities. I do not pretend to take on a broader understanding of their circumstances. However, the Nisga'a Treaty constitutes a significant expression of what the federal government and the government of British Columbia view as acceptable Aboriginal self-government. In this context, then, it seems to be fair for other Aboriginal people to ask themselves whether they agree with this view. The answer must be an emphatic no.[50]

As I have already stated, this treaty was originally a land claims settlement. One might characterize the self-government elements as coming along for the ride. However, the fact that land claims issues were a significant bargaining chip in these negotiations is instructive. One should also understand that the Nisga'a people had a number of other advantages as they undertook this exercise. Having negotiated this treaty for more than twenty years, they accumulated a great deal of experience at bargaining within the dynamic of a tripartite forum. This is seldom an easy task. It is often difficult to balance the interests of a third party to any negotiations. In addition, the community possessed sufficient financial resources to engage the services of highly skilled lawyers, researchers, and negotiators.

It is also important to appreciate that the legal position of the Nisga'a was secure, at least insofar as these matters can be secure in Canadian law (see the discussion of *Sparrow* in Chapter 8). Significantly, no previous treaties or surrenders compromised the Nisga'a claim. Where treaties have been signed in other parts of the country, Aboriginal claimants have to contend with the argument that many of their rights have already been bargained away. No such argument could be made in this instance. In addition, the Nisga'a were secure in their ability to illustrate passive occupation of their lands, and they could document their traditional harvesting practices on and uses of the territory.[51] Normally, such matters play an integral part in deciding the issue of compensation. Finally, this community was united in its support for these negotiations. This is not always the case and can prove to be an Achilles' heel for Aboriginal negotiators.

However, in spite of the security of their legal arguments, ample historical evidence of occupation, the availability of land as a bargaining chip, the capability to finance needed professional expertise, and the solid support of the community, the Nisga'a received so very little self-government authority. Their jurisdictional capacity is largely limited to areas of municipal competence, and in times of conflict Nisga'a laws may be overruled by federal or provincial laws. Even potential conflicts will be constrained by the requirement that Nisga'a law meet federal and provincial threshold standards. This sort of self-government authority in no way resembles the nature and scope of jurisdictions secured for Aboriginal communities in the Charlottetown Accord (these jurisdictional powers are explained at some length in Chapter 8).

Again it should be remembered that this was essentially a land claims package and not a self-government negotiation forum. Many more issues were involved in these negotiations than will be on the table in future self-government packages. Yet perhaps this emphasizes the weakness of the treaty option even more cogently. If the Nisga'a people, with all the advantages of their bargaining position, could only achieve meagre municipal-like authority, then what lies in store for those Aboriginal people who do not share these strengths? What will happen if an Aboriginal community has little with which to negotiate? Or, in cases involving previous treaties and land surrenders, how profitable will negotiations be for these Aboriginal communities? How productive will negotiations be for a First Nation that must contend with other First Nations with overlapping claims in the territory?[52] What can Métis people expect when their legal and perhaps even constitutional status is not as securely recognized as that of First Nations? Can they expect to achieve even as much as the Nisga'a? Aboriginal communities should be concerned about the implications of the Nisga'a Treaty for any future self-government negotiations.

Media coverage of the final Nisga'a Treaty included a number of federal government representatives expressing the belief that this treaty was not to be seen as a template for future negotiations with other Aboriginal communities. It is uncertain how individuals can make such a statement binding on the federal government. Indeed, other federal spokespersons seem to believe that this treaty will have a significant impact on future negotiations: "Catherine MacQuarrie, the director of Aboriginal governance policy in Ottawa's Department of Indian Affairs, says that more than eighty self-government negotiations are going on across the country. And all are looking at the Nisga'a treaty."[53]

Nevertheless, even if the federal government takes the position that the Nisga'a agreement is unique and should have little or no bearing on future treaties, there is no reason to believe that the provincial governments will follow suit.[54] Many provincial leaders view the limited Aboriginal jurisdictions recognized in this treaty as being much easier to sell to their non-Aboriginal constituents than the third order of government powers proposed for Aboriginal people at Charlottetown. It is reasonable to assume that many governments will use the terms of the Nisga'a Treaty as a template for future negotiations in their provinces. There is little that any federal spokesperson can say to reassure Aboriginal people that this treaty has not set a standard for future treaty-negotiated forms of self-government.

Comment

Treaty making as a vehicle for the entrenchment of Aboriginal self-government has many drawbacks, all of which make it a dubious choice. Although the federal government is entitled to enter into international treaties, it often requires the cooperation of the provinces if the terms of an agreement are to be fulfilled. In the context of current discussions of self-government, the provinces' acquiescence to the terms of any agreement would be required. Moreover, the subject matter of Aboriginal self-government is so mixed with provincial jurisdiction that the provinces would no doubt desire equal roles in the development of treaties. In addition, the provinces appear to lack the capacity to play a fully participatory role in an international agreement, the type of agreement that many Aboriginal people seek. Aboriginal governments share this disadvantage.

Should the treaty-making process be less international and more domestic, the Constitution appears to anticipate such agreements in Section 35. However, it is doubtful that this process was designed to entrench Aboriginal self-government (or that it could do so satisfactorily). Arguably, this constitutional legislation is intended to resolve disputes more properly the subject of simple land transfers, though nothing about this subject area is simple either legally or politically. Pacts such as the James Bay and Nunavut agreements fall within this context. Notwithstanding the recent Nisga'a agreement in British Columbia, it is almost certain that most Aboriginal people would refuse to negotiate the entrenchment of Aboriginal self-government at the cost of losing more land rights,[55] particularly in exchange for something that they believe they already possess. The recently negotiated Nisga'a agreement should indicate that the treaty option, even when used in conjunction with land claims resolution, will produce little more than municipal-like authority. A treaty agreement without the negotiating leverage of a land claim seems to be destined to provide limited self-government authority.

Perhaps the most telling weakness of the treaty option is the practical costs involved. Most Aboriginal communities would be at a huge disadvantage in negotiations with the federal and provincial governments, for these communities vary greatly in the kinds of resources they bring to the negotiating table. Uneven financial, professional, and cultural resources will no doubt produce unequal results. Why should this happen if these communities arguably possess the same inherent right of self-government? No Aboriginal community has ever argued that it possesses a more fundamental right to self-government than another Aboriginal community.[56]

Aboriginal groups may differ in opinion as to who actually occupied a certain territory, but they do not dispute each other's entitlement to self-government. The result of the treaty option would be a patchwork of agreements across the country in which few Aboriginal communities would share self-governing authorities. Finally, the problems presented by the issue of enforcement, with either the international model or the domestic proposal under Section 35 of the Constitution Act, are prohibitive. It thus seems that the treaty option for the entrenchment of Aboriginal self-government presents a myriad of difficult if not insurmountable problems. Perhaps it is appropriate, then, to consider an alternative approach.

4
Entrenching Self-Government: The "Principled Approach"

If treaty making is not the most useful method for the entrenchment of Aboriginal self-government, then there is still the alternative of simply entrenching the general principle through a constitutional amendment. This may be recognized as the more typical tried and true approach. Notably, it is common to both the Canadian and the United States constitutions. This mechanism has been used to entrench, or "constitutionalize," individual rights such as those in Sections 2 through 15 of the Canadian Charter of Rights and Freedoms. The principled approach seems to work well in setting out in usually clear yet general terms the normative values or practices to be enshrined in the Constitution. Such a statement of principle – one that recognizes the right of Aboriginal self-government – may be useful in the present circumstances.

This is not to say that there will be no need for the courts to interpret these rights and to determine their precise meanings. Indeed, not only will there be an ongoing need for the courts to further explain the meaning of each right, as well as corresponding responsibilities of governments, but also history has shown that much of the struggle to understand the scope of rights in general becomes clearer when these rights "collide."[1] Often the greatest illumination of rights is achieved when each competes against another for its respective authority.

The entrenchment of self-government in a principled fashion also provokes a difficulty similar to that presented by the treaty option. That is, how does one interpret the content of the right to self-government? Which wording would best characterize the aspirations of Aboriginal peoples for self-government while at the same time addressing the concerns of both the federal and the provincial governments? One might argue that this task is perhaps best left to the participants in the negotiations. For present purposes, I will put aside the merits of this suggestion and focus on how any wording may be interpreted by the courts.

The overriding concern of Aboriginal people is that the Canadian courts will not recognize the newly entrenched principle of self-government in a balanced fashion. Aboriginal people believe that their interests have never fared particularly well before Canadian courts.[2] Simply put, they want to be assured that when their rights are to be enforced, the judicial mechanism for enforcement will act fairly. An element of this fairness must include viewing these entitlements within the proper cultural context. Hence, the method of interpretation becomes almost as significant as the wording itself.

William Pentney has provided some guidance on how this issue might best be approached, at least initially. He argues in support of a "first principle of interpretation" that proscribes any impairment of an Aboriginal community's capacity to survive.[3] This is instructive. His argument is that such first principles would guide the courts in protecting the right of self-government from undue intrusion. Now it is unlikely that federal and provincial governments will rush to accept a first principle that prohibits "any" intrusion upon the exercise of Aboriginal self-government, if only because their respective jurisdictions will be forced to give way in the face of the Aboriginal expression of self-government. In addition, the courts, particularly the Supreme Court of Canada, have a history of ensuring a certain jurisdictional balance between federal and provincial authorities. It therefore seems to be reasonable, as Pentney argues, that the inherent disposition of the courts themselves would limit the meaning of any entrenched right. His first principles approach therefore attempts to ensure that an Aboriginal self-government authority would be protected by attempting to tie the hands of the courts when it comes to exercising their discretion.

In essence, these first principles would act as interpretive tools to assist the courts in understanding the intent of the right of self-government that has been entrenched. However, Pentney's approach is not without difficulties. Indeed, the weakness in the first principles approach is the very one that Pentney originally sought to overcome.

It is reasonable to expect that the courts will be called on to determine exactly which meaning and use this interpretive first principle statement will have. The courts will always need to examine such interpretive tools for their own meanings, no matter how many are included in the Constitution to assist in giving clarity to the right of Aboriginal self-government. This has been the history of judicial scrutiny of other principles of interpretation, such as the paramountcy test, the pith and substance test, and the double aspect theory (all constitutional tools). Thus, a court will be free to determine whether these interpretive tools themselves are to be interpreted broadly or narrowly, actively or passively. Any decision that results from such a review can have profound effects on how the first principles will be applied.

The difficulty for the position of Aboriginal peoples is that, if a court is inclined toward maintaining much of the present balance in the federal structure, then such a court would more easily be persuaded to choose an interpretation of the first principle statement that most closely ensures the continuation of the present state of the federation. Thus, even with Pentney's first principles, the integrity of the right of self-government may still not escape the historical interpretive inclinations of the court.[4] Notwithstanding the difficulties inherent in the first principles approach, Pentney's proposal brings into focus the weakness inherent in simply entrenching a barren statement that recognizes Aboriginal self-government. The threat to the interests of any party – federal, provincial, or Aboriginal – is in how their collective understanding will be reflected by the courts. There is little doubt that Aboriginal interests are in the most jeopardy.

Simply entrenching the principle of the right of Aboriginal self-government does not therefore guarantee for Aboriginal people the fairest interpretation of its content. Aboriginal people clearly have a compelling interest in ensuring, as much as possible, the integrity of the process that will interpret the nature and scope of this authority. Although one can never be certain of the outcome of a court's deliberations, perhaps the unique[5] circumstances of this situation warrant giving some thought to altering how Canadian courts currently consider this important constitutional issue. In particular, Aboriginal people would be highly motivated to have their understanding of the intention of the language used in any amendment given the precise meaning agreed to by the parties. A number of avenues are available.

Innovative Alternatives

Consideration may be given to reconstituting the courts themselves to deal specifically with this problem. Federal and provincial courts of appeal might be required to have a permanent sitting Aboriginal Advisory Committee. This committee, presumably with some Aboriginal membership, would have expertise in Aboriginal culture and law. Acting in a purely advisory capacity, it would be available to the court to provide explanations on matters of interest in the proceedings. The committee would be a significant resource in cases that address Aboriginal issues. It might prove difficult to have such a committee available to every trial-level court, as the number of cases it might be asked to become involved in could prove to be overwhelming. Thus one might consider having a resource of this kind at least available to appellate-level courts. Alternatively, an Aboriginal person could be appointed to the bench to hear cases that address matters of Aboriginal jurisdiction. Again, this person would be used principally as a court resource, similar in function to the committee, though he or she would participate as a full member of the court. If actively employed, either option would have a significant impact on any decision of the court.

Suggestions such as these might offend those who would argue that this constitutes little more than a lobbying of special interests, an advantage not shared by non-Aboriginal litigants. Many believe that the present judicial system offers every opportunity for all parties to fairly represent their respective positions. Neutral and impartial adjudicators then determine who has presented the best legal case.

Such a position is at best naïve and at worst wilfully blind to the history of how the courts have treated Aboriginal people, women, the poor, and people of colour. This is not the place to debate the merits of Legal Realism, but the opinions of prominent jurists and scholars agree that there is a dire need to level the judicial playing-field.[6]

Another approach designed to assist judicial interpretation might be to create a court whose principal purpose would be to hear Aboriginal jurisdiction cases. This court could be staffed by both Aboriginal and non-Aboriginal members. Awareness of and sensitivity to Aboriginal issues would be the fundamental requirement of membership. This court could be constituted by appointments from federal, provincial, and Aboriginal parties. Given the unique status of this court, perhaps an appeal from this forum should be directly to the Supreme Court of Canada.

Whether or not any of these suggestions is adopted, some might argue that the Supreme Court of Canada should also have an Aboriginal member. Otherwise, gains achieved through culturally sensitive mechanisms at the initial appeal stage might be ignored by this court. An Aboriginal appointment to the Supreme Court may be designated to hear only cases relating to Aboriginal jurisdiction, Charter disputes (described at greater length in Chapter 6), and so forth. This appointment would not only bring a unique and sensitive perspective to the court but also encourage relationships between Aboriginal communities and the federal and provincial governments. It would no doubt also encourage Aboriginal confidence in other government institutions.

With any of the above suggestions, the Supreme Court would have the benefit of a broadly informed discussion of the issues and their potential consequences. It may be claimed that courts, in particular the Supreme Court, already hear evidence from a broad range of sources, including those that inform cultural issues. True, but such an assertion is misleading. Today representation on matters of this nature is often wholly dependent on the expertise of legal counsel. Unfortunately, such counsel is drawn from a source of uneven competence and expertise. This may result in the omission or mismanagement of significant facts or issues being pleaded at trial. By the time the case makes its way through the legal system to the Supreme

Court of Canada, critical issues have been diminished or characterized in such a way as to be of little use to Aboriginal people. An Aboriginal perspective on the bench could provoke inquiries of counsel and perhaps precipitate a better understanding of the case.[7] Such proposals could help to ensure a thorough articulation and analysis of the problems for the Supreme Court.

Anticipating reluctance to implement any of the aforementioned suggestions, particularly regarding the membership of the Supreme Court of Canada, I must stress one fact. I acknowledge that these proposals for discussion – and that is all they are – must seem to be somewhat extreme. However, surely the seriousness of present circumstances warrants an extreme remedy. These proposals are not premised on an idea that all interest groups should have some direct control over judicial decisions affecting them. Nor am I arguing that every racial or ethnic group should have representation everywhere throughout the judicial process. Rather, these proposals are premised on the belief that what one is creating is a fundamentally new constitutional relationship between "peoples." Given the profound significance of this new relationship, rethinking some of the structures that underlie current relationships between Canadians is warranted. Revitalization would be intended to enhance the new constitutional relationship between Canada and Aboriginal people. Indeed, after reviewing the respective merits of these and other proposals for reform, if any were found to impede the development of this new constitutional relationship, no doubt it would be rejected by the parties. Often a new relationship demands new perspectives with new methodologies. This can only occur after a thorough review of all the alternatives together with their implications. If this task seems overwhelming, the thought of ignoring it seems irresponsible.

The Role of an Aboriginal Issues Court

Inclusion of an Aboriginal member on appeal court benches, whether full time or part time, is an option, but it may be unworkable. It may offend too strenuously the idea of the rule of law.[8] This option also runs the risk of becoming little more than a nominal or token gesture. If this resource is inadequately used, then its intention is easily frustrated.

These arguments are less applicable to the proposal of a separate Aboriginal court, briefly touched on in the final report of the Royal Commission on Aboriginal Peoples and discussed in Chapters 6 and 8. One purpose of an "Aboriginal issues court" would be to sensitize an essentially Eurocentric judicial system to Aboriginal values and practices. Issues involving jurisdictional conflicts between Aboriginal and Canadian governments might first be debated in this court, which could be empowered to initiate its own research on an issue, much like some tribunals do.[9] Disputes that pit the collective rights of Aboriginal communities against the individual rights of their citizens (discussed in the following three chapters) might also be addressed in this forum. Many of the conflicts between individual and collective rights will revolve around day-to-day issues.[10] Truly understanding the import of the issues involved in these disputes will necessitate an intimate appreciation of not only the theoretical issues but also of the dynamics of Aboriginal communities. This court could be constituted with the staff, financial resources, and the latitude for research that would accommodate these objectives.

Separate constitutional issues courts, intended to augment normal appellate structures, are not entirely uncommon. Some European countries have introduced such courts, usually to address human rights matters. Both Germany and Hungary actively employ constitutional courts to supplement their existing judicial structures. Hungary uses a constitutional court consisting of nine judges drawn from backgrounds of research, teaching, and legal scholarship. This court scrutinizes statutes and laws for breaches of human rights or other constitutional norms. Individuals may also petition the court to consider specific constitutional questions. When the court discovers a statute that violates constitutional guarantees, the Hungarian Legislature is obliged to amend or perhaps entirely redraft the offending legislation. Thus, an Aboriginal issues court in Canada should be viewed in the same light as these European constitutional courts. It is intended simply to supplement existing structures and to provide expertise and insight that can then be relied on by a court such as the Supreme Court. Alternatively, this court might serve an advisory function similar to that of federal legislators. That this court would share the same authority as its European cousins to disqualify legislation is doubtful.

Such an Aboriginal court might have a further function. The newly constituted Aboriginal governments will no doubt seek to implement their own structures of justice. Those that do so will include at least a trial-level court and in some instances an appellate court. For communities without an appeals court, the newly constituted Aboriginal court might well provide this additional function.[11] For communities that do institute their own appeals courts, they may subsequently decide to use an Aboriginal issues court as well, a number of which may be dispersed throughout Canada. Tribal court experience in the United States suggests that there may be good reasons to have an appeals forum somewhat detached from a community's influence (the issue of bias is outlined in Chapter 2). The Southwest Inter-Tribal Court of Appeal, described in Chapter 2, is an example of just such a court. It combines an understanding and sensitivity for Aboriginal culture with a certain objective detachment from local politics. The Aboriginal issues court could perform this appeals function in a similarly detached yet informed manner.

It would be important for the rules governing such a court to clarify which law would be applied in this forum. These rules could be flexible enough to accommodate the particular task handed to the court. For jurisdictional disputes, no doubt Canadian common law and constitutional rules of interpretation would prevail. However, they would now be augmented by a clearer understanding of Aboriginal communities. Where applicable, international law and its rules of interpretation might also apply. For example, currently there is little need to resort to a doctrine of laws where concerns are between international sovereigns. However, in resolving a dispute involving jurisdictional claims between Canadian governments and Aboriginal communities, there may be a greater need to use international legal standards. Notably, they might include principles of interpretation or procedure.

When trying to resolve disputes between community and individual rights, the legal reasoning of the court might be grounded in both Aboriginal customary law, which might include both traditional references and newly developed laws provided by local courts, and Canadian common law. On the other hand, when the Aboriginal issues court acts as an appeals court from an earlier tribal trial court decision, no doubt the basis for judicial review would include the appropriate local Aboriginal law. In situations where the local law is silent, the court may be given the latitude to apply Canadian laws or, when relevant, customary Aboriginal laws from another Aboriginal community.

As already stated, federal, provincial, and Aboriginal parties may agree that any appeal from this forum could be directly to the Supreme Court of Canada. However, this rule might be modified when the court performs the function of an appeals forum from an Aboriginal trial-level court. In these instances, where there are no jurisdictional[12] debates and no disputes between collective values and individual rights (i.e., Charter issues; see Chapter 6 for further discussion), perhaps the decision of this court should be final.

Although such a suggestion may strain the imagination of a judicial traditionalist, it achieves an important goal. It inherently expresses a profound respect for the ability of Aboriginal communities to govern their internal affairs. Since the purpose of appealing to the Aboriginal court is to benefit from its innate appreciation of Aboriginal communities and their laws, an appeal to the Supreme Court appears to offer no additional advantage to these communities. In such instances, the Aboriginal court seems to be the appropriate final court of review for these disputes. Again, if the dispute involves an issue of human rights or jurisdiction, then the decision would be reviewable by the Supreme Court.

There are those who assert that one has a better chance of winning a lottery than being able to predict the outcome of any decision from the courts.[13] What is nevertheless significant for Aboriginal communities, if they can achieve a certain sense of confidence or comfort, is how the courts interpret the content and scope of self-government. Establishing a first principle of recognition, as proposed by Pentney, is a reasonable first step. The above proposals regarding committees attached to courts of appeal, an Aboriginal appeals court, as well as reforms to the structure of the Supreme Court of Canada provide a starting point for discussion about how to ensure that the courts will interpret a proposed self-government doctrine in a manner mutually intended by all parties. But more can be done to add certainty to the process.

Domestic Dependent Nationhood as a Canadian Tool

Without a history of Canadian case law on the subject of Aboriginal self-government, there is little to guide a court in its interpretation of this notion. Currently, only Sections 25 and 35 of the Constitution refer to the idea of Aboriginal self-government or the rights of Aboriginal peoples, and these sections have received little interpretive comment from the courts. Thus, little in the way of judicial decisions from appeal-level courts provides much guidance as to how the courts would interpret these matters. In addition, much of the subject matter that might reasonably find its way before these courts, such as jurisdictional and rights conflicts, is not expressly addressed by these sections. Thus, any court asked to interpret a new constitutional statement recognizing this new third order of government, such as expressed in the Charlottetown Accord, would not be able to draw on Canadian case law in resolving the dispute.

However, in the United States Aboriginal self-government exists in a constitutional environment similar to that of Canada. American tribal government experience should provide Canadians with a sense of confidence that Canadian Aboriginal self-government is viable. Awareness of American tribal history should also help to ameliorate feelings of uncertainty or intimidation. However, for present purposes, the US experience may also serve as a stepping stone to legal certainty as Canadian courts attempt to interpret Aboriginal self-government.

Canadian law is filled with terms recognized as possessing precise meanings. Because of the acknowledged meanings of certain terms, they are used by legislative drafters time and again. The difficulty in the present instance is that Canadian jurisprudence does not have such precise meanings regarding Aboriginal self-government. Understandably, due to the absence of this legal concept in Canadian law, a set of expressions with clear meanings has not evolved to assist the current exercise.

In Chapter 2, I briefly described the origins and status of tribal governments in the United States. Since recognition of the tribal right of domestic sovereignty in the Cherokee Nation cases of the early 1830s, the term "domestic dependent nationhood" has often been used and refined by US courts. Their particular understanding and use of this term may provide a basis for elaboration of Aboriginal self-government in Canada.

For example, a degree of certainty may be achieved by adding to the original constitutional statement in Section 35, which recognizes that Aboriginal self-government is a form of domestic dependent nationhood. US courts have had over 150 years of experience addressing tribal sovereignty and domestic dependent nationhood. This history thereby provides both a picture of this entity and a long line of legal decisions that address issues with which the Canadian judicial system will be challenged. Thus, if the term "domestic dependent nationhood" were inserted into the Canadian Constitution, then arguably it would indicate a clear intention to adopt principles that have emerged from the history of American constitutional jurisprudence.

This position provides the parties to the amending process with some sense of certainty about how their efforts will be acknowledged by the courts. It would offer the Canadian judicial system clear indicators of how this new constitutional principle of Aboriginal self-government might be interpreted, and it would thereby ensure, as much as possible, certainty of understanding. However, such a statement need not be the only one made.

There is no prohibition against establishing multiple principles of interpretation for Aboriginal self-government. Any number of qualifying statements can be included to elaborate the content of this term. The only question is how these statements should be articulated to achieve the form of self-government desired by both Aboriginal people and the Canadian governments. If including in the Constitution some elaboration that would assist the courts in interpreting Aboriginal self-government is viable, then which specific references would provide a history of case law satisfactory to the parties to such an accord?

Again, the concept of domestic dependent nationhood may be of some assistance. The constitutional history of this concept has been evolving and will no doubt continue to evolve in a variety of ways. However, it is safe to say that this theory currently enunciates certain principles. It is therefore worth examining whether the fundamental principles inherent in this body of law are useful in the development of first principles that could be used in the establishment of a Canadian version of Aboriginal self-government. In particular, how amenable would these principles be to the aspirations of Aboriginal people in Canada?

The Charlottetown meetings went further than previous discussions regarding Aboriginal self-government. This agreement proposed recognition of Aboriginal self-government as a third order of government and provided for negotiation forums in which greater specificity would be given to the "implementation" of self-government. Since this agreement met with success among the federal and provincial governments as well as the Aboriginal parties, it is reasonable to assume that a similar approach may be taken in future first ministers' conferences to amend the Constitution. Therefore, to provide the following discussions with a context, I will offer observations on how the Charlottetown Accord proposed to deal with these same issues.

The principle of domestic dependent nationhood encompasses the following general tenets.

(1) Tribal communities possess an inherent right of self-government.
(2) Tribal communities possess an inherent jurisdiction over both criminal and civil law matters.
(3) Tribal sovereignty is limited to sovereignty of a domestic nature, and elements of self-government inconsistent with this nature are precluded from tribal jurisdiction (i.e., international relations).
(4) State governments have no criminal jurisdiction over Indians within Indian country but retain authority over non-Indians if no Indian person is affected as an immediate victim of a crime.
(5) State governments may have civil jurisdiction in Indian country provided no Indian persons are involved in the matter and no essential tribal interests are affected.
(6) The federal government can exercise authority over any matters and all persons in Indian country.
(7) Federal authority is paramount over both tribal and state jurisdiction in Indian country.

Tenet 1

Tribal communities possess an inherent right of self-government. This principle has been asserted for years by Aboriginal people in Canada. It varies substantially from the kind of authority delegated to band governments under the Indian Act and Métis settlements, pursuant to Alberta's provincial legislation. Delegated legislation is typically more confining in the types of activity that it prescribes. Moreover, unlike inherent authority, any delegated jurisdiction that Aboriginal communities exercise is only permitted at another authority's pleasure. Delegated authority does not exist as an innate right drawing its origins from the community itself. This last point is essential to the interests of Aboriginal communities. The Charlottetown Accord recognized the inherent authority of Aboriginal peoples to self-government. One might presume that a new agreement would provide for a similar recognition.

Tenet 2

Tribal communities possess an inherent jurisdiction over both criminal and civil law matters. The case of *Ex parte Crow Dog*[14] illuminated the content of tribal criminal jurisdiction. The Supreme Court of the United States held that the tribes possessed full criminal law jurisdiction. This subject matter jurisdiction was subsequently limited by the Major Crimes Act. Until then, however, the tribes were recognized as possessing plenary authority in this area.

In the area of civil law matters, the Supreme Court's decision in *Williams* v. *Lee*[15] is instructive. This case clearly established tribal authority over civil law matters on the reservation that affected Indian people or their interests. Thus, domestic dependent nationhood also clearly recognizes in the tribe full authority over all civil law matters.

Aboriginal peoples in Canada clearly seek to have recognized inherent authority over both civil and criminal law matters within their communities. Issues that typically find their way into discussions on this subject include taxation, education, resource allocation, child welfare, land use, marriage and divorce, and court administration. However, it is not clear from a reading of the Charlottetown Accord whether all these areas of jurisdiction would fall within the authority of Aboriginal governments. It is by no means certain that a third order of government would possess plenary authority over all these expressions of jurisdiction. Clearly, neither the federal nor the provincial governments currently possess such all-encompassing jurisdiction. The respective jurisdictions are now divided most particularly pursuant to the directions of Sections 91 and 92 of the Constitution Act, 1867 (other sections of the act, such as Section 93, are also relevant).

Notwithstanding that these authorities are shared between the two principal elements of Confederation, neither is seen in law as being anything less than a distinct order of government. Similarly, a third order of government, constituted by the Aboriginal people of Canada, could be construed by the courts as having jurisdiction over only a few of these elements. There would be no apparent inconsistency in being a third order of government and possessing only limited scope over certain jurisdictional matters. Thus, Aboriginal communities should be concerned that interpretation by the courts of the jurisdiction of a third order of government would be sufficient to protect the broad areas of governance exercised by tribal governments in the United States.

Furthermore, the Charlottetown Accord provided for a negotiation process that, if adopted, might concern Aboriginal parties. Article 45 of the agreement provides that Aboriginal governments negotiate with the federal and provincial governments to implement self-government, "including issues of jurisdiction." Certain federal or provincial governments may argue that this process of negotiation implies that Aboriginal governments do not possess full authority over both civil and criminal law jurisdictions. This realization should be troubling for many Aboriginal people.

However, the principle of domestic dependent nationhood appears to recognize broad authority of Aboriginal governments over both civil and criminal law jurisdictions. Surely, this authority would be the most appealing to Aboriginal peoples, if it is not somewhat more distressing for non-Aboriginal governments.

Tenet 3

Tribal sovereignty is limited to sovereignty of a domestic nature, and elements of self-government inconsistent with this nature are precluded from tribal jurisdiction (i.e., international relations). Areas of authority typically associated with non-domestic status include the capacity to declare and wage war with other countries, establish currency, keep a standing army, engage in international treaties, and so forth. These elements of jurisdiction are few and do not appear to have compromised US tribal powers in any substantial way. The realization by these tribal governments that their jurisdiction is limited to a domestic and local role seems to have precipitated little frustration. These communities recognize that the important issues concerning them are principally local. Health, housing, education, commerce, and so forth are all more relevant issues to these communities than engaging in treaties with foreign nations. Domestic governance provides enough of a challenge to dissuade tribal leaders from becoming involved in international matters.[16]

The Charlottetown Accord was silent on this matter, but presumably federal and provincial governments do not intend that Aboriginal governments are to assume international standing. Nor have there been any significant assertions from Aboriginal parties that they wish to exercise such an international role. One occasionally hears the claim that: "As nations, we should be able to have international relations with other nations." However, this statement is seldom given much priority, even within Aboriginal communities. Aboriginal nations simply have no need for such relationships, and it is doubtful that other nations would wish to cultivate them. Like US tribal communities, Aboriginal peoples in Canada seem to be willing to accept the limitations that come with domestic self-government. Thus, domestic dependent nationhood appears to be a valuable tool in establishing the domestic nature of Aboriginal self-government in Canada.

Tenet 4

State governments have no criminal jurisdiction over Indians within Indian country but retain authority over non-Indians if no Indian person is affected as an immediate victim of a crime. The general practice in US courts has been to accept the holdings in the Cherokee Nation cases as determinative on this point. Certainly, in regard to the involvement of Indians in a crime, this principle is secure. However, in cases in which both offender and victim were non-Indians, the court permitted state prosecutions.[17] Notwithstanding the apparent intrusion of state jurisdiction upon tribal authority in these cases, in practical terms these decisions have had only minor impacts on the jurisdiction of tribal governments.

Moreover, for present purposes, this is a moot point since provincial governments in Canada, unlike US state governments, do not exercise criminal law authority. In Canada, the federal government alone exercises criminal jurisdiction. The provinces limit their activities to policing and court administration in criminal law matters. The Charlottetown Accord did not propose any changes to this constitutional arrangement. Given the present circumstances, the implications of domestic dependent nationhood in Canada appear to be without substance one way or the other on this issue. Aboriginal communities would have no apparent reason to take exception to this principle.

Tenet 5
State governments can have civil jurisdiction in Indian country provided no Indian persons are involved in the matter and no essential tribal interests are affected. The seminal interpretation of the principle of domestic dependent nationhood on state jurisdiction over civil law matters found its expression in *Williams* v. *Lee.*[18] In this case, an Arizona state court was denied civil law jurisdiction over a matter involving two members of the Navajo tribe. The Supreme Court of the United States held that, in civil law matters in which the rights of Indians are jeopardized or essential tribal relations are involved, states have no jurisdiction. Thus, the court appeared to protect tribal governments from state intrusion upon their authority to govern themselves.

However, the later case of *McClanahan*[19] seems to have refined this principle. The court indicated that the proper reading of *Williams* v. *Lee* implied that states may have some civil jurisdiction in Indian country but that, if the laws interfered with either Indians or essential tribal interests, then state jurisdiction would be preempted. This is significantly different from the presumption of no state jurisdiction of any kind, which most observers believed was part of the doctrine of the domestic dependent nation established by the Cherokee Nation cases.

This principle was extended in *Washington* v. *Confederated Tribes of the Colville Indian Reservation,*[20] which involved only non-Indians. The court stated that "state jurisdiction is preempted by the operation of federal law if it interferes with or is incompatible with federal and tribal interest reflected in federal law, unless the state interests at stake are sufficient to justify the assertion of state authority." Thus, it appears that state governments can exercise jurisdiction over non-Indians in Indian country if essential tribal interests are not affected. Also, *Colville* appears to permit some state intrusion upon tribal interests when state interests are sufficient to justify such an intrusion and Congress has not occupied the field. Still in doubt is what constitutes "sufficient" state interests. Will this thinking be extended to cover incidents involving even essential tribal interests? (For a fuller discussion of this matter, see Chapter 2.)

For Aboriginal people in Canada, the doctrine of domestic dependent nationhood may not be secure enough concerning provincial civil jurisdiction. As already stated, Aboriginal people here seek to exercise comprehensive areas of civil jurisdiction, including health, education, child welfare, and so forth. Currently, much of this jurisdiction is exercised by provincial governments. Aboriginal governments, reasonably, would also wish to exercise jurisdiction in these areas. However, the Charlottetown Accord was not as clear as one might have wished on this issue. It only provided for a framework of negotiation in which these issues might be discussed. The contextual statement in the accord did provide for the exercise of Aboriginal jurisdiction over "languages, cultures, economics, identities, institutions and traditions." This may be a sufficient characterization for the courts to infer comprehensive civil law jurisdictions for Aboriginal governments. However, a problem remains. Even if Aboriginal governments are eventually found to possess this broad jurisdictional authority, is this to be a shared authority? There is no clear indication whether concurrent provincial authority would not also apply. Furthermore, if concurrent provincial jurisdiction is recognized, then which authority would prevail in times of conflict between Aboriginal and provincial laws?

Aboriginal peoples in Canada would probably require some clarification of or amendment to the doctrine of domestic dependent nationhood. The doctrine, as it stands, appears to ensure that Aboriginal people possess broad civil law jurisdiction. However, since it also permits states to exercise some civil law jurisdiction in Indian country, Aboriginal people will probably require a clarification of jurisdiction, which would outline not so much the scope of their own authority as the degree to which provincial laws would apply in Aboriginal communities – and particularly whose laws would prevail in times of conflict.

If domestic dependent nationhood were to be employed as a constitutional tool, then Aboriginal parties would probably wish to draft an amendment ensuring either that provinces have no civil law jurisdiction in Aboriginal communities or that provinces may exercise civil law jurisdiction provided that neither Aboriginal peoples nor Aboriginal governing interests are detrimentally affected. Aboriginal peoples may also wish to ensure that, when competing Aboriginal and provincial laws are in conflict, Aboriginal legislation will prevail.

This proposal may be the best middle ground. The clarification would permit the provinces to exercise some civil law jurisdiction in Indian country rather than prohibit it altogether. And Aboriginal peoples could accept this exercise of provincial jurisdiction within their communities knowing that Aboriginal interests would prevail in times of legislative conflict.

One may wish to elaborate within a constitutional document what is intended by Aboriginal "interests," or one may wish to leave such an exercise to the courts for perhaps more thorough consideration. However, Aboriginal parties may argue that this term should include nothing less than those "essential" government interests referred to in *Williams* v. *Lee*. Indeed, they may wish to lower this standard to include matters of "substantial" significance to Aboriginal communities. Requiring that the protected interests meet an "essential" level seems like a rather high threshold, while "substantial" perhaps suggests a more reasonable level of influence.

Tenets 6 and 7
The federal government can exercise authority over any matters and all persons in Indian country. Federal authority is paramount over both tribal and state jurisdiction in Indian country. It has been accepted law since the doctrine of domestic dependent nationhood that the federal government can exercise its jurisdiction over all persons regarding both civil and criminal law matters within Indian country. The will of Congress is plenary in this regard. Although Congress has been active in asserting its authority over criminal law matters, other than with regard to the Indian Child Welfare Act it has remained mostly silent on major civil law issues.[21] Nonetheless, its authority in Indian country remains broad and paramount.

Aboriginal people in Canada would have grave reservations about the inclusion of this tenet of the principle of domestic dependent nationhood. As previously stated, the Charlottetown Accord did not articulate exactly what authority the federal government would retain over matters in Aboriginal lands. Clearly, the second tenet of the doctrine permits Aboriginal governments to hold broad jurisdiction over matters now exercised by the federal authority. But the accord did not express whether the federal government would also retain concurrent elements of its jurisdiction within Aboriginal communities. Nor did the agreement explicitly provide for which authority, federal or Aboriginal, would prevail when laws conflicted.

Aboriginal people would no doubt require some amendment to the present doctrine of domestic dependent nationhood. Such an amendment would clarify the nature of residual federal jurisdiction and whose laws would prevail in the event of a conflict. This quandary may be resolved in the same fashion as a similar problem regarding provincial jurisdiction.

Accordingly, Aboriginal peoples may propose an amendment recognizing the concurrent authority of the federal government but stipulating that, in times of legislative conflict, Aboriginal interests would prevail.

Because the federal government exercises criminal law authority, and because of the unique nature of these matters, it may be worthwhile to clarify the nature of the shared jurisdiction. The intention is not that the federal government handle the more serious offences while Aboriginal communities exercise jurisdiction over the less serious crimes. Due to the uncertain process of negotiation proposed by the Charlottetown Accord, this is a possible outcome. But Aboriginal people might agree to an amendment that recognizes federal jurisdiction over all criminal activities in Indian country "unless acted upon" by the local government.

This proposal is different from that in which the federal government is precluded from exercising jurisdiction simply if a contrary Aboriginal law exists. A federal law would continue to be asserted until the Aboriginal government asserted its own jurisdiction. This definition could be triggered by an action either by a police officer or a prosecuting counsel and is not dependent on the courts prosecuting the person in question.

This qualification may be proposed to avoid potential chaos in Aboriginal communities that seek to exercise self-government but that may not have a refined criminal code or that wish to deal with an offender in some diversionary way short of having to go to court. It would thus provide for forms of dispute resolution unfamiliar to the Eurocentric system of justice.

This alternative may only be required for a transitional period of, say, ten years. A clause could be included with the amendment clarifying that once the ten-year period expires, and no Aboriginal criminal law has occupied the field, federal criminal law would prevail. Aboriginal communities would have until then to develop their own criminal laws and the infrastructure necessary to govern their communities (this period could be extended to some agreed-upon term). The notion of grandfathering this amendment is not uncommon in Canadian law. Indeed, the last major constitutional change, in 1982, included a five-year period in which the equality measures of the Canadian Charter of Rights and Freedoms were postponed.[22]

The wording could be articulated to clarify that, should an Aboriginal court eventually choose not to address the matter, the federal government would retain its authority to prosecute. It is important to recognize that this wording would not have to be stated within the Constitution Act itself. Rather, just as the Charlottetown Accord proposed, agreements could later be subsumed under the umbrella of constitutional protection. Section 35 of the Constitution Act, 1982, already recognizes such a process.

For present purposes, it is unimportant to focus on the precise wording of this phrase. An alternative phrase to "unless acted upon" may be more appropriate. Similarly, the exact grandfathering period may be lengthened or, for that matter, shortened. What is important is the need to recognize that on this issue the doctrine of the domestic dependent nation may not meet the needs of Aboriginal people.

Consequently, when approaching tenets 6 and 7 of the doctrine, one might anticipate amendments similar to that regarding the exercise of provincial authority in Aboriginal communities. Federal jurisdiction would be permitted unless it conflicted with the interests of or asserted an impact on significant Aboriginal government interests. In addition, federal authority over all criminal law matters would continue to apply "unless acted upon" by the local government. This authority would be permitted for a ten-year period, at which time this concurrent federal jurisdiction would cease if the Aboriginal community has invoked its own criminal law legislation.

Reflections of an Idea

Should Aboriginal peoples opt to use the doctrine of domestic dependent nationhood with the appropriate amendments to clarify the aforementioned questions, it might read as follows.

S.35.1
1. The Aboriginal peoples of Canada exist as domestic dependent nations.
2. In instances of conflict between Aboriginal governments and the laws of the federal or provincial governments, the laws of the Aboriginal governments will prevail.
3. The criminal jurisdiction of the Parliament of Canada will prevail in Aboriginal communities unless otherwise acted upon by the Aboriginal government.
4. Subsection 3 will remain in force for ten years following the enactment of this section.

Having considered the scope of the doctrine of domestic dependent nationhood, Aboriginal people may wish to employ it for the entrenchment of self-government. The doctrine clearly recognizes the right of sovereignty or self-government as inherent and not delegated. It also affirms the authority of these governments over both civil and criminal law matters. Although the Aboriginal governments' jurisdiction would be limited to a domestic application, this should not be a significant problem for these communities. A more serious difficulty is whether the federal or provincial governments would possess concurrent jurisdiction concerning matters in Aboriginal communities. In addition, should there be shared jurisdiction between federal or provincial governments and Aboriginal governments that will prevail in the instances of conflict? Aboriginal people may wish to draft an amendment to the general enshrining principle to clarify these uncertainties in the manner mentioned above.

This doctrine and its proposed amendments serve two purposes. First, they will bring to any forthcoming constitutional discussions an element of certainty in understanding what is intended by the recognition of Aboriginal self-government. This doctrine has clear jurisprudential meaning and, as such, lends itself more easily to prediction concerning the much-debated matters of jurisdiction. Second, the adoption of this doctrine together with certain amendments would probably be well received by Aboriginal people and their respective negotiating representatives. A clear and forthright position of Aboriginal consensus would assist in reconciling the present debate.

This doctrine, together with the suggested amendments, may fare less well in the eyes of the federal or provincial governments. The proposal under the Charlottetown Accord provided little specifically on matters of jurisdiction. Indeed, federal and provincial signatories might well have thought that significant elements of jurisdiction to be accorded to Aboriginal people would only be acquired through cooperative bargaining. They may have believed that they would play a significant role in determining the nature and scope of this third order of government, most probably by restraining its scope. Thus, it is not unreasonable to anticipate that federal or provincial governments may take exception to a third order of government possessing the combined jurisdiction of the other two levels of government, even if such jurisdiction were limited to a small locale. Since the doctrine of domestic dependent nationhood appears to create just this situation, to at least this extent, it may be less well received by these parties.

Furthermore, since the amended doctrine also gives Aboriginal governments paramount authority in instances of conflict, there may again be reluctance to use the doctrine for constitutional change. Nonetheless, the significance of rejecting such a doctrine would clearly indicate where these governments stand on accepting Aboriginal peoples as full participants in Confederation. Perhaps this clarification before both the Canadian public and the Aboriginal people of Canada would be useful.

Dworkin's Caution

Since the beginning of the last century, there has evolved a growing interest in understanding exactly how judges arrive at their decisions. The noted jurist Oliver Wendell Holmes founded and inspired the American form of Legal Realism.[23] Holmes and other "realists" believed that judges do much more than simply match the proper law with the facts of a case. They believe that the exercise of judicial discretion plays a much larger role in their decisions than most observers would imagine. However, some US scholars, acknowledging this kind of judicial discretion, nonetheless believe that it is significantly restrained by a particular conservative practice when it comes to interpreting constitutional documents. Ronald Dworkin is one such scholar.

A preeminent American legal theorist, Dworkin believes that in constitutional rights cases judges resolve "hard cases" through the application of rules, which may have a legislative or case law source, and the application of legal principles. These principles have evolved over time and are used by the courts to help interpret existing rules. A judge will then determine through the use of these tools who has a "right to win" the case.[24]

Dworkin asserts that "the origin of ... legal principles lies not in a particular decision of some legislature or court but in a sense of *appropriateness* developed in the public and [legal] profession over time. Their continued power depends upon this sense of *appropriateness* being sustained."[25] He also suggests that "a judge's responsibility is to fit particular judgements on which they act into a coherent program of action"[26] and "that will justify the settled rules."[27] Moreover, it is important to "find the moral principles that underlie the communities' institutions."[28] His description of a judge's approach to settling a case, though at odds with a "strict" construction of constitutional documents, strongly suggests that constitutional decision making will be conservative.[29]

Dworkin has also commented recently on the issue of judicial interpretation of constitutional rights. In *Freedom's Law: The Moral Reading of the American Constitution*,[30] he describes what he believes is the singular method of interpreting rights protected by the US Constitution. He observes initially that, for the most part, these guarantees represent moral statements as reflected by terms such as "the right of," "rights due to an individual," and "equal to."[31] Consequently, he argues that, when Supreme Court judges arrive at decisions regarding these matters, they are in essence making moral decisions in law. Dworkin also notes how judges are reluctant to admit that such a process occurs, for they would leave themselves open to the criticism that their decisions represent no more than the inclinations of current beliefs rather than the impartial analyses that reflect the sound intentions of the framers of the Constitution. This view suggests that law is "only a matter of which moral principles happen to appeal to the judges of a particular era."[32] In addition, subscribing to the "moral reading" of the Constitution would ostensibly portray these judges as philosopher kings with seemingly arbitrary authority, particularly when they receive their positions through political appointments. Many people living in a democracy would find this characterization unappealing.

Nonetheless, Dworkin states that judges, if only implicitly, recognize that these declarations of rights are moral statements that must be interpreted. The principal distinction that divides both the public and the court itself is whether such moral declarations deserve a liberal or a conservative interpretation. However, Dworkin also issues a caveat on the limits of a judge's discretion in his or her moral reading of these rights, and his comments on the qualifications imposed on a judge's discretion should concern Aboriginal people in Canada.

Dworkin asserts that judges are not free to read their own moral convictions into their judgments: "They may not read the abstract moral clauses as expressions of any moral judgement, ... no matter how much that judgement appeals to them, unless they find it consistent in principle with the *structural design* of the Constitution as a whole, and also with the *dominant lines* of past constitutional interpretation by other judges ... They must regard themselves as partners with other officials, past and future, who together elaborate a *coherent constitutional morality,* and they must take care to see that what they contribute *fits with the rest.*"[33] Thus, constitutional decisions regarding these rights are like strands of thread being woven into the constitutional fabric of the country. Supreme Court judges are free to make new interpretations of old declarations of rights, but they are not so free as to vary from the dominant colour and pattern of this fabric. New rulings must fit intimately with the preexisting structure.

If Dworkin's analysis has similar application in Canada, then Aboriginal people have much to fear. Such an approach indicates that decisions emanating from the Supreme Court of Canada will be premised only upon the historical structural design of this country's Constitution. Furthermore, these decisions will abide only by the existing dominant lines of jurisprudential thought. And, even if there is some movement toward the positions articulated by Aboriginal parties, these decisions can be expected to vary only in shading. The dilemma for Aboriginal people is that they wish to interweave a red thread within what has thus far been a white constitutional fabric.

It is unnecessary to review the long history of cases that have minimized or ignored the claims of Aboriginal people. Many of these cases have dealt with treaty claims, harvesting issues, and the broader issue of Aboriginal title. However, three recent cases are worth noting. They were decided by the Supreme Court of Canada since the 1982 amendment to the Constitution, and they specifically address the Aboriginal rights entitlements contained in Section 35 of the act. Consequently, these cases may indicate whether Dworkin's assertions have any validity within the Canadian context and, in particular, with regard to Aboriginal rights claims.

However, before I review these cases, I should address an anticipated observation. It may be argued that the common law doctrines of stare decisis or precedent will explain many of the Supreme Court's rulings.[34] Perhaps to some extent, but Dworkin might argue that this explanation is both naïve and limited. More importantly, this observation is less compelling when the rights in question are contained within a recent constitutional package that has clearly rewritten other areas of common law, at least in those areas concerning the civil liberties of Canadians (i.e., the Charter).

Therefore, one might be forgiven for believing that the new assertions of Aboriginal and treaty entitlements found in Sections 25 and 35 of the Constitution Act, 1982, were intended to be treated with gravity and consequence. Indeed, the assertion of these new rights was intended to indicate a break from the past and a fundamental restructuring of Canadian-Aboriginal relations. This does not, however, appear to be the view taken by the Supreme Court of Canada.

Sparrow, Van der Peet, **and** *Pamajewon*

In 1984, Mr. Sparrow, a member of the Musqueam First Nation, was charged with violating a regulation of the federal Fisheries Act that had been adopted by British Columbia. Sparrow argued in his defence that his Aboriginal right to fish for personal use was protected by Section 35 of the Constitution. Although this claim was initially rejected at the trial-level court, and the subsequent appeal was rejected by the county court, it was accepted by the British Columbia Court of Appeal. The Supreme Court of Canada was then asked to interpret the nature and scope of this right.[35]

The Supreme Court accepted Sparrow's assertions but, in doing so, characterized his Aboriginal right in what would prove to be, for Aboriginal people, a most unfortunate fashion. The *Sparrow* decision is reviewed in Chapter 8, but two points are worth noting here. First, the court agreed that Section 35 of the Constitution Act, 1982, does recognize that Aboriginal and treaty rights are constitutionally protected from intrusion. Second, the court also recognized that this protection was not absolute. However, it asserted that, although the section recognizes and affirms these rights, the phrasing implies that these rights are subject to qualification: "Rights that are recognized and affirmed are not absolute. Federal legislative powers continue, of course, the right to legislate with respect to Indians pursuant to 2.91(24) of the Constitution Act, 1867."[36]

The court did caution that regulation of these rights may only be undertaken if there are valid objectives to the legislation and provided that such regulation maintains the honour of the Crown.[37] "Conserving and managing natural resources"[38] appear to qualify as valued legislative objectives. In other similar situations, in order to achieve this level of justification, a government would be required to consult with Aboriginal communities and provide fair compensation when it could reasonably be achieved.[39] It is not clear which specific standards the court would require for the honour of the Crown to be met. However, if the Crown meets the standards of justification and there does not appear to be any obvious improprieties or conflicts, then a prima facie case may well exist that the Crown has acted in an honourable fashion.

The *Sparrow* decision is significant for a number of reasons. The most important, for present purposes, is how the Supreme Court chose to characterize Aboriginal and treaty rights as reflected in Section 35. The court could have chosen to view these rights in the same manner and with the same gravity as it views Charter rights. Indeed, it could have accepted the claims of the Aboriginal parties that these rights are superior to individual rights protected by the Canadian Charter of Rights and Freedoms. But the court rejected both views. Instead, it decided that the wording "recognized and affirmed" in Section 35 somehow imparts a lesser degree of constitutional protection than does the wording of the individual rights section within the Charter. The court offered no constitutional doctrine, reasoning, or case law in explaining how it came to this judgment. Once the court stated that this wording justified weaker constitutional protection of Aboriginal interests, the standards of justification and Crown honour were little more than procedural hurdles to be overcome provided that a government simply followed the new rules.

Section 35 did entrench Aboriginal and treaty rights – but in a very different way. The Court decided that the rigorous standards used by Charter-protected rights were not to be employed in these circumstances. The mysterious meaning of "recognized and affirmed" meant something else, something far less than anyone could have imagined.

Although the deficiencies of *Sparrow* are elaborated upon further in Chapter 8, a disturbing observation is worth mentioning here. When one compares the level of insulation provided to Charter rights and the degree of protection the Supreme Court accords Section 35 rights, the difference is profound. In the recent Mills case,[40] an accused in a sexual assault trial asked to see private personal therapeutic records regarding the mental health of the complainant victim. The victim sought to rely upon a section of the criminal code that would prohibit access to these notes.[41] The accused argued that this section of the code was unconstitutional as it prevented him from adequately and fairly responding to the charges against him, as guaranteed by Sections 7 and 11(d) of the Canadian Charter of Rights and Freedoms. The Supreme Court of Canada, in its judgment, pointed out that: "At play in this appeal are three principles, which find their support in specific provisions of the Charter. These are full answer and defense, privacy (both principles of fundamental justice) and equality. No simple principle is absolute and capable of trumping the others; all must be defined in light of competing claims. As Chief Justice Lamer stated in Dagenais ... 'When the protected rights of two individuals come into conflict ... Charter principles require a balance to be achieved that fully respects the importance of rights.'"[42]

The analysis in this and other Charter cases is quite different from how Section 35 rights are protected. In *Sparrow*, the court stated that any "infringement" of these Aboriginal and treaty rights was permissible provided only that the legislature met the procedural test of justification.[43] Thus an Aboriginal right may in fact be entirely extinguished provided simply that the government did so clearly and adequately (i.e., procedurally). Such procedural protection is hardly the equivalent of protection provided to those rights enshrined within the Charter. It is clear that the Supreme Court of Canada does not place Section 35 rights on an equal footing with Charter Rights. It is also clear that the absence of any action by Parliament to correct this inequity must be taken as an indication of how the federal government views the significance of the rights enshrined within Section 35.

In *Van der Peet* v. *R.*,[44] the appellant was charged with selling ten salmon while in possession of a licence that restricted him to personal food fishing. He claimed that the regulation was of no force since this commercial fishing right was protected as an Aboriginal right by Section 35 of the Constitution Act, 1982. The trial judge rejected this claim, but upon initial appeal that decision was overturned. Subsequently, the Court of Appeal overruled this decision, restoring the original decision of the trial judge. The Supreme Court of Canada agreed. The unanimous opinion of the court set out criteria for the establishment of an Aboriginal right under Section 35. One criterion was that the custom being claimed as an Aboriginal right must be distinctive to the particular community. It must be a practice that is both unique and integral to the distinctive Aboriginal culture. Another criterion was that the custom existed prior to contact with European settlers. If it is a custom that developed only after contact, then it does not meet this requirement.

The court cited the *Sparrow* case when it pointed out that Aboriginal rights must not be frozen in time.[45] Thus, the characterization of a right today may permit the practice to be updated, so to speak. In *Sundown*,[46] the Supreme Court said that a traditional lean-to used during hunting and fishing expeditions by the Joseph Big Head First Nation could today take the form of a log cabin.[47]

However, there appears to be a tension between a practice recognized at contact as an Aboriginal right and a practice that the court will accept as an updated expression of that right. As *Pamajewon* v. *R.* illustrates,[48] the Supreme Court has taken a rather narrow view of updating customary gambling practices. Absent a constitutional amendment clearly recognizing the ability of modern Aboriginal peoples to govern themselves in a contemporary fashion, what latitude will the Supreme Court extend to an Aboriginal expression of self-government today?[49]

The significance of the *Van der Peet* requirements for the recognition of an Aboriginal right is that both criteria are highly restrictive and consider such rights from a very narrow perspective. Notwithstanding the broad assertions of the Supreme Court to avoid a "frozen in time" approach, the "existing at contact" test locks the notion of an Aboriginal culture into a picture of what existed long ago. *Pamajewon* appears to reflect these limitations. Thus, *Van der Peet* does not appear to provide a great deal of latitude for the right of a culture, along with its customs, to evolve. Practices that have matured since contact appear to face a decidedly uphill battle to qualify as Aboriginal rights under Section 35.

But that's not all. The "integral to the distinctive culture" test indicates that, even if a custom existed at contact, it will survive only if it is shown to be central to the Aboriginal society. If it was also practised by many other cultures, then ostensibly it cannot be an Aboriginal right protected under Section 35. Such an approach would appear to impose profound limitations upon how broadly these entitlements may be viewed. Further decisions by this court may prove to expand their interpretation more liberally. However, until this occurs, the potential for a generous expression of Aboriginal rights seems remote.

Aboriginal people also find it at least curious that their rights are protected only if they are centuries old and then only if they reflect a unique and integral value to the community. No such limitations are imposed on individual Charter rights. A person's right to freedom of expression is not limited to forms of expression practised in either 1867 or 1982. Nor is this right left unprotected by the Constitution if it cannot be shown to be an integral element of democratic society. Yet the Supreme Court believed for some reason that such limitations must be imposed on the Section 35 rights of Aboriginal people. Dworkin might suggest that this view was meant to provide some substance to this new constitutional recognition of Aboriginal rights while not unduly disturbing settled jurisprudential tradition.

In the case of *Pamajewon v. R.*, the appellants were convicted of running illegal gambling activities within a reserve. They argued that the high-stakes bingo game was an expression of an Aboriginal social and economic right. As such, it should be protected under Section 35 of the Constitution.

The Supreme Court disagreed, holding, as in *Van der Peet*, that this activity was not integral to the culture of the community. Nor did it exist as a custom at contact. Thus, the court reaffirmed the time-period limitation imposed on such a right as well as the need for it to qualify as a unique and integral element of the culture. Once again these criteria take a narrow view of the nature of Aboriginal rights.

The decisions in *Sparrow, Van der Peet,* and *Pamajewon* are enlightening. These cases, together with a series of treaty cases such as *R. v. Badger*[50] and *Marshall*,[51] reflect an approach to both Aboriginal and treaty rights that the Supreme Court of Canada seems intent on pursuing. In every instance, the court has substantiated the claims of Dworkin. Although the court could have chosen to weave a new thread of judicial reasoning into the fabric of

Canadian constitutional law, it chose to maintain the same "structural design" and "dominant lines of past constitutional interpretation."[52]

In *Sparrow,* rather than raise Aboriginal and treaty rights to the level of Charter rights, the court effectively asserted that these were different and therefore less substantial rights. It used the wording of "recognized and affirmed" to rationalize a new and lesser form of entrenchment for these rights. In doing so, it provided some explanation for the presence of Aboriginal and treaty rights within the Constitution but in a fashion that continued to recognize the dominance of Parliament and past lines of judicial interpretation.

In *Van der Peet,* the Supreme Court further limited the scope of Section 35 rights by declaring that they may not mature from what they were at contact and that they must be unique and integral to the existence of Aboriginal communities. Such limitations appear to leave little room for new expressions of Aboriginal or treaty entitlements. *Pamajewon* appears to reinforce this observation.

Although the Supreme Court of Canada provided some recognition of Aboriginal entitlements in each of these cases, rights not recognized prior to 1982, such reasoning is unconvincing. Clearly, the inclusion of Section 35 in the Constitution Act, 1982, was intended to have some meaning. For the court to ignore this addition and simply mimic pre-1982 judicial reasoning in its handling of these cases would have been unacceptable and an insult to its integrity. The Supreme Court has in fact insinuated into these decisions a special status for Section 35 rights. However, Dworkin might suggest that the court's conservative findings, together with an absence of cogent supportive reasoning, indicate that the court intended to minimize Aboriginal entitlements and subsume them under the established structures of constitutional law. Little thought seemed to be directed toward exploring how the Section 35 entitlements were intended to reorder the underlying constitutional pillars. The "purposive approach" to interpreting constitutional documents, taken by the Supreme Court in *Van der Peet,*[53] begins with the assumption that Section 35, Aboriginal, and treaty rights must somehow fit within the bedrock of the original constitutional arrangement. Little serious consideration appears to have been given to viewing Section 35 rights as an intention by the framers of the legislation or the will of Canadians in general to initiate a fundamentally different relationship. Such consideration need not undermine the foundation of the present constitutional structure, but it would require the court to recognize that the Section 35 amendment was intended to be more than just a new coat of paint.

Aboriginal people believed that the failure of the first ministers' conferences of the 1980s and the Charlottetown Accord would be rectified by a less politically influenced institution such as the Supreme Court of Canada.

Dworkin suggests, however, that fundamental factors at work influence the court's decisions, perhaps in ways not fully appreciated. Until now, these factors have not been vigorously considered in the Aboriginal community. The recent decisions of the Supreme Court regarding Aboriginal and treaty disputes suggest that this court might not be the source of salvation longed for by the Aboriginal community. The irresistible conclusion is that litigating the constitutional recognition of Aboriginal entitlements under the current constitutional regime is a dubious venture.

Comment

It has never been a simple task for Aboriginal people to have their right of self-government recognized. As this chapter has illustrated, even when all levels of government support the inclusion of this principle within the Canadian Constitution, exactly how this is done presents its own set of problems.

Although many Aboriginal people would prefer recognition through a treaty process, as illustrated in the previous chapter, this option would seem to have little obvious merit. On the other hand, the entrenchment of Aboriginal self-government through the inclusion of clearly articulated principles in the Constitution also presents difficulties, not the least of which is how such principles will be interpreted by the courts. Canada has little jurisprudential experience in this area from which one might reasonably infer the outcome of a court's interpretation of this Aboriginal jurisdiction. Consequently, Aboriginal people should be concerned that the courts' interpretation of the newly entrenched principles of self-determination will be narrow and inconsistent with their understanding of these principles.

The first principles approach of William Pentney has merit but may suffer from the very problem that it purports to cure. Other proposals to assist the judiciary in its understanding of Aboriginal communities and culture also provide some advantages over the present judicial institutions. Although the doctrine of domestic dependent nationhood in its present form does not address all of the aspirations of Canadian Aboriginal communities, it does provide a useful starting point from which to add appropriate wording. It is crucial to understand that using this US doctrine arises from concern that, without the guiding principles implied by it, the courts would be unfettered in interpreting a constitutional amendment that ostensibly recognizes the inherent right of self-government.

A bare statement such as "The Aboriginal peoples of Canada possess the inherent right of self-government" presents serious reservations. If Aboriginal people were to assume that the federal and provincial governments had agreed to recognize by this statement a broad Aboriginal jurisdiction, like the third order of government agreed to at the Charlottetown summit, then they could ultimately be very disappointed. Since this wording is entirely new and without constitutional precedent in this country, the courts would be free to interpret it narrowly.[54] They might determine that such a constitutional amendment ensures Aboriginal communities little more than a modified form of municipal jurisdiction devoid of authority over criminal law matters and exerciseable only over their own residents. Such a limited scope of authority would fall far short of stated Aboriginal objectives. Ronald Dworkin has suggested that, at least in the United States, the Supreme Court is disinclined to stray very far from established constitutional norms. If his thesis holds true for Canadian courts, then Aboriginal communities should be concerned that a bare statement recognizing their right of self-government will be interpreted in a very limiting way.[55]

Recent comments by the Supreme Court of Canada in *Delgamuukw* v. *British Columbia*[56] would appear to reinforce Dworkin's caution. In commenting on how a court must view evidence in an Aboriginal rights case the court observed: "The justification for this special approach can be found in the nature of aboriginal rights themselves ... Those rights are aimed at the reconciliation of the prior occupation of North America by distinctive aboriginal societies with the assertion of crown sovereignty over Canadian territory ... In other words aboriginal rights are truly sui generis, and demand a unique approach to the treatment of evidence, which accords due weight to the perspective of aboriginal peoples. However that accommodation must be done in a manner which does not strain the Canadian legal and constitutional structure."[57] Such comments suggest that without very clear indications that a radical change is what is "intended," this court will be inclined to be quite conservative in its interpretation of aboriginal entitlements.

On the other hand, the wording "domestic dependent nationhood" imputes a general doctrine comprised of many clearly recognized principles. Consequently, it would impose on Canadian courts guidelines that they would be compelled to accept no matter how novel they may be. However, since this doctrine is still somewhat insufficient for Aboriginal purposes, further clarification is required. This complementary wording would sculpt the body of the doctrine so that it is compatible with both Aboriginal and non-Aboriginal parties.

For example, used in a Canadian context, the doctrine would ascribe to Aboriginal governments broad authority over both civil and criminal law matters. Other principles, such as a provincial government's authority to legislate over both issues and persons within Aboriginal communities, would be circumscribed. These elements of jurisdiction are clearly contained within the doctrine. Should the parties wish to alter this doctrine to either increase or reduce federal, provincial, or Aboriginal jurisdiction, the complementary language could do just that. Presumably, such language would clarify what would occur should Aboriginal and federal criminal laws conflict. It could also specify the exact circumstances in which federal or Aboriginal laws would prevail.

Of course, adoption of this doctrine will not eliminate disputes about its meaning. Such debates, no matter what wording a constitutional amendment employs, will always occur. However, using the doctrine would accomplish three tasks. First, it would establish a common basis for initial discussions. The history of these principles in American jurisprudence is clear. The Canadian parties would simply decide how best to adapt the doctrine in Canada. Second, assuming that the complementary language does not erode too much of the fundamental doctrine, Aboriginal parties would surely benefit from recognition of a broad jurisdictional authority. And third, all parties would benefit from knowing generally how the courts would interpret the constitutional amendment. The discretion of the courts would be constrained by the principles already established by well-known jurisprudential history. All parties would be able to take some comfort in this knowledge.

A final comment must be offered regarding this suggestion. The constitutional makeup of Canada and the United States varies in a number of ways. However, in this particular area the differences do not appear to be insurmountable,[58] for they can be accommodated by the complementary language proposed by this suggestion. Some observers might suggest that the language required to state a constitutional amendment, along with the complementary language necessary to qualify the doctrine, would be too lengthy. Indeed, any amendment recognizing Aboriginal self-government, whether or not it employs the American doctrine, could well be lengthy. Yet such observations seem to be unwarranted.

The Canadian Constitution is not comprised of just the Constitution Act, 1982, and the former British North America Act, 1867 (now the Constitution Act, 1867). The Constitution is an amalgam of both written laws and implied conventions. The written portions of the Constitution are contained in more than thirty separate pieces of legislation. When one considers the significance of the nation building to be achieved by an amendment recognizing Aboriginal self-government, a few more pages of print are a small price to pay.

Even if the use of this doctrine were constitutionally feasible, serious doubt remains that the federal and provincial parties would warm to the idea of recognizing such broad Aboriginal jurisdiction. The political climate has changed dramatically since the Charlottetown discussions, and it is unclear whether Aboriginal positions would be viewed as positively today as they were then.

If *Sparrow* and *Van der Peet* reflect Dworkin's assertions about the limitations on decisions from the Supreme Court of Canada, then Aboriginal people may have much to be concerned about. To begin with, they must realize that nothing less than a clear constitutional statement recognizing the right of self-government will achieve the significant political changes that they seek. Even though non-constitutional negotiations regarding local expressions of self-government (as are under way in Manitoba) seem to provide new beginnings for these communities, surely these opportunities are illusionary. Whenever a dispute occurs between Aboriginal and federal and provincial governments, as it surely will, Aboriginal interests will no doubt continue to be compromised. The history of constitutional jurisprudence already bears this out. And apparently even recent constitutionally recognized entitlements of Aboriginal people do not provide adequate security.

If Dworkin is correct in his analysis of the limitations imposed on judges interpreting rights within constitutions, then Aboriginal people should be troubled. They should be concerned that a constitutional document that clearly articulates recognition of the rights of Aboriginal communities may nevertheless be insufficient to prevent a judicial interpretation that seeks to preserve the "structural design" and "dominant lines" of old ideas.

Sparrow provided the Supreme Court with just such an opportunity – one that it chose to ignore. The court turned its back on the opportunity to protect the rights of Aboriginal communities through the normal application of the entrenchment function.[59] Instead, it characterized the wording "recognized and affirmed" as necessitating a new form of entrenchment protection. Without providing any explanation about why this wording required a new interpretation, the court forced these new Aboriginal entitlements to fit the old version of federalism. Thus, even language such as that found in Section 35 and thought to be unequivocal and sympathetic to Aboriginal interests will be interpreted in such a way as to maintain a "coherent constitutional morality."[60]

The warnings to Aboriginal people suggested by these cases seem evident. Anything less than a clear constitutional recognition of the right of Aboriginal people to self-government will fail to achieve their aims. The Nisga'a treaty has demonstrated that non-constitutional agreements will never achieve the degree of authority sought by Aboriginal people. In particular, when conflicts between jurisdictional authority arise, even recent case law indicates that Aboriginal positions will not be championed by Canadian courts.

This case law also suggests that, in instances such as the Charlottetown Accord, which proposed ongoing negotiations that might ultimately have to be decided by the courts, this too should be avoided. If the courts are not disposed to broaden the interpretation of Aboriginal entitlements, then as little as possible should be left to judicial interpretation. Permitting the courts to fill in the gaps seems to be unwise.

The recent judicial history of Section 35 interpretation might suggest something else to Aboriginal people. They considered the wording of this section to be clear, but the Supreme Court of Canada viewed it in a wholly surprising way. Hence, Aboriginal people may also seek to have structural changes made to the judicial institutions to ensure an equitable application of their rights. A number of possible institutional changes have been proposed in this chapter. The adoption of any of these proposals would likely improve the present judicial structure.

Perhaps the best alternative has yet to be proposed. Oliver Wendell Holmes once observed: "Many ideas grow better when transplanted into another mind than in the one where they sprang up." This has never been more true than in the present instance. However, that isn't going to occur unless greater attention is focused on the difficulties associated with the process of entrenchment and recognition. Unless these issues are resolved before a political commitment is made to recognizing Aboriginal self-determination, Aboriginal people may find that their right of self-government is notional at best.

5
Historical Aboriginal Collective Rights

The Initial Debate

The Charlottetown Accord initiated unprecedented public discussion in Canada of issues associated with Aboriginal self-government. Both the preliminary national discussion forums such as the Spicer Commission and the later pre-referendum debates often became public discussions of varied elements of the Aboriginal self-government proposal. Commonly, the concerns of "What does self-government mean?" and "How would self-government work?" were raised to prompt greater clarification of the content of Aboriginal self-government. Neither query was unexpected given that both federal and provincial governments had been making the same inquiries since the constitutional conferences of the early 1980s. However, now it was time for the Canadian public to pose these questions.

Once again these queries were met with the same reticence displayed by Aboriginal leaders for years. They believed – and were supported in this belief by most of their people – that it was both unnecessary and likely not possible to offer clear descriptions of self-government. When Aboriginal people replied by stating that, like any kind of community, there would be houses, stores, roads, schools, and an assortment of local government offices, their response was met with a request for greater specificity.

Aboriginal peoples took exception to such demands. Not every Aboriginal community had constructed a blueprint for its particular kind of self-government. Some communities were large enough that their members felt no need to reach beyond existing borders for any kind of association with others. In Ontario, the First Nation community at Six Nations near Brantford, with more than 20,000 residents, is an example of a large enough community to consider "going it alone." On the other hand, many small communities have always thought that joining together with similar local communities would make a great deal of sense, especially in terms of harnessing the benefits associated with economies of scale. Also in Ontario, the seven Anishnabek First Nations located on Manitoulin Island share a common cultural heritage. Each community, significantly smaller than Six Nations, might well consider amalgamating under a common tribal government. Both large and small communities of these sorts have also considered the merits of political alignment with regional communities that share a common history and culture and have similar aspirations. Regional non-governmental organizations such as the Federation of Saskatchewan Indians already reflect this approach, albeit in a much less governing-like format.[1]

Often Aboriginal people have stated that these and perhaps more traditional models were being considered. Precise decisions would be reached later by each community. However, such a response was usually treated as inadequate by those asking the questions.

Perhaps what is most surprising about the question "What would Aboriginal self-government look like?" is that it is treated as a reasonable inquiry. But is it? If the question is intended to probe the operational nature of government enacted under a self-government mandate, then such a query is pointless. Asking whether every home would be provided with gas and water, or whether specific tax forms and zoning codes would be enacted, is surely curious. If the question is intended to determine the legislative and judicial roles of the government, then it also seems to be a less than productive pursuit. How much more informed would one be, knowing that the government would mimic a parliamentary format or that there would be both trial- and appeal-level courts? Any responses to the question likely did little to address the concerns that prompted it. Perhaps the answers did not adequately allay these concerns because the right question was not being asked.

The Right Question
In the minds of some people, the compelling question remains "Can it be done?" One response is to point to the tribal communities in the United States. They exist, complete with schools, hospitals, roads, houses, and stores, in much the same way as towns and villages across the country exist. (Their governmental foundations and operations were explored in Chapter 2.) These communities clearly illustrate the potential operational feasibility of Aboriginal communities in Canada.

Another possible response to the question of feasibility raises a more ethical issue. Aboriginal people might point to the amalgamation of cities such as Halifax-Dartmouth and Metropolitan Toronto when responding to inquiries concerning their own communities. They would point out that no one asked the provincial governments, which created these amalgamated cities, exactly what such municipal governments would resemble. No one seriously asked how they would provide services or decision making. People were confident that, notwithstanding problems that might result from such amalgamations, the local governments would function adequately. Aboriginal peoples have the same confidence in their own ability to make such decisions. They are at once intrigued and offended by the realization that others do not share this belief.

If one needed a prism through which to view the ethical appropriateness of such a question, then one need look no further than the claims of sovereignty made by Quebec. Although most Canadians have no wish to see Quebec separate, none has dared to demand that Quebec first explain the nature or operations of a newly constituted government. Quebeckers are Canadians, too, at least for the time being. Surely any need to pacify the minds of Canadians regarding Aboriginal self-government applies equally to Quebec – perhaps even more so in light of its proposal to separate from the country. If one is concerned about protecting the rights and welfare of Aboriginal Canadians, then a similar concern is even more relevant to Canadians whose future within this country is in doubt. However, such a question has never been put to separatist leaders – nor is it likely to be considered.

Other questions more specific and arguably more relevant may address the real concerns of Canadians. More enlightened inquiries would ask how such communities would support themselves financially. How will Aboriginal governments, in whatever forms they take, relate to provincial and federal governments? How will non-Aboriginal people be affected by Aboriginal governments and their laws? Will such laws apply outside the territory of the Aboriginal government? Will principles of law such as due process, or the rule of law, be employed by such governments? Specifically, should the Canadian Charter of Rights and Freedoms apply to the governments of Aboriginal communities? Each inquiry addresses a tangible issue.

I want to focus on this last question but should first explain why such a question needs to be asked. Is there something unique about Aboriginal societies that would suggest that the individual rights protected in the Charter should not apply to them? This chapter will suggest that the answer to this inquiry is yes.

The debate about Aboriginal self-government that emerged from the 1980s and continued with the dialogue surrounding the Charlottetown Accord precipitated discussion of an equally volatile issue: equality of treatment for Aboriginal women within Aboriginal communities. Aboriginal women's organizations wanted some assurance that Aboriginal governments would not be able to pass laws or act in any fashion that would discriminate against them. Aboriginal women's leaders were in essence demanding equality of treatment as guaranteed by the Canadian Charter of Rights and Freedoms. They were asserting that the Charter should be imposed on the bodies governing their communities.

For years, Aboriginal women fought against a discriminatory Indian Act that denied them legal access to their communities and identities. As most Canadians are aware, the Indian Act demanded that those Indian women who married non-Indians lose both their status as an Indian as well as their membership in the local band. Men, on the other hand, were not only permitted to marry non-Indian women without losing either their status or band membership, but their non-Indian spouses automatically gained both status and membership. This discriminatory treatment lay at the core of Aboriginal women's outrage. This struggle has only recently resulted in significant amendments to the Indian Act, commonly known as Bill C-31, enacted in April 1985. By these amendments, women would no longer be treated differently than their male counterparts. They would retain both their Indian status and band membership, no matter whom they married. In addition, those Indian women who had been disenfranchised by discriminatory sections of the Indian Act regained their rightful places in their communities, and their children, subjected to similar disenfranchisement, also regained lost status. Still, even today, many women have not been able to exercise their right to full reintegration.[2]

Many Aboriginal women argued that their cause had not been championed by enough Aboriginal leaders, most of whom were men. Not surprisingly then, since the constitutional conferences of the 1980s, Aboriginal women have sought to have gender equality imposed on any form of Aboriginal self-government that might emanate from these discussions. Thus, when recognition of Aboriginal self-government found its way into the Charlottetown Accord, once again Aboriginal women sought to have entrenched some guarantee that they would not be discriminated against by their own governments solely because of their gender.

The other side in the debate feared that individual rights such as freedom from discrimination, guaranteed in and enforced by the Canadian Charter of Rights and Freedoms, would compromise the collective rights of the Aboriginal community. To many, the line was drawn between protecting the individual rights of women and protecting the collective rights of the community. Discussions ensued about the merits of requiring all Aboriginal communities to be bound by the Charter or none at all. A third alternative, an Aboriginal charter of rights, which would substitute for the Canadian Charter, was occasionally alluded to but never elaborated upon with very much specificity. Although some Aboriginal communities today do have a local tribal charter of rights, none directly takes on the challenge of reconciling those individual rights enshrined within the Canadian Charter with the concept of collective rights so often referred to.

As broad as one might expect a discussion to be when contrasting such conceptually divergent positions, the debate was surprisingly devoid of substance. It appeared that the opposing parties were already galvanized in their respective opinions. Hence, the debate was not broadened beyond the parameters of gender equality. This was unfortunate because the collective rights about which Aboriginal communities are concerned are much broader than individual rights such as gender equality. The ramifications of the Charter applying to Aboriginal communities are far more complex than this single issue implies and deserve more extensive dialogue.

Charter Rights and Human Rights

At this point, it is perhaps useful to clarify how a charter of rights is intended to function. It is not meant to resolve disputes between citizens. If an individual is treated in a discriminatory fashion by another person, such as being denied service in a restaurant due to his/her race, then the complainant can take a claim to a human rights commission. Such commissions have commonly been established by the federal government as well as by each province. If the discrimination is due to race, gender, or age, then a commission usually holds a hearing to resolve the dispute. Human rights charters are not employed for such purposes.

Rights entrenched within the Canadian Charter of Rights and Freedoms pertain to actions between a government and individuals. That is, federal, provincial, or municipal governments, as well as their administrative agents, are precluded in the exercise of their authority from discriminating against people on the basis of their religion, race, or gender. Similarly, these governments may not deny people freedom of thought, expression, association, and an assortment of other rights. The principal idea is that charters such as those employed in Canada and the United States (where the Constitution includes a Bill of Rights) are intended to protect individuals from government encroachments on these rights. It is this protective measure that Aboriginal women have sought to employ against the activities of Aboriginal governments. They simply wish to ensure that their own governments do not discriminate against them because of their gender.

There has been considerable scholarship about the ideological merits of collective rights as opposed to individual rights. However, little of this scholarship has a Canadian context, and even less of it focuses on Aboriginal societies. Individual rights theory has many rationales,[3] while collective rights theory has far fewer. Individual rights theorists commonly discuss whether rights are a reflection of nature or an expression of God's will. Is their purpose to achieve individual dignity or to provide the greatest amount of happiness for the greatest number? Others ask whether they create claims or entitlements, whether they are grounded in religious belief or can be known independently by simple reasoning. However, none of these inquiries is very helpful for Aboriginal concerns.

Although there is growing interest in the subject of collective rights, there is a significant lack of scholarship on the issue of Aboriginal practices as expressions of collective rights or values. Indeed, there is no significant treatment of which forms these collective rights might take (other than harvesting rights such as hunting, fishing, and trapping and, of course, self-government itself). Even less available is any expression of how such practices might conflict with the individual rights enshrined in the Canadian Charter of Rights and Freedoms.

Before further pursuing claims of Aboriginal collective rights, I should comment briefly on the nature of rights theory. Classical rights theory views individuals as possessing entitlements that establish particular relationships. If individual X has right A, then all other people have an obligation to respect or at least not interfere with X's enjoyment of right A. For example, if X has a right to freedom of speech, then others are prohibited from interfering with this right. Similarly, X's right to vote imposes prohibitions on others who would seek to restrict X's freedom to cast a ballot. This is the traditional understanding of the rights dynamic.

Such rights have been described as "negative" rights because in essence they create prohibitions against interfering with the exercise of these entitlements. But there is another perspective, referred to as "positive" rights theory, that this classical dynamic does not accommodate.

Much of the discourse on this positive rights perspective has centred on the individual's right to equality. The classical interpretation has been founded upon ensuring that no one interferes with X's guarantee of being treated equally. Others, in particular governments, are precluded from denying X the same fair treatment accorded to Y. If this treatment is provided, then X is viewed as being treated equally. In this respect, the right to equality is viewed as "equality of opportunity."

Others argue, however, that it is not quite that simple. Most proponents of a positive rights approach reason that individual dignity is at the core of what is protected when governments ensure freedom of association, speech, conscience, religion, and so forth. However, if a person's dignity is the real motivation for this exercise, then simply guaranteeing negative rights is insufficient to achieve this goal. Allowing X the same opportunity as Y to purchase a home does not achieve the goal of true equality. Not actively denying a person of colour the opportunity to purchase a home is a kind of equality of treatment; however, if this person has, through historical disadvantage, been denied the opportunity to become educated sufficiently to hold a job that in turn will give him or her the income to afford the house, then positive rights theorists would argue that this person has been denied equal treatment. Proponents of the positive interpretation of rights assert that equality also requires "equality of outcome."

Thus, equality is truly achieved only through additional efforts, usually by the government, to level the playing field. Often what is proposed to achieve this goal is a redistribution of income.

Another variation on the classical view of negative rights is reflected in recent international developments. The negative rights inherent in the Canadian Charter of Rights and Freedoms are in many ways a carbon copy of the American Bill of Rights. An American judge has provided his views on the reasons for such guarantees. Judge Posner has reflected that "the men who wrote the Bill of Rights were not concerned that the federal government might do too little for the people, but that it might do too much to them."[4] However, public attitudes have changed recently as people have come to believe that governments should be more actively involved in the well-being of their citizens. Although many would debate the extent of this involvement, few would doubt the need for some government intervention, such as in ensuring reasonable levels of public health and security.

In the 1944 "State of the Union Address," President Franklin Roosevelt introduced positive liberties to the American public. In what has become known as Roosevelt's Second Bill of Rights, he sought to ensure for Americans

- the right to a useful and remunerative job;
- the right to earn enough to provide adequate food, clothing, and recreation;
- the right of every family to a decent home;
- the right to adequate medical care;
- the right to a good education; and
- the right to adequate protection from the economic fears of old age, sickness, accident, and unemployment.[5]

Social and economic rights are also found in many European constitutions, such as in that of Sweden: "The personal economic and cultural welfare of the individual shall be fundamental aims of the activities of the community. In particular, it shall be incumbent on the community to secure the right to work, to housing, and to education and to promote social care and security as well as a favourable living environment."[6]

The United Nations Universal Declaration of Human Rights, adopted by the General Assembly on 10 December 1948, provides many statements of positive rights:

Everyone, as a member of society, has the right to social security and is entitled to realization through national effort and international co-operation and in accordance with the organization and resources of each State, of the economic, social, and cultural rights indispensable for his dignity and the free development of his personality.[7]

Everyone has the right to a standard of living adequate for the health and well-being of himself and his family, including food, clothing, housing and medical care and necessary social services, and the right to security in the event of unemployment, sickness, disability, widowhood, old age or other lack of livelihood in circumstances beyond his control.[8]

The rights enshrined in the Universal Declaration of Human Rights and in other European constitutions have not received the same legal status as the negative liberties protected by the Canadian Charter of Rights and Freedoms or the American Bill of Rights. Whereas negative liberties have received the benefit of legal enforcement through the courts, positive rights have not. Instead, these latter obligations imposed on governments have been viewed as "programmatic" rights. They are seen as goals to which the respective governments should aspire. It remains to be seen whether there are circumstances in which such constitutional declarations can receive judicial enforcement. In particular, can these positive guarantees be used to strike down new legislation that clearly abandons stated government objectives?

For present purposes, the enforceability of such positive rights is moot. I offer these comments to point out that classical rights theory is not the only approach. Today negative rights theory must make room for discussion of positive rights declarations. What these latter rights might be, how they can be achieved, and the difficulties encountered in enforcing them are all issues that deserve discussion. I simply seek to add to this debate about rights a further consideration of the collective rights of Aboriginal people. Although this collective rights form does not fit easily within the classical negative rights analysis, as I will illustrate, like positive rights theory it deserves serious consideration.

It is noteworthy that the Canadian Constitution, including the 1982 amendments, recognizes collective rights in a variety of subject areas, including separate school education, official languages, minority education, and multiculturalism. In addition, of course, the Constitution Act clearly recognizes certain collective rights of the Aboriginal peoples of Canada.[9] Yet this recognition does not provide any assistance in reconciling the debate precipitated by Aboriginal women. Section 35 of the Constitution Act recognizes the existence of the Aboriginal and treaty rights of Canada's three Aboriginal peoples, and Section 25 goes so far as to protect such rights from the Charter itself. But how these rights are to be achieved, and to what extent, remain unclear.

As mentioned above, too little has been written on the general debate about collective versus individual rights and on the particular implications of this debate for Aboriginal self-government. Excluding the debate about gender equality, the only other discussion of what has been characterized as a collective Aboriginal right revolves around the traditional gathering activities of hunting, fishing, and trapping. Although these activities are surely collective community rights, they do not precipitate the kind of confrontation between rights occasioned by the issue of gender equality. It is therefore somewhat surprising that both sides of the discussion are so entrenched in their beliefs when so few of the implications for Aboriginal communities have been discussed. It is therefore worth examining what some of these collective Aboriginal rights might resemble in practice and how they might conflict with individual rights guaranteed by the Charter.

Collective rights issues have long been recognized in Canada. Public order and morality, fair dealing in business activities, as well as guarantees of public health and safety all reflect the collective interests of a community. Unions are perhaps the most commonly provided example of how individuals both receive benefits and perform obligations within a collective context. Similarly, individuals in the military owe both duty and loyalty to their country. Failure to perform these obligations properly can lead to legal sanctions by a military court.

The Canadian Constitution also recognizes the existence of a collective's rights. The minority language rights provisions of the 1982 act are a clear reflection of a community's right to be educated in either of the official languages, notwithstanding the dominant language of use in a province.[10] There are limits, of course, to this right. The multicultural heritage provision articulated in Section 27 provides further evidence that members of a collective have certain rights as a consequence of their membership. Thus far, the case law seems to indicate that Section 27 is to be used by the courts largely as an interpretive tool in evaluating individual rights, recognized by the Canadian Charter of Rights and Freedoms, being considered under the Section 1 analysis[11] or in conjunction with other Charter rights being asserted.[12] The courts have not yet expressed the opinion that Section 27 imposes positive rights that can be enforced in law.[13] Nevertheless, this notion of collective rights is far from unknown in Canada.

In international law, the term "collective rights" has become known more popularly as "third-generation," or "solidarity," rights. The individual's right to life, and other rights of citizens against their government, as illustrated above, have become known as first- and second-generation rights, respectively. The right of a collective to life is now considered to be third generation. This is the kind of right that Aboriginal peoples seek as protection from the effects of the Charter. They claim the right to protect certain values and practices founded within their unique histories and traditions. They view the Charter as a threat to the existence of not only these rights but also community standards of behaviour that they believe flow from these practices (see Chapter 7). Out of deference to such concerns, it is therefore important for non-Aboriginal governments to understand

exactly what is being sought when Aboriginal leaders claim the need to recognize and protect these collective values and rights. Considering the issue
of rights and duties within an Aboriginal context may assist this understanding.

Rights versus Duties

In one sense, the term "individual right" has little meaning in many traditional communities. Few Aboriginal languages have a word or term for
"personal right." This is not a unique characteristic of Aboriginal communities, for many Asian countries, such as Japan, similarly lack a linguistic
conception of a personal right. Instead, Aboriginal communities have a
stronger appreciation of the word *duty.*

As described in Chapter 2, the Navajo Nation has a multifaceted judicial
structure, including both trial- and appellate-level courts with criminal,
civil, and family court divisions. These courts are similar in structure and
function to most provincial courts in Canada.

However, in addition to these Western-style courts, the Navajo have
developed another forum for resolving disputes. Drawing on their unique
cultural history, they have created another, more culturally sensitive, judicial structure. This forum is called the Peacemaker Court system and is
premised on traditional methods of Navajo conflict resolution, which in
turn are firmly grounded in Navajo values and traditions. The Navajo
peacemaking system has been described as being founded upon three general principles: freedom with responsibility, leadership among equals, and
traditional procedures.[14]

It is the first element of this triad that is of particular interest here.
Navajo tribal society is based on clanship. Consequently, the Navajo have
a strong sense of kinship, or *ke'e*. Each clan has its own role to play within
the larger community and is linked principally by birth and marriage. This
is in part the result of a prohibition against members from the same clan
intra-marrying. Thus, inter-clan marriages are the only alternative. Such
marriages not only help to solidify relationships between different families
and clans but they often become building blocks for a strong societal
framework. Traditional Navajo teachings describe the role each clan has to
play within the larger community. Within each clan, the family structure
and respective roles of women, men, and children are specifically defined.
This system has produced a community in which an individual's role and
obligations to family, clan, and community are clearly sketched out.[15] For
example, some clan members are required to teach Navajo customs and
values. Others are delegated the roles of political leaders, while still others
are required to preserve and teach religious practices.

However, the individual is not entirely forgotten within this paradigm.
Individuals are taught from birth that they are free to act in any fashion

they choose. However, this individual freedom is tempered by the teaching that they must have proper regard for their clan duties and obligations. Thus, for Navajo individuals, it is not always a question of which personal rights they have, since they are free to act as they wish. Rather, it is a question of which constraints are imposed on this freedom by an individual's duties and obligations to family, clan, and society at large.

The Peacemaker Court system operates within this cultural context and relies heavily on a process of quasi-mediation, though parties can agree to binding arbitration. One difference between the Navajo approach and Western styles of mediation is the unique role of the peacemaker. In most common processes of mediation, the mediator assumes a neutral role, but not so in Navajo peacemaking. The peacemaker draws heavily on cultural traditions and commonly reminds the parties of these traditions and their respective historical roles. Thus, it is often a peacemaker pointing out not an individual's rights so much as his or her duties that helps to resolve the dispute.

This system has proven highly successful as an alternative to the more common adversarial structure used by their tribal courts (peacemaking has also been used in criminal law matters). Furthermore, peacemaking is testimony to the community's understanding of and respect for Navajo values, used in a culturally meaningful fashion, to resolve local problems. It is through a like-minded use of traditional values and customs that Aboriginal people in Canada may choose to enact a judicial system that has greater cultural relevance and application.

Values reflected in the Navajo Peacemaker Courts are not limited to tribal communities with clan structures. Many of these cultural elements are common to other tribal communities throughout North America, including those not based on clan systems. Both the Peacemaker Courts and other tribal court systems in the United States value the restoration of cultural harmony in the community (Pueblo and Hopi examples are given elsewhere in this book). Some people argue that the Peacemaker Court system is ideally suited to this task because it is a voluntary structure grounded in traditional values and methodologies. Other tribal courts similarly engage in unique quests for the restoration of community balance and harmony through the expression and utilization of their respective values. It is important to recognize that in the majority of circumstances these processes of dispute resolution are concerned equally with individual rights and community responsibilities.

It would be inaccurate to characterize Aboriginal communities as having no interest in protecting individual rights. The Canadian dispute over gender discrimination in Aboriginal communities indicates that this is clearly not the case. However, to understand the perspective of Aboriginal peoples regarding community rights, one must appreciate that civil libertarian urges do not attract all people equally. Many Aboriginal people wish not only to have their individual rights respected but also, more importantly in some instances, to preserve the recognition of duty within a community, a duty directed at care and consideration for others. They ask only that this recognition also be protected by law.

Democracy and Aboriginal History

Fundamentally, the debate concerning the protection of collective rights versus individual or Charter rights is not a dispute between democratic rights and antidemocratic concerns. Although some observers may characterize it this way, this view is misleading. Moreover, such an approach brings nothing substantive to the discussion concerning how the values of Aboriginal and non-Aboriginal societies can exist in harmony. In some sense, this is not a debate about the competing values of each society so much as it is a discussion of methodologies.

It is somewhat ironic that the collectivist approach of tribal communities has, in some discussions, been cast in these terms, particularly in regard to conflicts with the Canadian Charter of Rights and Freedoms. Elements of the Canadian political structure and particularly the Charter were created with a clear appreciation of US constitutional history. Canadians have learned much from the American experience, especially in regard to recognizing constitutionally protected guarantees of individual rights – so much so that many of the rights enshrined in the US Constitution are clearly reflected by the Canadian Charter. It is therefore worth noting some of the precipitants of the American model.

In the genesis of the American government, many of the democratic structures and civil liberties were adopted directly from local Aboriginal tribal values and practices. Two of the principal framers of the American Constitution were Benjamin Franklin and Thomas Jefferson, both of whom studied Indian tribal life extensively and had numerous contacts with these communities.[16] Not surprisingly, then, significant elements of the founding American political document were drawn from their knowledge of tribal structures and values. Professor Robert Miller has described how Benjamin Franklin was favourably impressed by the sociopolitical dynamic established within the Iroquois Confederacy. He notes: "Due to Franklin's experiences with Indians, it is generally well accepted that the Iroquois Confederacy was a model and a significant influence on his Albany Plan and the Articles of Confederation. As a result, Franklin, and subsequently the United States, were influenced and affected by his contact and familiarity with Indian tribes."[17]

Jefferson also greatly admired the democratic ideals inherent in many tribal communities. Miller writes: "Jefferson found among the Indians a modified state of nature – pre-civil society. He praised Indians for having 'no law but that of Nature.' They lived, according to Jefferson, without government but enjoyed *peace, justice, liberty,* and *equality.* Furthermore, when Indians adopted government, they adopted a republican form, a fact that reinforced Jefferson's belief that republican government was natural to mankind. Jefferson, as a student of nature and its experiences, learned much from Indians and 'freely acknowledged his debt to Indian teachers.'"[18]

Much of their knowledge of Indian tribes came from their association with tribes of the northeastern United States,[19] which included the Iroquois Confederacy, Shawnee, Ottawa, Delawares, Algonquians of Virginia, and Miami of Ohio. Several of these tribes recognized a woman's right to vote on tribal matters, including the appointment of a tribal chief. Indeed, some tribes, such as the Mohawk, have a clan structure whereby clan mothers choose the tribe's various chiefs and have the power to replace, at any time, the appointed chief with someone else. As well, some of these tribes recognized the right of a woman to be appointed chief centuries before women were given the right to vote in elections in either the United States or Canada.[20]

Many tribes have traditionally exercised internal checks and balances against the concentration of too much power in any single tribal function. Separating the roles of war chief and peace chief in Mohawk communities was an early reflection of this separation of powers. Franklin and Jefferson later borrowed the separation and balancing of centres of power in the development of American government structures. Many decisions in tribal communities had to be ratified by clan structures or, in some instances, "councils" or "senates." This kind of consultation not only acted as a check on the concentration of too much authority in a single person but also provided a broad representation of opinion in the governing process. Thus, the very structure of Aboriginal communities historically has been not only inherently democratic but also wisely balanced. It was such a structure that Franklin and Jefferson borrowed and that subsequently found its way into the development of the American government.

Western society is commonly characterized by a hierarchical structure resembling a pyramid. On the other hand, Aboriginal communities traditionally had only a two- or three-tiered structure. Mark Dockstador has described this phenomenon lucidly in his seminal treatise on Indian law making.[21] He describes how Aboriginal communities were commonly characterized by a flat political structure that maximized the involvement of individuals within the spectrum of decision making. He illustrates how most community decisions were made through the exercise of consensus building. In this way, everyone, including men, women, and children, had an opportunity to express an opinion on an issue. These expressions of opinion could occur during family or clan meetings, at spiritual or cultural events, or even at full tribal councils. In one fashion or another, everyone was given the opportunity to express his or her thoughts on issues of importance to the tribe. The result was often a decision that attempted to balance the various interests expressed. This consensus building could be a lengthy process, but the results were broadly accepted in the community. Thus, the harmony and balance within this society was the benefit of a highly democratic decision-making process.

Another inherent element of democracy in tribal communities was respect for individual freedom for both men and women. In essence, this freedom constituted a form of gender equality. As mentioned above, the right to elect chiefs was often shared by all members of the tribe, including women. Although not all of these rights were practised equally by every tribe, many of the aforementioned democratic practices were commonly shared. Thus, it is clear that the ideas of democracy were not foreign to tribal communities prior to European contact. Today American tribes can boast a long history of association with both the ideals and the practices of democracy. To assume therefore that Aboriginal communities are indifferent to such values or that these notions are without broad support within these communities is a serious misreading of both history and present circumstances.

Comment

No society exists in a vacuum totally insulated from external pressures. Notwithstanding the efforts made by a community to set itself apart from the values of communities around it, such an endeavour is fraught with great difficulties. One need only consider recent international developments to recognize how Western ideas of democracy and economics have forever changed the sociopolitical environments of what for centuries were isolated societies. Both the disintegration of the former Soviet Union and the events leading up to the Tiananmen Square incident can be attributed, at least in part, to the introduction of Western political ideas into these societies. Exposure to such values is no less influential in tribal communities in North America.

In the United States, the Hopi community at Old Oraibi, Arizona, is worthy of notice. It is the longest-existing tribal community on the continent (though a similar claim is made by the Acoma Pueblo community located on the First Mesa in New Mexico). Documentation exists to show that Hopi people have lived at Oraibi since the early twelfth century. Among Hopi tribal communities, Oraibi is recognized as being the most "traditional." Its government and social structure are still premised on an active and vital clan structure. Traditional religions and other cultural ceremonies are still practised there daily.

However, the maintenance of cultural values and traditions has not been achieved without cost and effort. Neither still-picture or video cameras nor voice-taping machines of any kind are allowed within the community. In this way every effort is made to respect and preserve the Hopi culture within. Knowledge and traditions are passed from generation to generation verbally through the Hopi language. Any written account of traditional customs is prohibited. The Hopi believe that through these efforts Oraibi's culture will be protected from external influences and therefore preserved.

Moreover, Oraibi has neither electricity nor running water. Adoption of Western conveniences was initially thought to threaten the preservation of Hopi traditions simply through bringing with them a necessary association with the outside world. It was thought that the introduction of these amenities would be the thin edge of the wedge that would introduce values associated with a non-Hopi lifestyle. Thus, Oraibi precludes by law the introduction of electrical lines or running water into the community.

However, these efforts to prevent the Westernization of the community and its values have not been entirely successful. It is somewhat curious to see the traditional mud and stone houses equipped with generators that provide electric power for televisions, whose antennas protrude from these homes. Apparently, the laws attempting to insulate local culture have been no match for the allure of Western convenience and Hopi ingenuity. The values of the surrounding non-Hopi culture have also found their way into these homes. Changes in the social structure of this most traditional Hopi community are already evident.

Nonetheless, the values of Hopi culture are still preserved in Hopi language and custom. The unique perspectives and attitudes of the Hopi still prevail. What Old Oraibi has found is a balance between the old and the new, with some of the cultural accoutrements of each. Indeed, the type of balance maintained by the Hopi is perhaps what most Aboriginal communities seek in their quests for unique expressions of self-government.

It thus seems that, where Western amenities and values find their way into a highly traditional Aboriginal community, as in Oraibi, notions of individual rights will inevitably be expressed. Indeed, the debate about gender equality in Canadian Aboriginal communities has ensured that discussions of individual rights will continue to occur within the context of collective rights.

6
Aboriginal Values versus Charter Rights

As mentioned in the previous chapter, there has been a great deal of general comment about the conflict between individual and collective rights. However, little has been said about exactly what these collective rights might resemble in practice.[1] Thus far, the debate has been largely theoretical.[2] The issue of gender equality represents the principal exception to this observation. The absence of tangible examples from such a discussion is unfortunate since there are a number of areas of potential conflict between an individual's rights as enshrined in the Canadian Charter of Rights and Freedoms and the collectivist values and customs of various Aboriginal peoples. Hence, a discussion of practical examples of potential conflict would illuminate much of what is currently vague and unfamiliar terrain. Indeed, the discussion of such examples could achieve a great deal in reassuring non-Aboriginal people that Aboriginal communities have legitimate cultural concerns in this area. These concerns deserve to be addressed.

There are a number of such potential conflicts. For example, the Charter guarantees that every citizen has the right to vote in federal and provincial elections.[3] Many Aboriginal communities, however, are constituted along clan lines and may have difficulty with this provision. As described in the previous chapter, traditional Mohawk communities have used a different method of choosing leaders. The traditional practice does not reflect this concept of one person, one vote. Instead, the decision rests exclusively with clan mothers (as explained in Chapter 5). Thus, in such circumstances, not every tribal member is permitted to vote for community leadership. Similarly, not all tribal members may be eligible to stand for office. Since the clan mothers choose who is most appropriate to lead the community, individuals cannot actually decide to stand for public office, at least not in the same sense that provincial or federal politicians decide to become candidates for their positions. If the clan mothers decide not to consider an individual, then that person cannot really choose to run for office.

If the Charter guarantees of Section 3 were to be imposed on such a community, ensuring everyone the right to vote or stand for public office, then this would clearly offend the collective values at work as expressed by the clan mothers' decisions. In such circumstances, the application of Section 3 would surely constitute an attack on the clan system. The imposition of the Charter would not only threaten a traditional practice but also, perhaps more importantly, significantly undermine one of the most cohesive elements of this society. The clan system, which helps to articulate rules and duties for all members of the community, lies at the heart of this culture. Charter rules that undermine the future of integral elements of such a structure surely represent an intrusion upon the culture itself.

In the area of legal rights, the Charter ensures that an individual cannot be compelled to give evidence against himself or herself.[4] Many Aboriginal communities find this protection offensive. These communities believe that honesty and responsibility for one's actions can only be maintained as cultural values if an individual is required to speak on his or her own behalf and explain his or her actions. In some communities, these values may be centuries old. One often has a duty to explain one's actions to other members of the community, particularly to other members of one's clan. Sometimes this explanation is required as part of one's role within the clan or larger societal structure (perhaps as a spiritual leader). Other times the necessity to perform obligations is motivated by the liability that one clan has toward another clan, whose member may have been injured by the accused.[5]

However, by enforcing subsection 11(c) of the Charter, persons may avoid their responsibilities to their communities. Not only are the values of truth and duty jeopardized, but so are the fundamental pillars of the society. Clan structures, traditional elements of cohesion within a community, are undermined by the potential enforcement of the Charter. Hence, the very cultural integrity and cohesion of the community may once again be seriously jeopardized.

Similar community values promoting honesty, personal responsibility, and group obligations would be offended by the Charter guarantee that incriminating evidence given by individuals in one judicial forum cannot be used against them in another.[6] Once again the collective values of the community are at odds with this interpretation of the Charter's guarantee of an individual's rights. An Aboriginal civil adjudication, wherein clan obligations may be sought to be harmonized, would be precluded from hearing the admissions of the accused made in a criminal trial. The Charter right could prevent the resolution of a problem that may have broad cultural implications.

Aboriginal communities have always had their own methods of dealing with societal offenders.[7] Incarceration was seldom an option that they exercised. An alternative common to many Aboriginal cultures was the sanction of banishment. If counselling or warnings were not successful in changing a person's behaviour, then the offender might well be banished from a community as a last step in addressing the problem. In the future, however, this recourse may no longer be available to an Aboriginal court.

Should such a practice be adopted by an Aboriginal community today, this punishment could well offend Section 12 of the Charter. It prohibits any cruel or unusual treatment or punishment of an offender. Banishment of a person from an Aboriginal community might well be viewed by the Eurocentric courts of Canada as too cruel a punishment for the crime committed. If this were to be the finding of the court, then once again a traditional cultural practice would be undermined by the Charter.

There are other potential conflicts with the Charter. Subsection 11(d) ensures that an individual will be tried by an independent and impartial tribunal. This guarantee includes being tried by members of a jury who are just as independent and impartial. Yet this guarantee would ostensibly prevent those members of an Aboriginal community who may know the accused best, who may be highly acquainted with his or her personal history and family background, from being able to contribute to the successful resolution of the dispute. They would be prohibited from sitting as members of a jury out of concern for potential bias in any decision. Historically, this rule about bias has been followed by provincial courts in deciding the members of juries. However, this approach does not appeal to all Aboriginal communities.

In certain US tribal courts, such as those of the Pueblo, community members familiar with the accused are sometimes sought as jury members. The peacemaker appointed under the Navajo Peacemaker Court system is anything but impartial in his or her role in the resolution of the dispute. Indeed, peacemakers often perform this role specifically because of their intimate knowledge of the disputes and the parties to them. In some circumstances, the intention is to find jurors who will effect a reconciliation that balances individual and community interests. It is thought that this balance can best be achieved through a more personal understanding of the accused.

Clearly, all of these scenarios may constitute conflicts with a narrow interpretation of subsection 11(d) of the Charter. Should such a challenge prove successful, traditional practices of dispute resolution and the inherent values that they promote will once again be undermined. Surely methods of dispute resolution go to the cultural heart of a community. The integrity of any community that has its unique approaches to achieving fairness and justice undermined would be in serious jeopardy.

One should always remember that a trial is simply a forum for the resolution of a dispute. For Aboriginal communities, the prevailing perspective is that not just an individual but also the entire community has been injured. Certainly, any victim of an offence, as well as the community in which the offence occurs, have interests in the favourable resolution of the conflict. However, in Aboriginal societies, it is not just some vague "community at large" that has some obscure interest in reconciliation. Rather, traditionally, there has been a tangible collective concern regarding community disputes.

No doubt the generally small size of an Aboriginal community fosters familiarity among members and heightened concern regarding the outcome of any dispute. A smaller community obviously increases the likelihood that any person may be more closely connected to this dispute. However, perhaps size alone is less a determinative factor than is culture in this regard. In Aboriginal communities, as opposed to non-Aboriginal communities, the importance of the outcome of a dispute is more culturally grounded. Usually, traditional values, customary practices, and societal structures (i.e., clanships) create a dynamic not mirrored by the general Canadian public. The traditional need to maintain harmony within these societies is often achieved only through a recognition of historical roles and personal responsibilities.

Another area of potential conflict with the Charter concerns subsection 11(h), which provides protection for the individual from double jeopardy – that is, in simple terms, an individual cannot be tried twice for the same offence. Again an Aboriginal community's right to resolve a dispute consistent with its own values may be compromised. For example, if an Aboriginal couple who were married pursuant to Aboriginal law took up residence outside their community, then they would fall within the jurisdiction of federal and provincial laws. If the wife were subsequently assaulted by the husband, then Canadian criminal laws would no doubt be engaged to resolve the situation. However, what if the wife were to move back to Aboriginal territory, perhaps as a consequence of the assault, and the husband were soon to follow? The Aboriginal community might wish to deal with this problem in its own unique way.

Typically, a provincial court would address the assault in terms of the couple and any of their children. Alcohol and anger counselling may play some part in the sentence. However, this is as far afield as most courts will commonly go. On the other hand, an Aboriginal community may wish to expand this review considerably. It may wish to address the motivation for the assault, which may lie within the accused's community history. Without addressing the motivation, this person's likelihood of rehabilitation lies in doubt, and community members (especially the spouse) may remain in peril.

If, for example, the offence is a form of pedophilia, for which treatment is often problematic, banishment from an Aboriginal community might be a punishment that urban Canadian courts would not consider. Alternatively, this person may have a specific cultural role to play within the community – a role that may have been tarnished by this behaviour. For example, this person may, by cultural obligation, perform the role of a community teacher or religious leader. Clearly, this person must be counselled and made to understand the cultural significance and impropriety of his actions. This would be particularly important if the crime offended a vital local teaching. Such a crime would offend the entire community, but perhaps more importantly it could threaten to destabilize the societal balance. Thus, more may be required than just the rehabilitation of the accused to reharmonize the community.[8] None of these considerations would be reflected in the decision of a Canadian criminal court. To address and balance these concerns adequately, the community must have the ability to adjudicate the issues. Yet the double-jeopardy provision of the Charter would prohibit such readjudication.

Perhaps a less inflammatory example will illustrate the significance of this issue more clearly. In the spring of 1994, two members of a Pueblo tribe got into a fight while drinking in a local bar in Albuquerque, New Mexico. One of them sucker-punched the other, presumably to emphasize his point concerning their debate. The more eloquent of the two was subsequently tried and convicted of minor assault in an Albuquerque court (an unreported case). However, when the aggressor returned to his Pueblo community, he found that his ordeal had not quite ended. This tribal member was now charged with breaking Pueblo law. He was once more tried and convicted.

How the accused was dealt with by this traditional court enlightens the present issue. The court determined that the victim of the assault was a teacher within the community. His responsibility, within the context of his clan duties, was to instruct tribal members on Pueblo history, cultural practices, songs, legends, teachings, and so forth. He was also obliged by custom to share Pueblo practices and beliefs with outsiders who visited the community (e.g., anthropologists, government officials, and tourists). The clan-designated role of teacher within this community was important. The problem was that the victim had incurred a broken jaw and now could not perform his duties.

The tribal court addressed the issue by requiring the defendant to work with the victim and perform his duties for him. In this way, the role of the victim as a community teacher was maintained. The consequence of the court's decision was that the immediate victim of the assault and his assaulter were reconciled. Similarly, and perhaps more importantly, the community's interests were also addressed and remained in balance. The accused did not serve any jail time or pay a fine to the Pueblo court; that

wasn't the point of the exercise. Rather, the court simultaneously reconciled a dispute between individuals and maintained the harmony and balance within the community. All of this was accomplished in a sensitive
and culturally relevant way.

Aboriginal communities in Canada may wish to address a similar situation in the same way, but they would likely be prevented from doing so.
The double-jeopardy provision of the Charter would prevent any Aboriginal court from revisiting an assault case once it had been dealt with by a
provincial court. Such a stipulation would deny an Aboriginal community
the right to resolve local disputes in a culturally sensitive way that would
also promote its unique culture. Surely this would be a tragedy.

American courts have addressed the double-jeopardy issue to the general
satisfaction of Indian tribes. In *United States* v. *Wheeler,*[9] the Supreme Court
of the United States declared that, when an individual was convicted of a
criminal offence in federal court, this did not bar a subsequent prosecution
by the tribal authority. The court declared that, since tribal governments
possess an inherent right to sovereignty, their judicial authority does not
derive from the federal authority or the US Constitution. Consequently,
the double-jeopardy provision in the fifth amendment of the Constitution
would not be offended, since the person is not being tried a second time by
the same sovereign authority.

Although Canadian courts might well adopt this reasoning, there is no
guarantee that this outcome would be inevitable. However, if the Charter
were imposed on Aboriginal governments, then this kind of community
reconciliation would not be possible. The double-jeopardy provision of the
Charter would demand that a community's collective rights surrender to
this individual rights guarantee.

The Charter also protects an individual's right to what is often called
"due process." Sections 7 through 11 address what are commonly referred
to as due process guarantees.[10] These protections essentially ensure that an
individual will receive a fair process when charged with an offence that
threatens his or her general freedoms of life, liberty, and security (this definition extends to property interests). As laudable as these protections are,
there are potential difficulties in the application of some elements of due
process for an Aboriginal community.

Historically, the application of these rights has resulted in delays. The
guarantee of due process all but ensures that the time line will wind itself out
to a length usually inconsistent with a community's desire for an expedited
healing process. For example, the guarantee of legal representation, which
in the Canadian context would mean a qualified lawyer, could impose great
delays on the resolution of a dispute.[11] When a community is remote and
no lawyer is readily available, counsel may have to be transported a great

distance to ensure compliance with the Charter guarantee.[12] An early resolution of the problem is obviously undermined. In a situation in which an individual's essential role within the community is compromised, resolving the conflict quickly can be of great importance to the community.

An alternative to this strict requirement may be to ensure that an individual has access to advice from someone other than a lawyer. The Navajo Peacemaker Courts provide a unique type of counselling through their particular forms of mediation. The peacemaker assists in the adjudication of both civil and criminal law disputes through a reliance on knowledge of traditional Navajo laws and customs. Some US tribes employ advisors familiar with techniques of dispute resolution as well as local cultural history (some Pueblos, such as the Acoma, engage the services of lay advisors). They may advise both the accused and the court, yet they are not lawyers.

In the future, Aboriginal communities in Canada may wish to take a similar approach to the resolution of a criminal law dispute. However, a defendant's claim that such a process would compromise due process would probably be sustained when reviewed by a court. This culturally sensitive process of dispute resolution would then be greatly undermined.

One should recognize that a tribe's rejection of these due process guarantees is not unmindful of the potential costs to individual liberties. Many tribes use punishments other than a fine or imprisonment. Warnings, counselling, and other forms of teachings are typical alternatives. Due process originated from the concern that punishment would be imposed without an adequate opportunity for the accused to defend himself or herself. Where the penalties that impinge on civil liberties are less prevalent, perhaps the need for due process guarantees is less compelling.

In Canada, for example, human rights tribunals can compel parties to either perform or refrain from performing certain activities. Fines are also commonly imposed by such tribunals. Yet these are not criminal law matters, so appeal courts have not held them to the same high standards of natural justice.[13] Perhaps, in similar instances, Aboriginal courts could provide less strict standards of due process, particularly since they may choose to treat offenders in a less criminal law-like manner.

Once again US tribal experience suggests a workable alternative for the Canadian context. In some tribal courts, an accused individual can choose to waive due process rights in favour of a tribe's more traditional process of dispute resolution.[14] Perhaps all or some of the due process guarantees in the Charter could be subject to a similar waiver. This option may be particularly relevant when the dispute forum is less confrontational and the alternative structure is strongly grounded culturally. Thus, something akin to a Peacemaker Court or a similar alternative process of mediation may be less needful of strict due process guarantees as required by the Charter. When due process requirements are inconsistent with or perhaps even harmful to the successful resolution of a dispute, an Aboriginal justice system may stipulate that the accused can waive these rights. However, the imposition of the Charter as it currently reads would rarely permit this measure to be employed by an Aboriginal community.

The Charter also ensures, through Section 15, that all persons are to be treated equally by the federal and provincial governments. The form of discrimination most often highlighted by Aboriginal women's advocates is gender bias, which is certainly anticipated by the Charter. However, Section 15 appears to cover nearly every type of discrimination, and the application of this section of the Charter could prove troublesome for Aboriginal communities that practise certain traditional customs.

The people of the Laguna Pueblo tribe in the United States are subject annually to the terms of the Myadormos Ordinance.[15] It can be described generally as a law that requires each person to participate, over a one-week period, in community-enrichment programs as well as cultural and sometimes spiritual ceremonies. Significantly, roles in these activities are largely based on gender, age, and religion. A person's failure to perform a traditional role could result in loss of tribal membership. With that disqualification, one may have to forfeit all rights pertaining to employment, voting, standing for public office, and even residence within the Pueblo community. The Myadormos Ordinance is strongly tied to both spiritual and cultural beliefs in this community. Indeed, many members of the Pueblo believe that these yearly practices provide a strong sense of community cohesion through the reinforcement of cultural values.

An Aboriginal community in Canada might wish to revitalize its culture through a law similar to the Myadormos Ordinance. It might also require participation in community activities determined by distinctions of gender, race,[16] age, or religion. Failure to comply with such a law might result in the loss of membership rights similar to those articulated in the Pueblo ordinance. Would the application of the equality guarantee in Section 15 of the Charter prohibit such a law?

If an individual refuses to participate in community activities, perhaps not accepting the responsibilities associated with his or her role (which may have been assigned according to age, gender, or religion), and is penalized as a consequence, then it is reasonable to assume that such a law would be in conflict with the Charter. In such an instance, although an individual's right to equality may be protected, the community's right to preserve its cultural values and practices would be undermined. Some would argue that membership in an Aboriginal community of this kind may require a personal undertaking of certain responsibilities as required by a law such as the Myadormos Ordinance. Is it unreasonable to expect that certain individual liberties might have to be compromised to maintain membership in such a society, particularly when the purpose of such an exercise is the preservation of a culture and its values? It is doubtful that the Charter would accommodate such a viewpoint.

It is important to acknowledge that the Supreme Court has made it clear that the equality guarantee in Section 15 of the Charter does not insist that everyone be treated identically. The court has been much more sensitive to the variety of individual circumstances and backgrounds from which people come. Thus it has taken a much more textured approach and clearly rejected the idea that equality means everyone is to be treated the same way.[17] Would such an approach also permit the various kinds of discriminatory treatments that may be reflected in a Myadormos Ordinance? Perhaps. But one caution is worth noting. The cases that recognized that equality in Section 15 is not always offended by differentness were cases in which the different treatment of an individual was defended in order to acknowledge other "individual" rights. For example, in Andrews,[18] the individual sought protection behind Section 15 by arguing that his differentness should be permitted and the law that prohibited it should be ignored.[19] The Supreme Court agreed. But in so doing, it was also defending his differentness on the basis of protecting other "individual" rights guarantees. In this instance, the court defended his right to be different in order to protect his individual right of political citizenship. But would this court defend the Myadormos-like ordinance if it denied individual equality for a reason other than to preserve another individual liberty? It would be asked to preserve the new law in deference to the rights of the collective. There is simply insufficient case law available to infer how the court would treat such a conflict. It is because of this uncertainty and the fear that Aboriginal communities will emerge with the short end of the stick that Aboriginal people must be concerned.

The issue of free speech is also of concern to Aboriginal people, particularly those in more traditional communities. Aboriginal peoples often possess what are commonly described as oral traditions. Many of the cultural values and customs of the community are passed on to its members not through a written text but through the spoken word. Not only does this provide a vibrant cultural context for the teachings, but it also ensures that only those who should know about these teachings receive them. In effect, an oral tradition prevents "outsiders" from becoming privy to some of the more sensitive customs and beliefs of the community.

Over the years, Aboriginal cultures have attracted increased interest among non-Aboriginal people. One might say that Aboriginal cultures and values have even become fashionable. The Western world has come to recognize the merits of many Aboriginal perspectives on the environment, medicine, spirituality, and life in general. Indeed, many books written about Aboriginal culture include descriptions of legends, stories, and songs. Unfortunately, not all such texts have portrayed Aboriginal cultures with the accuracy or respect that some Aboriginal people may have desired. Moreover, of greater concern to many in more traditional communities is that certain teachings intended to be kept within a particular community have been shared with outsiders. Many Aboriginal peoples have come to believe that their cultures are being misappropriated.[20]

This concern is focused not so much on the history of totems in a community or how crafts are made as on the more important and sensitive teachings. These teachings include false face mask society practices, Kachina customs, or Sun Dance ceremony traditions, all of which deal with significant cultural and often spiritual matters within Aboriginal communities. Many believe that these teachings and practices are uniquely theirs, that they have been given directly to them by their Creator and are not intended for non-members.[21] Hence, more traditional people are typically offended when these teachings are shared by other community members with outsiders. These actions are all the more offensive when done primarily for profit.

Some observers have characterized the sharing of particular cultural teachings as "cultural defamation."[22] Recently, some US tribal governments have expressed interest in enacting laws that would allow the prosecution of tribal members who breach the practice of secrecy concerning certain tribal customs and beliefs. Some leaders argue that this would be an effective way to curtail the sharing of tribal secrets.[23]

The difficulty for like-minded Aboriginal communities in Canada is the resulting conflict with the Canadian Charter of Rights and Freedoms. Subsection 2(b) protects freedom of expression and would therefore challenge the legitimacy of any Aboriginal law that limits this freedom for both individuals and the media. Any effort to protect a community's interest in privacy could be challenged by an individual's right to share information indiscriminately with others.

The community's right to protect its culture is certainly a broadly based concern. Should a community not have some control over how, or with whom, its important cultural elements are shared, particularly if sharing them impairs the community's ability to preserve and practise its culture?[24] Is there no room for the argument that expression should be limited by some cultural parameters? If there is support for such an idea does any reasonable person believe that the Charter would permit such a liberal interpretation? Probably not.

It is improbable that the Charter would permit Aboriginal laws of cultural defamation to survive scrutiny. Rights regarding privacy are few and far between in Canadian law,[25] and there certainly is no constitutional guarantee of privacy that would protect this Aboriginal interest. Should there not be limits to the right of free expression when it becomes a threat to cultural survival? No such protection for the cultural survival of any Aboriginal community in Canada currently exists.[26]

Understanding the Context of Due Process

To suggest that any of the rights guaranteed by the Charter should be suspended to accommodate Aboriginal concerns may initially offend some people. Although the Charter itself is a relatively new constitutional institution in Canada, the rights that it articulates and protects are very familiar. Democratic rights such as the right to vote or the legal right to be free from double jeopardy in the courts have been recognized under the common law for generations. As well, the abundance of movies and television programs depicting police, lawyers, and politics has contributed to a sense of protectiveness concerning individual rights. On the other hand, the issues associated with the collective rights of a community are less well understood. Therefore, some comments about individual rights guarantees within a historical context may be appropriate here, particularly those rights closely associated with the term "due process."

There is no universal definition or definitive statement of what due process means. Certainly, in the history of Canadian jurisprudence, there is no fixed idea of what constitutes due process. It is widely accepted that the essential purpose of due process is to protect the individual from a government acting adversely and arbitrarily against him or her. The origins of due process can be traced as far back as Chapter 39 of the Magna Carta. This document, written in 1215, is widely accepted as having established the seminal notions of the doctrine: "No free man shall be taken and imprisoned or disseised or exiled or in any way destroyed, nor will we go upon him nor send upon him, except by the lawful judgement of his peers and by the law of the land." From this statement evolved the concept that no person could be arbitrarily denied freedom or property except "by the law of the land." Such wording was thought to ensure that the English subject would be protected from the oppressive misuse of government authority. Over the years, "law of the land" became interchangeable with "due process of law." James Madison, one of the fathers of the Constitution of the United States of America, included a due process clause in Amendment V: "No person shall be ... deprived of life, liberty or property, without due process of law."

However, it was still uncertain what exactly was intended by this due process guarantee. It was argued that the only assurance that flowed from this right was that a person and his or her property could be compromised only if done so in accordance with a clear and properly enacted preexisting law.[27] This bare statement was an early Canadian interpretation of the concept of due process, and the principle was to undergo considerable expansion.

In 1961, American courts held that the due process clause included guarantees against unreasonable searches.[28] In 1962, the courts included protection against cruel and unusual punishment.[29] The Supreme Court of the United States held in 1964 that a person could not be forced to give evidence against himself or herself in a criminal proceeding.[30] And in 1966 the Supreme Court determined that due process ensured that an individual could confront witnesses testifying against him or her.[31] In addition, the courts interpreted due process as the individual's right to counsel and protection against involuntary confessions.[32] The rights to a speedy trial, trial by jury, and protection against double jeopardy were also guarantees that originated in the due process clause.[33] Clearly, the 1960s comprised a decade of evolution for this concept.

Canada also has a significant judicial history with the due process clause. The Canadian Bill of Rights incorporates many of these guarantees:

> Section 1. It is hereby recognized and declared that in Canada there have existed and shall continue to exist without discrimination by reason of race, national origin, colour, religion or sex, the following human rights and fundamental freedoms, namely,
> (a)   the right of the individual to life, liberty, security of the person and enjoyment of property, and the right not to be deprived thereof except by due process of law;
> (b)   the right of the individual to equality before the law and the protection of the law.[34]

Section 2 of the Bill of Rights expressly incorporates the same due process guarantees that evolved through the judicial decision making of the US courts:

> Section 2. Every law of Canada shall, unless it is expressly declared by an Act of the Parliament of Canada that it shall operate notwithstanding the Canadian Bill of Rights, be so construed and applied as not to abrogate, abridge or infringe or to authorize the abrogation, abridgement or infringement of any of the rights or freedoms, herein recognized and declared, and in particular, no law of Canada shall be construed or applied so as to:
> (a)   authorize or effect the arbitrary detention, imprisonment or exile of any person;
> (b)   impose or authorize the imposition of cruel and unusual treatment or punishment;

(c) deprive a person who has been arrested or detained
   (i) of the right to be informed promptly of the reason for his arrest or detention.
   (ii) of the right to retain and instruct counsel without delay. Or
   (iii) of the remedy by way of habeas corpus for the determination of the validity of his detention and for his release if the detention is not lawful;
(d) authorize a court, tribunal, commission, board or other authority to compel a person to give evidence if he is denied counsel, protection against self crimination or other constitutional safeguards;
(e) deprive a person of the right to a fair hearing in accordance with the principles of fundamental justice for the determination of his rights and obligations;
(f) deprive a person charged with a criminal offence of the right to be presumed innocent until proved guilty according to law in a fair and public hearing by an independent and impartial tribunal, or of the right to reasonable bail without just cause; or
(g) deprive a person of the right to the assistance of an interpreter in any proceedings in which he is involved or in which he is a party or a witness, before a court, commission, board or other tribunal, if he does not understand or speak the language in which such proceedings are conducted.

The Canadian Supreme Court had the opportunity to interpret the due process clause in 1972. In *Curr* v. *The Queen,* Judge Ritchie stated that due process means "according to the legal processes recognized by Parliament and the Courts in Canada."[35] Judge Laskin equated this phrase with "a fair hearing in accordance with the principles of fundamental justice."[36] In the early 1970s, Canadian courts grappled with the meaning of the due process clause and eventually came to believe that it meant no more than procedural rules to ensure fairness and protection for the individual from a government's arbitrary misuse of authority.[37] This phrase has more recently become known in Canada for reflecting the principles of "natural justice."

This principle has two primary rules: *memo judex in sera causa* represents the proposition that those with judicial or quasi-judicial power be free of bias; and *audi alteram partum* may be defined generally as a guarantee that a person is able to make his or her point of view or defence known. It is this second principle that has produced much of the law that characterizes due process.

To give effect to the *audi alteram partum* rule, certain principles evolved. It became necessary to ensure that, whenever a person's interests (both personal and private property interests) were in jeopardy, one would be ensured the rights to a formal hearing, to representation, to cross-examine witnesses, and so forth. Clearly, these elements of the general rule evolved to guarantee fairness in the process.

These due process, or fundamental rights, guarantees have been included in Section 7 of the Canadian Charter of Rights and Freedoms. As well, Sections 8 through 14 articulate essentially the same due process guarantees that have evolved in the American courts. Thus, the road to ensuring due process guarantees in Canadian law has been very similar to that in the United States. It's been one of measured steps. There has never been a consensus in Canadian jurisprudence as to which rights are protected by the concept of natural justice or due process. They continue to comprise an evolving area of law.

Importantly, even when recognized in Canadian law under both the Canadian Bill of Rights and the Canadian Charter of Rights and Freedoms, these rights have been less than secure. Both the Bill of Rights and the Charter provide opportunities for Canadian governments to override these rights of the individual through the use of a "notwithstanding" clause (Sections 2 and 33, respectively). Consequently, if a government clearly states that the law it intends to enact is to apply "notwithstanding" conflicts with either code, then the offending legislation will nevertheless prevail. Moreover, Section 1 of the Constitution, the "general limitation clause," permits a law to survive conflicts with these natural justice guarantees if it is found to be a reasonable abridgement that can be "justified in a free and democratic society." Professor Janet Hiebert illustrates how this phrase encompasses "non-enumerated" standards articulated by the Supreme Court that will have the effect of imposing limitations upon protected Charter rights.[38] It may also be argued that the criminal law practice of plea bargaining offends both due process and the rule of law. It therefore seems that, despite the apparent respect that these individual rights guarantees enjoy publicly, even today Canadian law permits them to be overridden in certain circumstances. Apparently, these laws are not as sacrosanct as one might at first believe.[39]

Perhaps then the Aboriginal proposal to balance individual rights with collective rights should not be viewed with too much suspicion. In light of the relatively recent evolution of these principles in Canadian jurisprudence and the fact that they have received constitutional recognition only even more recently, how offensive should one find the proposal that they might receive an abridgement within an Aboriginal context? In particular, since these rights are still subject to qualifications by Canadian governments and judicial interpretations, perhaps the Aboriginal position is not so extreme. Consequently, when Aboriginal people suggest that they too would like to discuss reasonable abridgements of some of these principles, surely one should at least consider the merits of such a proposition. To dismiss it out of hand suggests that two standards are being employed – one for federal and provincial governments, and one for Aboriginal governments.

Understanding the Motivational Ethic

As just explained, due process rights have only recently been entrenched in the Canadian Constitution as the supreme law of the land. Their evolution in the American judicial system crystallized in their present form only since the 1960s. However, neither fact diminishes the general public belief that these rights deserve universal respect and observance. Accordingly, when collective rights practices conflict with these expressions of the Canadian Charter of Rights and Freedoms, there is little initial sympathy for the Aboriginal position. Without further insight into the motivation behind the Aboriginal proposal, there is little likelihood that the position of the non-Aboriginal community will change. Therefore, it may be useful to understand the ethic that commonly informs the Aboriginal perspective on this issue.

Historically, Aboriginal communities have been defined in a context of relationships sustained by a philosophy of care and responsibility. This philosophy of caring for others and the concomitant value of duty are commonly expressed in the creation stories of Aboriginal people. Often these legends have been supplemented with stories of day-to-day life in these communities, all expressing a concern for the welfare of others. Aboriginal legends, songs, and stories offer clear examples of the sense of responsibility that derives from this value of caring for others. The harshness of the environments in which Aboriginal people existed only served to reinforce the merit of such principles. Whether the messages of the early teachings or the physical elements had the most impact on these communities is unknown, but these values remain an integral part of most Aboriginal communities today.

The value of care and the sense of responsibility have created communities bound together by a complex web of relationships. Out of such relationships have evolved various roles and duties prescribed for both families and individual community members. Clan systems are a clear reflection of such relational structures. This ethic of care and responsibility has also shaped the sense of justice that has evolved in these communities.

Although the Canadian Charter of Rights and Freedoms is a recent addition to the Canadian Constitution, and the Canadian Bill of Rights has existed only since the 1960s, the notion of individual rights has prevailed in the common law for much longer. "Rights theory" has a long history within the common law judicial system, and today it is firmly embedded within the Canadian psyche. However, Aboriginal people have been less enamoured of such notions. Aboriginal societies premised on an ethic of care and responsibility have traditionally been interested less in rights than in concepts of personal obligation.

The Canadian justice system, which is inherently rights oriented, derives from notions of classical liberalism. The concept of individual liberty is at the core of this philosophy.[40] The idea of equality is a more recent value that has also emerged as a separate political concept from these early writings wherein each person shares roughly the same legal status. The classical interpretation of rights ascribes to the individual certain assurances. She is free to move about, express herself, and associate with others. In turn, others owe her a set of obligations. They are obliged not to interfere with her freedom of movement, expression, or association. Much of individual rights theory is based on a belief in the dignity of the individual. That is, respect for the dignity of a person can truly be achieved only if he is accorded certain fundamental rights that respect his freedom of speech, religion, association, and so forth. In turn, other rights have also evolved, arguably as a method of ensuring respect for these "rights to dignity." The right to vote and freedom of the press are often considered necessary to give effect to the rights to dignity. Without respect for these democratic freedoms, it has been asserted, there would be little likelihood of achieving the individual rights to dignity. Notwithstanding the merits of these ideas, it is inescapable that their focus is on the individual apart from the community.

The Aboriginal perspective is somewhat different. The ethic of care and responsibility that has characterized Aboriginal communities establishes an environment of understanding and sensitivity to the situations of others. An individual is not viewed as separate from the community but as an integral element of a much broader association. The liberalism of Locke and Mill began with a view of people alone within nature. Initially we were separate and isolated from one another. Thus a society premised on an ethic of individual rights inevitably leads to the conceptual isolation of a person, whereas Aboriginal communities espouse an ethic of care, which teaches inclusiveness. Everyone belongs and has a role to play. This ethical perspective fosters compassion for others, which in turn establishes an environment of tolerance. Such beliefs occasioned the moral codes for these communities.

An Aboriginal ethic of care and responsibility has understandably generated a greater appreciation for equity[41] than for equality. Equality seems to be strict in its application and divisive, if only because of its emphasis on the individual. On the other hand, Aboriginal equity is flexible, contextual, and inclusive. The ethic of care and responsibility, which informs Aboriginal equity, recognizes imbalances in life. Rather than deny them within a thesis of equality, Aboriginal equity seeks to manage them within a local context. It permits differing roles and duties to coexist within a community, and taken together they establish and strengthen relationships. By recognizing a dispute but reacting to it within the context of interrelationships, a flexible hand can often temper justice with fairness. An example seems appropriate.

In the summer of 1994, a Hopi man was brought before a Hopi tribal court charged with being intoxicated and possessing alcohol within the boundaries of the reservation. Both acts were in violation of the Hopi tribal code. The facts, as recounted to the court by the arresting tribal police officer, were that the accused had been drinking off the reservation in a local town for most of the day. His fourteen-year-old daughter and a younger sibling had waited for their father in the car; subsequently, the accused had instructed her to drive them home since he was too intoxicated to drive. The daughter had no driver's licence, and her erratic driving had soon attracted the attention of the police. The arresting tribal officer also found a case of beer in the trunk of the car. These facts were not contested by the accused.

Initially, the Hopi court resembled any provincial trial-level court found in Canada. In attendance were a presiding judge, a tribal prosecutor, police, witnesses, and the accused. No defence counsel was present. Although the setting was typical of most Canadian trial-level courts, once the charges had been read and preliminary declarations made, what followed was anything but common to Canadian law.

After the arresting officer gave a description of the arrest, the forum began to resemble a roundtable discussion. Without taking the stand, the accused was asked by the judge what had led him to this behaviour. He was cautioned by the police officer about the implications of his actions for his children. The prosecutor reminded him of his tribal obligations and how his actions would reflect on his duties. He was told that it was better to be dealt with by this court than by the Kachinas, who might have taken great exception to his activities.[42]

Throughout the "trial," the accused was reminded of his traditional duties to both the community and his family. He was questioned about the motivation for his actions. He was cautioned about the implications of repeating this behaviour. All of this was done through reference to local cultural teachings. However, at no point did this forum take on an adversarial atmosphere, at least as I observed it. The accused responded freely and receptively. He was subsequently convicted, given fifteen days in jail, and ordered to make a public apology for his actions.

There are many salient points to be noted in such proceedings. Without a doubt, a rights theorist would draw attention to the wholesale abandonment of due process guarantees. The point is well taken, but such an analysis would miss the whole purpose of this exercise. This "trial" reflected recognition of a problem much larger than that represented by just the accused, his children, and a legal prohibition. The court understood that cultural values, practices, and duties were also intimately involved. It recognized that the individual could not be separated from the context of his relationships if he were to be dealt with fairly. Hence, the court, compelled by the values of care and responsibility, articulated its own form of Aboriginal equity in addressing the situation. The individual was dealt with in a fashion cognizant of his family and community responsibilities. The proceedings exhibited an air of both reproach and tolerance. At the end of the "trial," the accused seemed to be receptive to the verdict as he expressed his gratitude to the court. Thus, it appears that an ethic of moral concern and duty, translated from cultural norms into a legal structure, achieved a judicial standard of equity apparently to the satisfaction of everyone involved.

Historically, the values of care and responsibility have established within Aboriginal communities networks of relationships. Out of these interrelationships has often evolved a clear sense of roles and duties, which are often expressed through cultural practices. When given the opportunity, Aboriginal communities have often articulated a preference for notions of equity rather than for a justice system whose tenets are often based upon the concept of rights.[43]

Understanding the Silence

An appreciation of the ethic of care and responsibility may also explain the history of the Aboriginal response to gender discrimination in the Indian Act. Until this act was amended in April 1985, women who married non-Indians lost their Aboriginal status. They were thus denied access to community membership and an assortment of government programs.[44] Although gender became the basis for the legal discrimination and the consequences that resulted, criticism was often levelled at community leaders who were, for the most part, male (typically, chiefs and council members). It was argued that their refusal to endorse an amendment to the Indian Act to remove the offending sections was a clear case of gender discrimination.

Consequently, the dispute was often depicted as one between men and women. Yet such an assertion was not entirely accurate. Many Aboriginal women were also unsupportive of those women who "married out" and then later complained of this unequal treatment. When this issue arose at national and local meetings, it was often Aboriginal women who spoke out against the return of these disenfranchised women.[45] To assert that the unequal treatment of these women was solely the consequence of male indifference does not explain why other Aboriginal women articulated the same position. However, in light of the ethic of responsibility, it is perhaps easier to understand what motivated both men and women who remained silent regarding this gender discrimination.

Many within the Aboriginal community, both male and female members, viewed marrying out as an abandonment of the community. These women were seen as voluntarily leaving Aboriginal communities and therefore forsaking networks of relationships that sustained these societies. Some viewed these women as abandoning not only these cultural relationships but also, more importantly, specific roles and duties that they were culturally obliged to honour. Viewed in this context, the reluctance of members of these communities to sympathize with the plight of the ostracized women and their families is easier to understand. However, understanding this motivation does not necessarily justify it.

Clearly, a value structure premised on an ethic of care and responsibility can have uneven consequences. For a judicial system that seeks a balanced response to problems affecting both an individual and the community, the flexibility inherent in such a process can be rewarding, as illustrated by the Hopi and Pueblo cases noted earlier in this chapter. On the other hand, these values may well have fuelled the lack of generosity inherent in the position taken by many Aboriginal people in regard to gender discrimination in the Indian Act.[46] These values can cut both ways and do not always ensure the most satisfying results. Nonetheless, if Canadians are to appreciate more fully the Aboriginal position regarding collective rights, then they must understand differences in values that underlie the respective societies.

The Aboriginal assertion that certain collective rights should have pre-eminence over some individual rights, at least in certain instances, belies a fundamentally different way of looking at an individual's place in society. All societal laws are expressions of a certain morality or ethic (though legal positivists might argue otherwise), and Aboriginal people construct laws upon a different philosophical foundation. Moreover, the specific morality or ethic may differ between one Aboriginal people and another. But what they all truly wish is the opportunity to practise their own unique forms of communal expression. Canadian governments, by reviewing the appropriateness of imposing the Canadian Charter of Rights and Freedoms on these communities, would take a large step forward in achieving a balance between rights and duties.

Collective Rights as a Right in Law: A People's Culture

Personal obligations in an Aboriginal community may be difficult to recognize at first as expressions of a collective right of the community. It may be argued that such practices do not fit comfortably into the typical rights analysis of Western thought. However, rather than attempting to force the Aboriginal expression to fit the classical context, approaching the issue from a different perspective might be helpful.

Collective rights have received the greatest recognition in international law, especially following the First World War in the case of minority schools in Albania.[47] This case, heard by the Permanent Court of International Justice, offered an enlightened opinion regarding minority rights guaranteed by certain European treaties:

> The idea underlying the treaties for the protection of minorities is to secure for certain elements incorporated in a State, the population of which differs from them in race, language, or religion, the possibility of living peaceably alongside that population and co-operating amicably with it, while at the same time preserving the characteristics which distinguish them from the majority, and satisfying the ensuing special needs.
>
> In order to attain this object, two things were regarded as particularly necessary, and have formed the subject of provisions in these treaties.
>
> The first is to ensure that nationals belonging to racial, religious or linguistic minorities shall be placed in every respect on a footing of perfect equality with the other nationals of the State.
>
> The second is to ensure for the minority elements suitable means for the preservation of their racial peculiarities, their traditions and their national characteristics.
>
> These two requirements are indeed closely interlocked, for there would be no true equality between a majority and a minority if the latter were deprived of its own institutions, and were consequently compelled to renounce that which constitutes the very essence of its being as a minority.[48]

Some years later, the first UN-sponsored human rights treaty that maintained the right of cultural groups to exist was agreed to in the Convention Against Genocide.[49] Since then, the UN Declaration on the Rights of Persons Belonging to National Ethnic, Religious, and Linguistic Minorities[50] and the 1966 UNESCO Declaration of the Principles of International Cultural Cooperation[51] have reiterated the right of a people and their culture to exist. The latter UN instrument clearly states that

1. Each culture has dignity and value which must be respected and preserved.
2. Every people has the right and duty to develop its culture.
3. In their rich variety and diversity, and in the reciprocal influence they exert on one another, all cultures form part of the common heritage belonging to all mankind.[52]

All of these documents speak to the cultural integrity of a people. These tenets also apply, of course, to Aboriginal people. In particular, however, the International Labour Organization Convention No. 169 (ILO 169)[53] and the

Draft United Nations Declaration on the Rights of Indigenous Peoples[54] express perhaps the broadest parameters of these ideas. These documents not only prohibit cultural discrimination against Aboriginal people but also stipulate that governments must undertake positive action to eliminate incidents of such discrimination.

Many of these documents express the intention to protect a variety of collective rights. Here it is useful to recognize only one: the right to the protection and continued expression of a people's culture. It is against the background of these international documents and standards that Aboriginal claims of self-government and the protection of collective rights are being made. If a country were to pass a law prohibiting the expression of a people's language or religion, then claims may be made that this state is violating one of these international documents.[55] Similarly, Aboriginal people in Canada may argue that application of the Canadian Charter of Rights and Freedoms offends an Aboriginal community's collective rights.

For example, enforcement of a Charter right that impairs the role of clan mothers in a Mohawk community could damage the traditional functioning of a clan structure. In light of the vital function that clan systems perform in a society, particularly in stabilizing social norms, it would seem obvious how the Charter can threaten a people's right to cultural protection and expression. By prohibiting these traditional practices, the Charter endangers the very existence of an Aboriginal culture.

In some ways a culture is not unlike a house. If one loosens a significant number of cinder blocks in the foundation, then the whole structure may collapse. Cultures also have foundations, which are commonly expressed through their values and related customs. If enough customs are undermined or significant community values interfered with, the entire culture of a people can come tumbling down. It is from this perspective that Aboriginal customs must be viewed when considered in the context of Charter rights.

This perspective should apply equally to Aboriginal communities not structured along clan lines. In communities that have developed other customs that attempt to instil principles of care, honesty, and personal responsibility, to undermine these customs would surely constitute an assault on the very essence of the culture.[56] Language and religious institutions alone do not constitute a culture; as described earlier in this chapter, other practices, which reflect the integral values of a community and help to keep it vital, are no less worthy of protection. Consequently, where established practices such as clan mothers exercising traditional customs affect values essential to the integrity of a culture, these customs deserve the collective rights protection as articulated in international covenants. Aboriginal people argue that these practices must be recognized as elements of a people's expression of their culture.

However, does every practice, no matter how significant, justify the exclusion of the Charter? Arguably, most practices, even those of little immediate impact, reinforce a community's inherent values. But does the protection of any value that may preserve or stabilize a culture warrant compromising a person's individual rights? Surely not.

If an innocent individual is charged with violating a law, civil or criminal, then is a simple plea of "I didn't do it" enough to ensure that he or she is not found culpable? If not, then which other safeguards guaranteed by a charter will be required to ensure that the accused is not wrongfully convicted? Or will such safeguards be rejected simply because they may compromise a traditional cultural practice? Is conviction of an innocent person the price that must occasionally be paid to preserve a culture?

Obviously, there must be some balancing of these potentially conflicting interests. The Canadian Constitution balances the interests of the individual with other democratic values.[57] Similarly, there will be a need to create mechanisms to balance collective and individual rights within an Aboriginal community. However, enunciating what they might be is not the purpose of this book.

The articulation of these expressions of collective rights is intended to clarify the argument of Aboriginal people in seeking recognition of their collective rights. It is important to understand how the claim for collective rights protection must be viewed within the context of the application of the Charter. It is not the intention of this book to suggest how these conflicting rights should be resolved. For present purposes, it is sufficient if the profile of these potential conflicts is raised among the Canadian public. Then, perhaps, the difficult issues associated with it can be tackled in a balanced and constructive fashion to the satisfaction of all Canadians.

A Final American Caution
The foregoing discussion indicates some of the perils faced by Aboriginal people when their collective rights practices are ignored. However, there is a further and perhaps more important consideration. Two decisions of the Supreme Court of the United States offer insights into the perils that may confront Aboriginal people in Canada in seeking collective rights protection. The danger is presented by any decision-making body – be it a group of first ministers, a legislature, or a court – permitted to make significant decisions affecting Aboriginal peoples about whom they know little.

In 1978, the case of *Oliphant* v. *Suquamish Indian Tribe* came before the US Supreme Court.[58] As explained in Chapter 2, that case raised the issue of whether a tribe could exercise criminal law jurisdiction over a non-Indian who committed a crime on an Indian reservation. The court found that the defendant, a non-Indian, was not subject to the authority of a tribal court. The court determined that the exercise of criminal law jurisdiction by the tribe over non-Indians was inconsistent with its domestic dependent status. Since the accused was not able to vote, stand for public office, or sit on a jury in a tribal community, the court found that those communities' governments should not be permitted to exercise criminal law jurisdiction over his activities. In such instances, it was determined, the federal government would exercise this jurisdiction.

Until this decision of the Supreme Court, it was presumed that the tribe could exercise full criminal authority over anyone who committed a criminal act in Indian country. Effectively, this decision insulated from tribal prosecution a significant number of non-Indian people who regularly spent time on reservations. Today, consequently, an Indian community has no immediate way of protecting itself from non-Indian criminals. Moreover, the failure by federal district attorneys to prosecute offences and the inadequately staffed Federal Bureau of Investigation's reluctance to investigate some crimes have amplified this problem.

But this is not the end of the story. In May 1990, the US Supreme Court again offered its opinion on the scope of a tribe's criminal law authority. In *Duro* v. *Reina*,[59] Albert Duro, an Indian though not a member of the Salt River tribal community, shot and killed a member of the tribe while on the reservation. Presuming to exercise its criminal law jurisdiction, the Salt River tribal court moved to try the accused, who sought a writ of habeas corpus from the federal district court, arguing that the decision of the Supreme Court in *Oliphant* applied in this instance. Consequently, he argued, the tribe lacked the jurisdiction to try him.

The Supreme Court found, as in *Oliphant,* that, since the defendant could not vote in a local election, stand for public office, or sit on a local jury, he was not subject to the authority of a tribal court. The court felt that the limitations on Duro's rights were no different than those of the non-Indian in *Oliphant.* Here was simplicity unencumbered by reason.

The thinking expressed by the Supreme Court in both *Oliphant* and *Duro* is suspect. One need only consider its application in a similar situation. If a Canadian citizen visiting New York City robbed a local bank, then how well would this Supreme Court reasoning be received? Clearly, the Canadian defendant is not able to vote, run for public office, or sit on a jury. Would this defence deny the state jurisdiction over the Canadian defendant? And, since the Canadian has no federal rights either, he or she should be insulated from federal prosecution. The Supreme Court achieved uniformity but at the expense of distortion.

However, what is important here is not so much the integrity of the legal reasoning as the dire consequences of it for tribal communities. Until *Oliphant,* the pattern of criminal law jurisdiction in Indian country was straightforward. The federal government exercised criminal law jurisdiction over all "serious" criminal offences committed by either Indians or non-Indians. This authority was determined by cases that interpreted the federal Major Crimes Act. Tribes exercised criminal law authority over both Indian and non-Indian perpetrators of less serious criminal offences, and states had no criminal law jurisdiction in Indian country (the respective criminal law jurisdictions of these governments are outlined in Chapter 2). *Oliphant*, however, gave the federal government complete authority over all criminal activities of non-Indians while precluding that of the tribe. States continued to lack criminal law jurisdiction in Indian country unless both the accused and the victim were non-Indian. Nevertheless, tribal courts continued to exercise criminal law jurisdiction over *all* Indians for non-Major Crimes Act offences.

But *Duro* changed this dramatically. Now tribal courts could exercise authority only over their own tribal members for non-Major Crimes Act offences. The federal government retained the authority that it received as a result of *Oliphant* over all non-Indians, and the states were still without criminal law jurisdiction in Indian country unless both accused and victim were non-Indian. But this division created a problem arguably unforeseen by the court: a gaping hole in the law. No authority had jurisdiction over Indians from other tribes who committed non-Major Crimes Act offences. These "from-another-tribe Indians" could commit an offence not listed in the Major Crimes Act and not be subject to punishment by any court in the land.

Many offences covered by the Major Crimes Act are indeed serious, but not all serious offences are covered by this legislation. Outside its scope and therefore within the competence of a tribal court are offences such as fraud, sexual assault, drug possession and distribution, firearms possession and use, certain forms of robbery, and an assortment of other significant offences. Thus, *Duro* left tribal communities vulnerable not just to "less serious" offences but also to those that are really quite serious. Tribal communities were left without any way of protecting themselves from these various forms of serious harm.

For Canadians, perhaps the key lesson derived from *Oliphant* and *Duro* is that decisions affecting Aboriginal communities should not be made in an intellectual vacuum. No person familiar with life in a tribal community, where Indian people from other communities freely come and go, would have reached a decision such as that in *Duro*. Clearly, the court did not appreciate the nature of the tribal community about which it was making such a significant determination. This kind of decision making must not be permitted to reoccur in Canada when Aboriginal self-government is debated, particularly in regard to the impact of the Charter on an Aboriginal community's collective rights.

Lack of appreciation of the merits of collective rights or community values supporting such rights must not be permitted to cloud the discussions that will ultimately decide the status of these rights. Any decisions affecting the rights of Aboriginal people must be informed. Only a commitment to both understanding and tolerance by all parties in the debate will ensure that the results of this dialogue are fruitful.

Comment

It is clear from the foregoing discussion that the debate concerning collective rights challenges many areas of application of the current Canadian Charter of Rights and Freedoms in Aboriginal communities. The Charter's impact on self-governing Aboriginal communities could have profound implications for many traditional values and customs. It is important that the argument for Aboriginal collective rights be viewed in its proper context. It would be both inaccurate and unfair to say that Aboriginal communities have no interest in the protection of individual rights. The rising number of complaints made by Aboriginal people to both federal and provincial human rights commissions clearly reflects a respect for the merits of individual dignity and self-worth. However, Aboriginal people hope that the non-Aboriginal community will understand that there are other values to be cherished and protected if Aboriginal cultures are to survive.

This same idea was expressed, perhaps more eloquently, by Tevye in the movie *Fiddler on the Roof*: "Because of our traditions everyone of us knows who he is and what God expects him to do." The implications of our traditions are no less significant for Aboriginal people.

Should an Aboriginal community seek to impose limits on the application of Charter rights, some would argue that in doing so this community would actually be defending fundamental democratic values. Both the American Bill of Rights and the Canadian Charter of Rights and Freedoms in effect restrain democratic decisions of the respective legislatures. Both constitutional codes effectively overrule the will of duly elected legislators to enact laws presumably passed on behalf of those who have democratically elected those legislators. Some cultural practices, outlined earlier in this chapter, may block access to certain civil liberties. But no one can claim that such decisions offend a "classical" view of democracy.[60] In all instances, it would be the democratic decisions of these communities that would determine whether they intend to exercise any of the traditional practices. If these practices ignore certain civil liberties, then presumably they would only be enacted by community consensus, clearly a fundamentally democratic exercise.

It would also be inaccurate for Canadians to believe that multiple Aboriginal systems of justice will necessarily result in confusion or the failure to prohibit certain crimes. If one were to drive across the United States, one would likely drive through seven or eight different criminal law jurisdictions. Unlike Canada, with its provinces and territories, every state has its own criminal code. Including the federal authority, there are more than fifty criminal codes of behaviour in the United States. There is no sense of chaos there, because reasonable people generally agree that murder, kidnapping, fraud, and similar crimes must be prohibited. Aboriginal people are no different. Activities such as these will always be prohibited by Aboriginal communities.

However, it is the other two functions of criminal codes that will reflect the greatest differences with the present Canadian judicial system. In addition to listing the kinds of behaviour that are prohibited, the Canadian Criminal Code sets out both rules of evidence and court procedures as well as the appropriate penalties to be invoked. It is in these two areas that the Aboriginal ethic and rules of justice will have their most significant expression.[61]

American tribal justice provides examples of these differences. The tribal court at Isleta Pueblo will sit at night to accommodate an accused who is unable to attend during the day. If the defendant has limited resources, then a fine may be paid on instalments. If the defendant misses a payment, then he or she is mailed a reminder rather than arrested under a warrant for being in default. The Acoma Pueblo court has accepted pottery in lieu of a fine from persons who are convicted of a less serious offence but who are unable to provide immediate payment in cash. This pottery is then sold by the court to pay the fine. Drivers' licences are sometimes suspended only during evening hours and on weekends if a defendant needs to drive off the reservation to maintain employment. All of these situations reflect the compassion and flexibility demanded by an Aboriginal ethic of care.

But these tribal governments have not abandoned the penalty of incarceration when it is warranted. Research undertaken at the University of New Mexico Indian Law Center indicates that traditional healing measures are not always effective. In particular, in instances of pedophilia, customary healing practices have been less than successful. Thus, tribal courts have chosen to incarcerate offenders for these and other offences when the community would otherwise remain at risk and traditional practices of reconciliation are ineffective. Clearly, these communities are not bound exclusively to past practices.

Whenever the Canadian policies of multiculturalism are criticized, usually from the right, the value of tolerance is often held up as a justification for these programs. It is commonly argued that multicultural habits and practices teach, if only implicitly, an understanding that leads to tolerance of others. If such a learning process indeed occurs, then what are the values being taught by the emphasis on an individual's rights?

Aboriginal communities in both Canada and the United States view the introduction of individual rights with trepidation. Aboriginal people are concerned that doctrinal individualism will create feelings of separateness and isolation. Classical liberalism has placed very little emphasis upon the individual within the context of society.[62] This doctrine has seldom recognized the individual as a social actor intimately tied to her community. Since the Charter is a clear expression of this liberal thought, there are many who feel that the lessons that will be taught through its enforcement may lead to behaviour associated with self-interest, self-indulgence, mistrust, insensitivity, arrogance, and disrespect. These attitudes are commonly reflected today in the personal behaviour of many within non-Aboriginal communities in North America.

Aboriginal communities may wish to continue practising, or perhaps to revive, traditional customs such as a Myadormos Ordinance. Or they may wish to maintain the unique involvement of elders and clan mothers in their societies. Perhaps they wish to introduce approaches to justice similar to Navajo peacemaking. These practices emphasize collective values such as caring for others, tolerance, patience, humility, sacrifice, discipline, gratitude, and responsibility. These are all values of inclusiveness that use consensus building and provide proportion and balance within a community. Traditional Aboriginal communities have always valued harmony through cooperation rather than competition. Surely such aspirations are not without merit.[63]

If certain Aboriginal customs and rituals offend Charter sensibilities, one might ask, then how difficult would it be to simply update them? Could the underlying values not be transmitted through more Charter-compatible practices? This may be a reasonable alternative in some instances. There is a certain charm in the simplicity of this suggestion, but a caution is worth mentioning. It should be appreciated that, historically, Aboriginal people have learned by remembering. Aboriginal people have always relied heavily upon teaching values through the use of custom and ritual. These practices remind them where they came from and who they were so that they might better understand who they are and what it is they must do. In a sense the traditions of Aboriginal people permit them to remember tomorrow. Hence by recalling their history they are able to appreciate their dignity and self-worth. If they are required to sacrifice a custom because it may offend the Charter, can the essence of who these people are be maintained? Perhaps pulling a single thread from a sweater would make little difference. But how many threads can be pulled before the sweater completely loses its shape and falls apart? Cultures are no different.

On the other hand, Aboriginal communities are not locked in the past. These are vibrant societies that need to evolve like any other. There is no denying that these once largely insulated and collectivist societies have been challenged by the introduction of new ideas of individualism – to the extent that Aboriginal perspectives on the merits of a rights charter are changing. Perhaps what is really sought by Aboriginal people, then, is "a theory of everything."

Today scientists agree that the general theories concerning quantum mechanics and Einstein's general theory of relativity do not fit well together. The principles of astrophysics, which seem to work well on a large scale, simply break down at the nuclear level. Similarly the scientific discoveries of the physical world at the quantum level don't seem to divulge much that can be useful at the macro level. Hence, a number of scientists, perhaps most notably Stephen Hawking, are now searching for a way to reconcile the inconsistencies between the macro- and micro-levels of the universe. They are in essence seeking a "theory of everything."

Perhaps a similar challenge confronts Aboriginal communities in Canada. It appears that they too must find a theory of everything that will reconcile apparent inconsistencies between the rights of the individual and those of the community. Both approaches have their merits, but both also have drawbacks. The reconciliation of the two perspectives may appear to be a daunting task. Since Hegel[64] first popularized the seminal ideas of what is today called "Communitarianism," finding the proper tension between these two value systems has been difficult.[65] However, if this is to be a nation-building exercise, then what better time to undertake such a challenge?

Finally, an appreciation of recent criminal case law developments in the United States should provide a useful warning. *Duro* reflects what can happen when those who are either unaware or possess only a theoretical understanding of the problems facing Aboriginal communities make important decisions. The *Duro* decision was a formal and stylized exhibition of reasoning that lacked any substance or appreciation for Aboriginal reality. Such an approach should be avoided in Canada. Therefore, Aboriginal people must continue to play an active role in resolving self-government issues. Without their contributions, any results would produce little more than the sound of one hand clapping.

7
A Metaphorical Charter: An Aboriginal Response

Prior to 1985, there was much consternation about gender discrimination in the Indian Act. Clearly, the act contained provisions that discriminated against women. The most prominent was subsection 12(1)(b), as it was then worded, but other sections of the act, such as Section 11, were also discriminatory. Simply stated, a woman recognized as an Indian under the Indian Act lost both her Indian status and her band membership if she married a non-Indian. No such disenfranchisement occurred if an Indian man married a non-Indian woman. Moreover, in what seemed to many disenfranchised Indian women the height of injustice, the non-Indian female spouse immediately gained both Indian status and band membership upon marriage to her Indian husband. Children from the marriage of a disenfranchised Indian woman received equally unjust treatment: they had no claim to either Indian status or band membership. The ensuing debate over the unjust and arguably hypocritical treatment of women became a focus for discussions as to whether the Canadian Charter of Rights and Freedoms should apply to Aboriginal communities under any new scheme of self-government.

Aboriginal women argued that they could not rely on Aboriginal governments dominated by men not to occasion further discrimination against them in the future. In discussions regarding whether the Charter should be enforced against future Aboriginal governments, some participants point out that the offending sections of the Indian Act were neither inspired nor drafted by any segment of the Aboriginal community. They argue that this legislation was imposed on Aboriginal people by a government historically oppressive in its treatment of them. Hence, it is asserted that Aboriginal people should not be painted with this brush of discrimination. This argument, however, conveniently ignores more recent and equally distressing treatment of Aboriginal women across Canada.

Bill C-31 contained amendments to the Indian Act that eliminated the discriminatory elements focused on gender. Women who "married out," along with their children from these marriages, would no longer lose their status and band membership. The legislation also rehabilitated women and children who had lost their legacy due to an earlier application of the Indian Act. Non-Indian women were now precluded from gaining Indian status or band membership simply by marrying an Indian man.

However, these amendments were not widely embraced by First Nations leaders prior to their becoming law. Indeed, discussion of the need to address this gender bias in the Indian Act was almost exclusively the task of Aboriginal women's organizations in Canada. Few First Nations chiefs, most of whom were men, spoke up to correct the gender bias, and some even defended the legislation. One reason commonly offered for this position was that the limited resources of a First Nations community could not reabsorb these women without undue stress, both physical (e.g., housing) and financial (e.g., education). In addition, some chiefs commented that the women knew the implications of marrying out and that they would just have to live with the consequences (see Chapter 6 for the motivation behind this attitude).

Significantly, during the first ministers' conferences of the 1980s, the Native Women's Association of Canada (NWAC) repeatedly asked the Assembly of First Nations (AFN) for the opportunity to address the gender bias issue through one of the AFN's speakers' chairs. They were denied this access, ostensibly on the ground that AFN chiefs speak for all First Nations people, including women. Hence, there was no need to have NWAC use the chair.

This explanation is unconvincing. Not one of the chiefs spoke from the AFN chair about gender discrimination against Native women and their families. Marlyn Kane, then president of NWAC, finally had to request access to a seat through one of the provincial government delegates. Her subsequent expression of the continuing problem of gender bias in First Nations communities was both eloquent and compelling.

The recent history of gender bias in First Nations communities highlights the potential for individual rights conflicts in future self-governing Aboriginal communities. This conflict appears to cry out for Charter protection for members of these communities. Yet potential conflicts between the Charter and collective rights suggest that the Charter could create equally enormous cultural problems for these communities. Some observers suggest that the only response is to apply the Charter wholesale to Aboriginal communities, while other observers advocate the complete absence of individual rights protection in these communities. Even the Royal Commission on Aboriginal Peoples took the one-dimensional position that current Charter protections should apply to all Aboriginal governments (the shortcomings of this position are discussed in Chapter 8). But there is another alternative that may balance individual rights protections and Aboriginal cultural concerns.

Before proceeding further, I should comment briefly on Aboriginal perspectives regarding the concept of democracy. As recounted in Chapter 5, Aboriginal communities have historically been premised on broad notions of democracy. It is notable that Western origins of democracy were never premised on the idea of one person, one vote. From the seminal thoughts of the Greeks to the relatively recent writings of John Locke and John Stuart Mill, no author anticipated that everyone in a community would have the right to vote. The Greeks would never have accorded this right to lower-caste citizens, let alone slaves. Even the English democrat Mill never anticipated that everyone would have the right to vote. He believed that working-class citizens would only be permitted to vote if they paid their taxes and passed a literacy test. Even then, wealthy citizens or those who worked in professional or managerial positions would possess the right to vote multiple times. During his own life, Mill, lacking property, never expected the privilege to vote without first acquiring land. Finally, none of these bastions of democratic thought seriously anticipated that women should have the right to vote in any election.[1] The fundamental exercise of choosing community decision makers was commonly considered to be the right of only a select minority of community members.

This was not the case in most Aboriginal communities in North America, in which men and women were fundamentally regarded as equals. This is not to say that role distinctions were not made; clearly, they were. Men, women, and children all had their respective parts to play in contributing to the community's well-being and survival. But making distinctions is not in itself undemocratic. Nor is it necessarily unfair. In Canada, the notion that to achieve equality all people must be treated in the same way has commonly been referred to as the "similarly situated principle." The Supreme Court of Canada clearly rejected this principle in 1989 – and arguably so.[2] That people have different roles to play in society does not necessarily indicate inequality or some rejection of fundamental democratic ideals. Aboriginal people have known this for centuries. More recently, the Supreme Court of Canada clarified that "the interests of true equality may well require differentiation in treatment."[3]

Aboriginal people have commonly treated men, women, and children differently within their respective cultures. Indeed, Aboriginal values have shaped traditions around these very distinctions. However, at the heart of these communities has always been a sense of egalitarianism. It is reflected not only in those practices mentioned in Chapter 6 that have maximized community consultation and consensus but also in the unique perspective regarding the nature of the community itself.

North American Aboriginal communities commonly have creation stories. These narratives are traditional teachings that usually explain what this community is, where it came from, certain tribal responsibilities, and perhaps even laws. Importantly, no Aboriginal creation story has ever placed the right to make decisions or govern the community in the hands of anyone but community members. There has never been recognition of a monarch or oligarchical body that governs the community. Nor has there ever been a creation story suggesting that the people have been delegated any authority or personal rights other than from the Creator. The people have always been recognized in these teachings as possessing a sovereign will with inherent responsibilities and liberties. It is therefore not surprising that democratic ideals and practices have long flourished in Aboriginal communities. It is worth remembering that Canadian democracy is premised not on the sovereign will of the people (as it is in the United States) but on the sovereign right of Parliament.

Since the first ministers' conferences of the 1980s and even more frequently since the Charlottetown conference, First Nations have expressed much interest in an Aboriginal charter of rights. Little explanation has been offered as to what such a charter might look like, though the apparent intention is for it to operate as does the current Charter. This Aboriginal charter would safeguard certain individual rights while presumably maintaining and protecting the cultural contexts of the respective communities. It would thus balance individual rights with collective concerns and values.

Consequently, should a community wish to pass a law similar to the Myadormos Ordinance of the Laguna Pueblo (see Chapter 6), they might consider drafting the Aboriginal charter so as to insulate this practice from the application of the equality guarantee of this charter. To achieve this goal, the draft could exempt certain religious or cultural practices from application of the local charter. Alternatively, an interpretive context section might be employed, as in the Canadian Constitution. Section 1 of the Constitution Act, 1982, provides a context within which to interpret the rights contained in the Canadian Charter of Rights and Freedoms: "The Canadian Charter of Rights and Freedoms guarantees the rights and freedoms set out in it subject only to such reasonable limits prescribed by law as can be demonstrably justified in a free and democratic society."[4] These "unenumerated" principles thus help to shape the scope of the Charter's individual entitlements. Thus, either a section that lists specific exemptions or a more general interpretive approach, like Section 1 but more consistent with Aboriginal values, might be borrowed by Aboriginal communities in creating their own charters. The "reasonable limits" in this section could refer to some collectivist standard such as an ethic of care and responsibility rather than one of democracy.

However, neither approach seems to be entirely adequate. Articulating clearly which practices would be exempt from application of the Aboriginal charter is fraught with difficulties. The primary problem is that this approach provides little flexibility for the growth of customary practices. Presumably, only those customs specifically designated for exemption from the local charter would be insulated from its application. Any practice or custom not clearly articulated would not be protected from charter review. Conceivably, then, any expansion of customary practice may not be exempt from review by the Aboriginal charter. This could be unfortunate. Insofar as all cultures evolve and mature, any subsequent expression of communal values would not be protected from charter scrutiny. If one views community customs and practices as teaching tools, since they express values thought to benefit the community, then arguably a community may wish to protect both currently evolving practices as well as more traditional customs.

An alternative may be to borrow the approach used by the Canadian Constitution – that is, an interpretive context section. This method may offer more flexibility than does articulating each practice that is to be exempt from the Aboriginal charter.

The Canadian Charter of Rights and Freedoms prohibits certain discriminatory practices by governments. However, even if certain actions or laws are found to be contrary to the Charter, they may be saved by Section 1 of the Constitution Act. This section states that rights and freedoms protected by the Charter may be limited if such limits can be "justified" in a free and democratic society. Thus, the Constitution provides that, even where a government law[5] offends an element of the Charter, it may be lawful if it meets the standards set by Section 1.

A similar section might be drafted in an Aboriginal charter to establish a context for reviewing laws and customary practices. This section could stipulate that all laws or customs promoting certain traditional values or beliefs be exempt from charter application.[6] This stipulation would address the lack of flexibility in the first option by permitting present customs to evolve into culturally relevant forms as required. Similarly, traditional customs, perhaps currently unknown to a community, may also be protected when rediscovered. Arguably, both kinds of practices would be permitted to survive provided that they complied with the interpretive section.

However, this approach is not without its own difficulties. To state simply that practices promoting certain Aboriginal values or beliefs are not to be infringed upon by individual rights guarantees does not offer much context. Such a stark statement arguably does little to promote a historical context within which to evaluate the impinging laws. Since the collective rights of a community as expressed by these customs and practices are largely a new element in the exercise of protecting domestic rights,[7] surely a court would appreciate guidance in understanding the content of these rights. Moreover, the proposed interpretive section provides no clear cultural character, which some may argue should be contained in such a statement. Or they may assert that it should contain at least a tone by which other expressions of culture will be judged. Thus, adopting an interpretive statement similar to that of Section 1 of the Canadian Constitution may provide little specific context for communities arguing that any Aboriginal charter of rights must be culturally sensitive.

Perhaps a more significant concern is that this kind of contextual statement permits too much flexibility. Arguably, a broad interpretive statement that insulates so many laws and practices, both new and old, misses the point of the exercise. If the wording protects virtually every local discriminatory custom or law, then individual rights will have little protection. This, too, would be unacceptable.

Aboriginal people have usually defended their collective rights as traditional practices. Thus, some would argue that, if certain customs or laws are to be insulated from charter principles, the goal of which is to protect the rights of individuals, then these collective rights must relate in some way to Aboriginal history and traditions. Arguably, an Aboriginal charter would protect that which has been recognized as important, if not essential, to Aboriginal societies. That something, be it viewed as practices, principles, or values, is so strongly attached to an Aboriginal society that it is believed that it should be protected from the intrusions of an individual rights charter. Protection of traditional practices espousing collective rights has been argued from this general basis.

A broadly based statement similar to Section 1 of the Constitution Act, 1982, would likely include a wide variety of new laws and practices under its umbrella. But members of Aboriginal communities may object to such a broad level of protection. No doubt it would be argued that the collective rights paradigm is intended to preserve selected customary practices from more modern individual rights guarantees. However, even proponents of this position would agree that the contextual statement must not be so broad as to protect every new evolution of collectivist ideas. Flexibility is fine, but it must not become an excuse or tool with which to deny individuals their rights and freedoms.

Clearly, not having some charter of individual rights within an Aboriginal community would fail those whose experience with gender discrimination has taught them that Aboriginal communities are not above ill treatment of their own people. At the same time, the imposition of the Canadian Charter of Rights and Freedoms on Aboriginal communities would result in conflicts between valuable collective rights practices and individual rights protected by the Charter. If an individual rights charter is to have any value, then in most instances Aboriginal customary practices would have to give way. As illustrated in the preceding chapter, this could be highly detrimental to Aboriginal societies. In light of these observations, perhaps a third choice is worth considering.

A Metaphorical Aboriginal Charter

The two options described above have difficulties that cannot easily be overcome. Perhaps the dilemma can be addressed by more innovative wording in an Aboriginal charter. It may be possible to draft an Aboriginal charter that recognizes both the individual rights and important customary ceremonies and practices of a traditional people.

The Navajo Nation has a code of judicial conduct that governs the behaviour of members of its judiciary. Canon 1 of the code states that "A Navajo Nation Judge shall promote Navajo Justice."[8] This canon is to be interpreted by the principle that "a Navajo judge should decide and rule between the four sacred mountains. That means that judges as Navajos should apply Navajo concepts and procedures of justice including the principles of maintaining harmony, respecting freedom and talking things out in free discussion."[9] In addition to guaranteeing due process, the canon, as interpreted by the Navajo judiciary, ensures respect for clan relations, general beliefs about harmony, traditional leadership roles, and the proper treatment of all victims. Decisions concerning this as well as other such judicial canons have become part of Navajo common law. This canon is most striking in its wording, for clear reference is made to Navajo spiritual traditions that *imply* certain laws and obligations.

This technique might be particularly useful in Canada when drafting an Aboriginal charter that overcomes the deficiencies of the alternative options. Aboriginal communities could list individual rights that they wish to protect. No doubt some of these rights would be the same as those in the Canadian Charter of Rights and Freedoms. Indeed, the wording in some instances may be identical. Alternatively, Aboriginal people might phrase these protections so as to make specific traditional references necessary for the interpretation of each individual right. Such a cultural context would be useful when interpreting how collective rights customs might be preserved in the face of these individual rights guarantees.

Yet there is no reason why a particular collective right cannot be included for protection in the Aboriginal charter. The Canadian Constitution includes recognition of collective rights, such as minority language educational rights in Section 23, in addition to more familiar individual rights. Hence, the Aboriginal charter could be drafted so as to protect both collective and individual rights concurrently.

If Aboriginal communities choose what might be described as the "metaphorical" approach to an Aboriginal charter, then they would retain advantages not shared by the first two options. Such a charter would have an immediate cultural context concerning the people whom it most directly affects. Also, the collective rights to be protected would have the flexibility carried by the historical context. There would be limits, of course, to this flexibility, as imposed by the cultural teachings themselves. Not every new law or practice would come under the umbrella of protection provided by that section of the Aboriginal charter. If the new law or practice did not conform to the historical context, then it would not be permitted to impinge on the individual rights protected by the charter. Consequently, protected collective rights would need to have some traditional relevance. Without this historical association, individual rights guarantees would prevail over a collective law or practice.

Another advantage of a metaphorical Aboriginal charter is that, because of its historical nature, its meaning would be more accessible to members of Aboriginal communities. The Canadian Constitution refers to protected rights, democracy, and the rule of law, but these references can usually be understood only by those with legal training. The most fundamental Canadian document is all but inaccessible to the average Canadian. There is no reason why such mysteries should also have to be endured by Aboriginal communities. Surely a metaphorical statement of rights lends itself more readily to an Aboriginal public's understanding of its freedoms and duties. The references in such a charter would be drawn from the immediate history of the community itself. This alone should allow more people to understand both how it works and the role that it plays in their lives.

The prospects of a metaphorical code should engender significant public participation in the initial development of that code. It would be more immediately accessible to the public and consequently of greater community interest and, ultimately, would result in community compliance. Indeed, the development of such a code could only be undertaken through the cooperation and participation of the community. Each community's songs, stories, and history will form the basis for the particular wording of its code, and their teachings will express the values to be protected. It is thus unimaginable that this task could be undertaken without a community's full involvement. The outcome would be a code of rights that a community could understand and honour.

However, it is important to appreciate that drafting a metaphorical charter would not necessarily preclude litigation over its interpretation. No doubt there will always be a need to clarify individual rights and duties, particularly when they collide with collective ones. Nonetheless, with this type of charter, there should be fewer abstract assertions and more pragmatic references for the litigants than is the case under the current Canadian Charter.[10] But the greatest strength of this type of Aboriginal charter would be its ability to balance individual and collective rights within a meaningful cultural context.

Applications of a Metaphorical Aboriginal Charter

A metaphorical Aboriginal charter might be expressed in two ways. Following the format of the current Canadian Charter of Rights and Freedoms, there could be an interpretive section against which the rest of the charter guarantees could be measured. Section 1 of the Charter currently performs this role. As mentioned above, it states that "the Canadian Charter of Rights and Freedoms guarantees the rights and freedoms set out in it subject only to such reasonable limits prescribed by law as can be demonstrably justified in a free and democratic society."

Before using this section, courts ask whether a certain law offends a Charter guarantee such as the right to be secure against unreasonable search or seizure or the right not to be arbitrarily detained. If the court finds that the law does offend one of these guarantees, it then asks whether such a law can nevertheless be justified as a reasonable limit within "a free and democratic society." If the court finds that the law can be thus justified, then it will not be struck down by the Charter. If the law cannot be justified in this manner, then the Charter will prevail, and the law will not survive.

An Aboriginal community might draft a similar section into its own charter. If this community were the People of the Six Nations, then it might wish to draft the following: "Section 1. The rights, obligations, and duties ensured by this charter shall be interpreted in a fashion consistent with the Great Law of the Confederacy of Nations." Thus, when interpreting any right borrowed from the Canadian Charter, such as "Everyone has the fundamental freedoms of thought, belief, opinion and expression,"[11] it would have to be weighed against this new section before it could be fully enforced against an Aboriginal law.

As this example section reads, it is dramatically different from the present Canadian Charter in two ways. First, Aboriginal community members explicitly have "obligations" and "duties." No such reference exists in the Canadian Charter for Canadian citizens. Clearly, the wording introduces a sense of communal, or collective, rights that individuals owe to other parties. However, this wording does not precisely define these obligations and duties. Instead, it leaves to the courts (no doubt, Aboriginal courts with knowledge of local cultures) the task of definition. In many Aboriginal communities, it is common to undertake personal responsibilities through clan structures or other family paradigms. The wording in Section 1 would presumably recognize and preserve some element of this practice.

Second, "the Great Law of the Confederacy of Nations" has a rich history and body of interpretation. It is held close to the hearts of most Iroquois people, and its central purpose is to teach people how to live together peacefully. It was conceived at a time when the Iroquois Confederacy had many internal and external disputes. The development of this law brought peace and harmony to its own members as well as to external tribes with whom they had contact.

With the Great Law came a number of separate teachings that elaborated its full meaning. Some of these teachings stress a sound mind and a healthy body. The law also teaches peace and harmony among both individuals and groups, righteousness in conduct, and honesty in speech and thought. As well, it demands the fair resolution of disputes, including the settlement of conflicts between personal rights and obligations. Strength of character and respect for civil authority are also stipulated by this law, as is respect for the spiritual power of the people, their rituals, and their institutions. All of these teachings add to the meaning of the Great Law. It is against these teachings that the protection of individual rights would be interpreted.

It is now possible to see how the proposed section 1 of a metaphorical charter could influence rights currently protected by the Canadian Charter. For example, subsection 11(c) states that "any person charged with an offence has the right not to be compelled to be a witness in proceedings against that person in respect of the offence."[12] In essence, this right prevents a person from being forced to testify against himself or herself in a court of law. Such a section could also be included in a metaphorical charter to protect the rights of the Aboriginal individual. However, this right would be interpreted against the revised section 1. The effects of the analysis could differ dramatically from the present Charter design.

Subsection 11(c) of the Canadian Charter is arguably so strong that there is virtually no situation in which a person relying on the right against self-incrimination would be forced by a court to testify against himself or herself. This protection is fairly absolute.[13] Thus, if a proposed amendment to the Criminal Code requires individuals to give evidence against themselves under certain circumstances, then the defendant could invoke the protection of subsection 11(c) and have the law struck down. The current Section 1 of the Charter would not overrule this interpretation; indeed, it might reinforce it.[14] However, under the metaphorical charter with the proposed section 1 wording, which refers to the Great Law of the Confederacy of Nations, this restraint against self-incrimination is more tenuous. The reasons are twofold.

First, as already mentioned, unlike Section 1 of the Canadian Charter, Section 1 of the metaphorical charter states that the individual possesses not only rights but also obligations and duties. Thus, any right of protection from self-incrimination must be balanced against personal responsibilities to the community. Conceivably, the individual's duties to the community could override any apparent protection from self-incrimination. This would depend, of course, on just how compelling these responsibilities were.

Second, and in a similar fashion, some of the individual teachings of the Great Law, quite apart from the element of personal responsibilities, could diminish the general scope of protection from self-incrimination. One of these teachings concerns righteousness of conduct and truth in both thought and speech, and it could diminish the initial ambit of constitutional protection from self-incrimination. For example, if a serious crime creates severe unrest and disharmony within the community, perhaps between clans, it is conceivable that a court might overrule the right against self-incrimination. The court might reason that certain responsibilities to a clan are integral to the functioning of the general clan structure. The court might also find that ongoing relationships between clans would be greatly imperilled if it were to recognize the protection against self-incrimination. Thus, the court might uphold the responsibility to honour truth as the only way to restore harmony within the greater community. In such a situation, the prohibition against compelling individuals to give evidence against themselves might justifiably be overruled. If no such perilous situation exists, then no doubt the right against self-incrimination would prevail.

The challenge, as with the current Canadian Charter of Rights and Freedoms, will always be to balance rights. This balancing occurs when Section 1 analysis determines that a law ostensibly in conflict with a Charter right is nonetheless deemed to be justified. Perhaps more relevantly, this balancing exercise occurs whenever different Charter rights collide.[15] There will always be a need to determine which right will prevail in particular circumstances. The Aboriginal charter would simply interject a different set of values (i.e., a different context) against which to evaluate familiar individual rights in a more culturally relevant fashion.

Collective rights would not always prevail over individual rights as articulated within an Aboriginal charter. For example, if an individual committed a relatively minor offence that did not impinge on personal obligations to the clan or duties to the community, then the individual rights protections within the Aboriginal charter would probably prevail. In addition, the Great Law itself may require that subsection 11(c) protection against self-incrimination be honoured. A teaching from the Great Law requires that, for the fair settlement of any dispute, both equity and justice must be respected. In this situation, it may successfully be argued that the protection against self-incrimination is an integral part of both concepts. Thus, this individual right might be protected not only as a Charter right but also as an expression of the Great Law itself. Thus, when community rights are only minimally affected, individual rights protection would likely prevail. In some instances, principles such as the Great Law may indeed demand their protection.

Comprehensive versus Individual Rights

The foregoing discussion explored the use of a single interpretive section to assist in the application of individual rights guarantees of the metaphorical charter. However, with a more expansive approach to this methodology and, perhaps, one more consistent with the term "metaphorical charter," there is yet another alternative. One need not limit metaphorical references to a single interpretive section of the charter. It is feasible for a community to attach a specific metaphorical reference to each individual right mentioned in its charter. Doing so would clearly indicate how each right is to be interpreted. This approach would be more effective than would a single interpretive section.

Drafting each section of the charter with a different metaphorical reference would be repetitive; however, if a community insists that this would be the most effective way of ensuring a balance of everyone's interests, then it may be the best approach. It would be less cumbersome to draft metaphorical references for groups of charter rights. A number of individual rights currently protected by the Canadian Charter have common purposes.[16]

Accordingly, a section of an Aboriginal charter addressing the democratic rights of the individual in a traditional Mohawk community might read as follows: "Each citizen has the right to stand for public office and the right to vote for that office, subject only to those limitations as prescribed by the local clans and clan mothers." Although this section does not refer specifically to Mohawk traditions, it does allude to certain traditional practices. Such a section would ensure the individual right to vote except when a Mohawk Nation retains the role of clan mothers in choosing council chiefs. Where this custom is no longer practised, or where a vote is held for a public office not impinged on by this custom, an individual's democratic right would be preserved.

Another section of the charter might address rights related to due process within a metaphorical context. Due process has commonly included the right to legal counsel, the right to determine habeas corpus, the right to be immediately and properly informed of an offence, and so forth. The following section might be drafted regarding these rights: "Everyone has the right to rely on the rules of natural justice, including not to be arbitrarily detained or imprisoned, to be secure from unreasonable search and seizure, unless to do so would be in conflict with the Great Law. Every person has the right to lay himself or herself at the tree of the Great White Root and to take away the rights of equity and justice, which are to be properly preserved." Once again the teachings that flow from such a metaphorical reading of rights would balance an Iroquois tradition that honours community customs against a Eurocentric tradition that respects due process protections. The metaphorical references would be culturally meaningful for the community, while the collective values would be balanced against the protection of individual freedoms. Importantly, this balancing of collective and individual rights would have a culturally meaningful context for the community, a context that is lacking within the confines of the present Canadian Charter of Rights and Freedoms.

Introducing Aboriginal Charters

Those involved in constitutional revision in this country view the need for Aboriginal charters of rights as a key element of any constitutional package. Aboriginal women's groups, concerned about gender equality, want to ensure that the Section 15 guarantee of equality in the present Charter also applies to Aboriginal governments. The Charlottetown Accord proposed that the entire Charter as it currently reads should apply to any new Aboriginal third order of government. This proposition was supported by civil libertarian authors and organizations. It is less clear, however, how the Canadian public felt about this proposal, since the issue did not receive public debate other than within the context of gender equality. Nevertheless, in the next round of constitutional dialogue, application of the Charter will once again be of much interest to Aboriginal communities.

Surely these communities must be consulted on the drafting of laws regarding Aboriginal self-government. As illustrated in earlier chapters, these communities are in many ways different from Eurocentric Canadian communities. In Aboriginal communities, personal duties and obligations have always existed alongside individual rights. Many traditions still honour this relationship. Any discussion of the application of the Charter to these communities must therefore respect these time-honoured values.

In any such discussion, there must be a full disclosure of issues and interests. Moreover, since the cultural teachings of Aboriginal peoples vary from region to region across Canada, these discussions would yield a variety of results. Present circumstances suggest that most Aboriginal communities would wish to develop their own charter of rights. These charters may or may not adopt the metaphorical style just reviewed. Some communities may simply adopt the same set of rights articulated by the Canadian Charter, while other communities may borrow some of these rights and add to them to create a hybrid charter. Nevertheless, out of deference to these communities and respect for democratic principles, they should be able to decide for themselves.

If a constitutional amendment were to reconcile the aforementioned concerns, then Aboriginal communities would not likely be able to implement immediately their own charters of rights. It would not be fair to expect these communities to implement codes without first engaging their members in the kind of consultative process appropriate to the development of such a significant document. Such a process of production and refinement would take time, but recognizing self-government before a charter of rights can be implemented is not without precedent in the Canadian

Constitution. Such a methodology was employed regarding introduction of the equality provision of Section 15 of the Charter.

While drafting the Charter, legislators believed that, because of the apparent inequities of treatment in various pieces of existing legislation throughout the country, if Section 15 were to come into force concurrently with the rest of the Charter, then large pieces of legislation would be struck down as unconstitutional. Hence, they agreed that, in order to address the inequities of existing legislation and to lessen the impact on individuals, governments, and programs of the wholesale striking down of laws, Section 15 would not come into effect until three years after the introduction of the rest of the Charter.[17] This provided time for the respective legislatures to get their houses in order and to minimize any turbulent effects caused by the introduction of the equality section. A similar device might be employed for the introduction of an Aboriginal charter.

Perhaps there could be a moratorium on the application of the Canadian Charter to Aboriginal communities. It could be decided that, out of deference to the right of self-determination by Aboriginal communities, and due to an abiding respect for their collective values, the Canadian Charter would not be imposed on them until five years after any constitutional recognition of their right to exercise self-government. Within this five-year period, each community could develop its own charter. This procedure would also permit adoption, in whole or in part, of the Canadian Charter. If no charter has been established by a community after five years, then the Canadian Charter of Rights and Freedoms would automatically apply in its absence. However, such an approach would initially leave these communities without any charter of rights.

An alternative approach might be for the Canadian Charter to apply to Aboriginal communities until they adopt their own charters. If no local charter has been introduced after five years (this span is always subject to further consideration), then the Canadian Charter would become the permanent community charter.

Either approach would stimulate discussion concerning interests vital to the community and establish a closure period for these discussions. To some degree, the latter proposal would placate the concerns both of those who proposed the Charter's application in the Charlottetown Accord and of civil libertarians across the country.

Comment

The merits of applying the Canadian Charter of Rights and Freedoms to Aboriginal governments in Canada, with emphasis on the debate over collective versus individual rights, should be fully discussed before any final decision is made. *Duro* illustrates the risks that are run when choices are left to the courts or to any decision-making process that renders decisions without the benefit of informed opinions.[18] All parties to this debate should make concerted efforts to understand both the essence and the implications of arguments on each side of the debate. This understanding appears to be missing from present discussions. The merits of the individual rights paradigm are perhaps easier for many to comprehend, but the collective rights position deserves equal consideration. If Canadians are truly committed to the goal of Aboriginal people instituting their own forms of self-government, then they must give appropriate regard to Aboriginal expressions of this authority. Moreover, Aboriginal people are not unmindful of the value of protecting fundamental individual rights. Such liberties are perhaps most relevant to young people in Aboriginal communities. Thus, any self-government paradigm will no doubt include some form of individual rights protection – but it must also include some form of collective rights recognition.

8
The Royal Commission on Aboriginal Peoples and Self-Government: Just Another Lump of Coal

The Royal Commission on Aboriginal Peoples (RCAP) was established by the federal government on 26 August 1991. The commission was handed a broad mandate: "The Commission of Inquiry should investigate the evolution of the relationship among Aboriginal peoples (Indian, Inuit and Métis), the Canadian government, and Canadian society as a whole. It should propose specific solutions, rooted in domestic and international experience, to the problems which have plagued those relationships and which confront Aboriginal peoples today. The Commission should examine all issues which it deems to be relevant to any or all of the Aboriginal peoples of Canada."[1]

The commissioners subsequently undertook four years of research and consultation with a large number of people and organizations, both Aboriginal and non-Aboriginal. In the fall of 1996, the commission submitted its final report to Parliament. This report was far reaching in the scope of its subject matter as well as in the depth of its specific topics. Of particular interest to many people were the opinions regarding Aboriginal self-government. Many submissions had been made to the commission by Aboriginal peoples, and the final report's comments were greatly anticipated. Unfortunately, the commission's opinions on Aboriginal self-government seem to have been hardly worth the wait.

The commission premised its recommendations on prevailing constitutional law, federal legislation, Canadian common law, and aspects of international law. However, principal in the commission's analysis of self-government was the Supreme Court of Canada's decision in *R. v. Sparrow*.[2] It was upon the court's reasoning and its own inferences from this case that the commission premised many of its recommendations. *Sparrow* should therefore be explained to set the context for the commission's recommendations on Aboriginal self-determination that follow.

Sparrow and Its Legacy

The case of *R. v. Sparrow* came before the Supreme Court of Canada from the British Columbia Court of Appeal.[3] Sparrow was charged with a violation of the Fisheries Act: namely, fishing with a drift net larger than that allowed pursuant to the relevant regulations. The defendant argued that his right to fish for food was protected by subsection 35(1) of the Constitution Act, 1982, which states that "the existing aboriginal and treaty rights of aboriginal peoples of Canada are hereby recognized and affirmed."[4] Sparrow argued that his Aboriginal fishing right recognized by this subsection invalidated the regulation. Unsuccessful at trial, the defendant appealed to the BC Court of Appeal, which also refused to recognize the appellant's constitutional argument. In addition, it found insufficient factual evidence introduced at trial to overturn the conviction. The Supreme Court of Canada was then asked to reconcile the relevant constitutional issues. Significantly, its findings dramatically revised the jurisprudential perspective of the courts toward Aboriginal rights. However, most importantly for Aboriginal self-determination, the court may have also undermined many of the Aboriginal community's aspirations.

The Supreme Court agreed that the appellant's Aboriginal right to fish was recognized and protected by subsection 35(1). In this instance, this right was extended to fishing for both consumption and ceremonial purposes. However, the court took this opportunity to describe some of the limitations imposed on this right, asserting that subsection 35(1) applies to the protection of all Aboriginal rights in existence in 1982 when the Constitution Act came into existence. However, this subsection does not revive rights that may have been extinguished by then. Clarifying this concept, the court stated that there must be a "clear and plain intention" to extinguish such rights. That a right is "regulated" does not imply that it has been extinguished. Thus, a "policy of behaviour" alone does not extinguish an Aboriginal right without a clearly expressed intention. In addition, whether or not such a right still exists, one must consider the particular circumstances in a flexible context that permits a right's "evolution over time."[5] From the point of view of Aboriginal people, so far, so good.

However, the Supreme Court went on to describe the unique nature of this entitlement and the circumstances in which it could be limited. The court stated that Aboriginal rights are not subject to the interpretive section of the Constitution Act. This section states that "1. The Canadian Charter of Rights and Freedoms guarantees the rights and freedoms set out in it subject only to such reasonable limits prescribed by law as can be demonstrably justified in a free and democratic society."[6] Nor are Aboriginal rights protected by Section 52, which states that "(1) The Constitution of Canada is the supreme law of Canada, and any law that is inconsistent with the provisions of the Constitution is, to the extent of the inconsistency, of no force or effect."[7]

This is the entrenching section. Professor Monahan describes entrenchment this way: "We say that rights or norms are entrenched when they are set out in a fundamental constitutional document that takes precedence over all other laws and that cannot be amended through the ordinary process of law making."[8] He then describes Section 52 of the 1982 Constitution Act: "Section 52 states that the documents falling within this definition are the 'supreme law of Canada' and that any Canadian law that is inconsistent with these entrenched constitutional documents will be ruled invalid by the courts."[9] At first reading, Section 52 would seem to indicate that the Section 35 rights are protected through the entrenchment function of the section. Like the Charter sections, they too are part of this constitutional document. Therefore, one might reasonably assume that, since there is nothing on the face of this document that suggests otherwise, and that there is no constitutional history or doctrine that might disagree, then the Aboriginal interests would seem to be equally protected. But such was not to be the case. Instead of relying on Section 52 for the protection of Aboriginal and treaty rights in the same way that the rights in the Charter are protected through entrenchment,[10] the court decided that the protective mechanism for Aboriginal rights is in the unique nature of subsection 35(1) itself. The court reasoned that, although this subsection recognizes and affirms Aboriginal rights, it "does not promise immunity from government regulation."[11] The court stated, without any explanation why, that "rights that are recognized and affirmed are not absolute."[12] Since Section 35 rights cannot rely upon the Section 52 entrenchment function, simple legislation that affects Aboriginal rights, even to the extent of extinguishing them, may be valid.

The court did require, however, that any such legislation be justified. Thus, the Crown would have to prove that the legislation has a valid objective and that the action is justified in relation to the resulting infringement on the Aboriginal right. As well, the Crown, in keeping with its special trustlike relationship with Aboriginal peoples, must maintain an honourable relationship. Hence, such legislation must infringe as little as possible on the subsection 35(1) right.[13]

The result of the court's reasoning[14] was that the Crown failed to illustrate sufficient justification for its infringement on the Aboriginal right of Sparrow to fish. The court went on to describe exactly which subsection 35(1) rights Aboriginal people have in such circumstances: "Any allocation of priorities *after* valid conservation measures have been implemented must give top priority to Indian food fishing."[15] One recognizes from this statement that subsection 35(1) does not protect Aboriginal rights so much as it establishes a system of priorities in dealing with them. Unfortunately, for Aboriginal people, it is also clear from this statement that their interests are of secondary importance.[16]

Ironically, before *Sparrow* was heard by the Supreme Court, Aboriginal people were very concerned about how the court was going to interpret the meaning of the word "existing" in subsection 35(1). Since enactment of the Constitution Act, 1982, Aboriginal people had argued that the section recognizes and protects all Aboriginal rights, including those not yet recognized in law. This was known as the "full box" theory of Section 35. Government parties, however, argued that, unless these rights had been recognized in 1982, when the act came into existence, they did not exist. Consequently, they argued, such rights should not receive the protection of Section 35. This was known as the "empty box" theory, or "frozen rights" theory. Although the Supreme Court eventually supported the position of the Aboriginal litigants, perhaps in retrospect greater concern should have been devoted to how the court would interpret the words "recognized and affirmed."

The disappointment of Aboriginal people over the *Sparrow* decision resulted from the characterization of their collective rights (many of which are discussed in Chapter 6) in such a way that the court gave with one hand and took away with the other. Although recognizing that Aboriginal rights are protected by subsection 35(1), the court diminished the protection of those rights by permitting legislation rather easily to minimize or even extinguish such rights.[17] Aboriginal people believed and argued that subsection 35(1) rights were entrenched in the Constitution in the same manner as Charter rights. Thus, they claimed that, like these Charter rights, Aboriginal and treaty rights should be protected by the terms of Section 52 of the Constitution Act.[18] Subsection 52(1), known as the "supremacy clause," is the most powerful tool used in the protection of all Charter rights. For reasons unexplained, the court decided that Aboriginal and treaty rights, clearly articulated in subsection 35(1), do not deserve the same protection. Instead, the Supreme Court simply asserted that the process of "recognizing and affirming" rights somehow exempted Aboriginal rights from such protection.[19] This finding was devastating to Aboriginal interests because it meant that Aboriginal rights were far less "entrenched" than were an individual's Charter rights. The court's assertion meant that Aboriginal entitlements could be limited even to the point of extinguishment provided only that it was done in the proper fashion. It is this new approach to the "entrenchment" of Aboriginal and treaty rights that, among other deficiencies, poses such serious problems for the resulting recommendations of the Royal Commission on Aboriginal Peoples.

Through the Looking Glass

The report of the Royal Commission on Aboriginal Peoples begins its thesis by asserting that the Aboriginal right to "self-determination"[20] exists in law based on any one of three foundations. First it argues that the right is recognized in international law.[21] This recognition has evolved over the years as a consequence of emerging international norms. The commission documented the many international instruments that have evolved, mostly since the end of the Second World War, to recognize the right of Indigenous peoples to self-determination. However, RCAP did not base its recommendations on this evolving area of law.

The commission went on to argue that Aboriginal self-determination has been recognized in federal common law at least since the case of *Connolly* v. *Woolrich*.[22] After a brief review of the history of jurisprudence in this area, the commission found that the Aboriginal right to self-determination can also be successfully argued as existing within current Canadian common law.[23] Notwithstanding this finding, the commission moved on to another thesis on which to base its theory of Aboriginal people's right to self-determination.

The RCAP report states that the Aboriginal right to self-government can now be asserted as a consequence of the findings in *Sparrow* and the Supreme Court's interpretation of subsection 35(1) of the Constitution Act, 1982. Based on the court's decision regarding recognition of the Aboriginal right to fish pursuant to subsection 35(1), RCAP asserted that the right of self-determination is now established: "The Commission concludes that the inherent right of Aboriginal self-government is recognized and affirmed in section 35(1) of the Constitution Act, 1982 as an Aboriginal and treaty protected right. The inherent right is thus entrenched in the Canadian Constitution, providing a basis for Aboriginal governments to function as one of three distinct orders of government of Canada."[24]

Thus, RCAP concluded that subsection 35(1) recognizes that Aboriginal people possess the right of self-determination, that it is an inherent right, and that it is currently entrenched in the Constitution. The commission then went about the task of characterizing both the nature and the scope of this right. It stated that the jurisdiction of this right is divided into two aspects: "core" and "peripheral." Both are inherent and entrenched.[25] The "core" area of Aboriginal jurisdiction includes matters over which an "Aboriginal group has the right to exercise authority and legislate at its own initiative without the need to conclude self-government treaties or agreements with the Crown."[26] The "peripheral" area includes all matters that fall outside the core area. However, the commission required that peripheral issues, unlike core subjects, must first be negotiated for and agreed to by the appropriate federal or provincial government before this jurisdiction can be exercised by the Aboriginal government. The terms of these negotiations are to be articulated in agreements or treaties, which in turn will be constitutionalized through the use of subsection 35(3) of the Constitution Act.[27]

The commissioners went on to outline principles that they thought naturally flow from *Sparrow* and that outline the parameters for the core and peripheral areas. The report states that core areas of jurisdiction for Aboriginal governments are restricted to all matters that

1. are of vital concern to the life and welfare of a particular Aboriginal people, its culture and identity;
2. that do not have a major impact on adjacent jurisdictions; and
3. that are otherwise not the object of transcendent federal or provincial concern.[28]

"With respect to these matters, an Aboriginal group has the right to exercise authority and legislate at its own initiative, *without* the need to conclude federal and provincial agreements."[29] Any subject matter that does not meet *all* of these standards will fall outside the definition of core issues and fall within the ambit of periphery issues. Consequently, an Aboriginal government would first have to negotiate with the relevant federal and provincial governments before it could exercise any jurisdiction in this area.[30] Although it is not entirely clear how such jurisdictional distinctions emanate from *Sparrow,* the implications of the defining terms of this description of self-government should be troubling for Aboriginal people.

The Vital Threshold
The initial concern emanates from the requirement that the area of authority for unilateral Aboriginal government action is limited to matters deemed "vital" to the life of an Aboriginal community. When one first considers the concept that Aboriginal peoples should be able to exercise unilateral jurisdiction over matters vital to their communities, it certainly sounds reasonable. However the recommendation would confine unilateral actions to only those areas deemed to be of a vital nature. Surely this threshold is too high.

For example, if a matter is of "some concern" to a community, then can it exercise authority unilaterally to address the issue? Clearly not. Similarly, if an issue is "significant" or "important" to a community, then is it free to act independently? Once again, no. These matters simply do not rise to the vital threshold, at least not until they are shown to have more serious consequences for the community. Until this level of seriousness commensurate with the term "vital" is reached, the matter would not fall within the parameters of the core area as outlined by RCAP. Accordingly, these communities would not be free to address these issues unilaterally.

In practice, this would mean that minor labour laws addressing hours of work or overtime pay would not meet the threshold of being vital to an Aboriginal community. Unless labour laws can be shown to have very serious consequences for a community, they would not meet the vital threshold. Similarly, landlord and tenant issues would seem deficient in meeting the threshold of vital. In fact, the Aboriginal government would be so limited by the interpretation of the word "vital" that it would not be able to legislate unilaterally even highway traffic laws.[31] Apparently, even a left-hand turn would first have to be negotiated as a periphery item with the appropriate levels of government.

One should understand, though, that the proposed RCAP recommendations will not necessitate scrutiny of every individual law as to whether or not it is vital before it can be legislated. Presumably, the areas or matters would receive the required scrutiny as to whether the laws are vital to a community's interests. Surely not every law would have to be scrutinized, though the report fails to elaborate the particulars of any such review.

Criminal law matters or highway traffic issues would likely be easily assessed under the RCAP criterion of vital. Such matters are discrete and easily recognizable. However, other general subject matters, such as family law, include diverse subgroups of issues such as divorce, separation, child support, alimony, and so forth. These issues are not so clearly set apart from one another. A federal or provincial government might concede an Aboriginal government's authority to legislate in one area but not in another, depending on whether the government considers the area vital to the community. Unlike federal or provincial governments, which can unify related areas of law under a single piece of legislation,[32] Aboriginal governments will be prevented from unilaterally doing so unless each area is deemed vital. If it is not, then negotiations will have to occur before a comprehensive effort can be made to tackle what are nonetheless serious matters for the community.

An Aboriginal government may in fact be required to review each piece of legislation to determine whether it is vital to the integrity of its community. Although such a task is daunting, there is nothing in the RCAP recommendations that would clearly relieve an Aboriginal government from such an undertaking. One might claim that such a process is what federal and provincial governments must now endure when they have a dispute regarding their respective jurisdictions, but they have the significant advantage of much clearer assistance from the Constitution[33] as well as existing constitutional tools.[34]

The American Lesson

Canadian jurisprudence provides few clues as to how the term "vital" will be interpreted by the courts. There is no similar situation in Canadian law from which to draw insights. However, jurisprudence in US common law may be helpful.

Indian tribes in the United States have been recognized as "nations" since the early 1800s. A series of Supreme Court decisions determined that these tribes were "domestic dependent nations" possessing inherent "sovereignty." Since then, courts have had many opportunities to express their opinions on the scope of this jurisdiction. Although many of the early cases dealt with issues concerning tribal criminal law jurisdiction, more recently the subject of civil law jurisdiction has occupied these courts.

In 1959, the case of *Williams* v. *Lee*[35] established parameters for the civil law jurisdiction of a tribe. It was recognized that, under the doctrine of the domestic dependent nation, Congress could at any time limit a tribe's civil jurisdiction. With regard to state governments, *Williams* reaffirmed that state laws apply in Indian country only "where *essential* tribal relations were not involved."[36] For present purposes, it is important to note the similarity between the term "essential" as used in *Williams* and the term "vital" as used by the Royal Commission on Aboriginal Peoples.

Since *Williams* v. *Lee,* the term "essential tribal relations" has come under increased scrutiny in the courts. State governments have consistently argued that the areas in which they wished to exercise jurisdiction did not affect essential tribal matters. These arguments have been made with increasing success.[37] The consequence for US tribes has been a court-imposed limitation on the scope of tribal civil jurisdiction.

This development is instructive for Aboriginal people in Canada. Arguably, both federal and provincial governments will mount similar attacks on the term "vital." They may argue that, as with the US term "essential," the word should be accorded a narrow interpretation. The Canadian governments may claim that there are few areas or matters that should be considered vital to an Aboriginal community's welfare. Indeed, common sense indicates that the term "vital" can only refer to a limited number of areas; most subjects, it would be asserted, fall outside the scope of the term. Thus, it might be argued, most matters should be relegated to the jurisdiction or area termed "periphery." Consequently, they must first be negotiated for by the Aboriginal government before they can be enforced in law.

If there is any doubt about the plausibility of such a forecast, then one need only consider the positions taken by the same Canadian governments concerning the term "existing" in subsection 35(1) of the Constitution Act, 1982. Not one Canadian government supported the position taken by Aboriginal people that the term referred to a full box of Aboriginal and treaty rights. Instead, they argued the empty box theory, implying a much more limited recognition of rights.[38] The presence of the term "vital" in the RCAP recommendations will once again provide these governments with the opportunity to argue a very limited scope for Aboriginal jurisdiction.

Cultural Concerns?

definition of core matters presents another difficulty for
. The recommendation states that the core jurisdiction
'of vital concern to the life and welfare of a particular
:, its *culture* and *identity*."[39] The dilemma that arises from
this stat..... this: Does such wording imply that the area of core matters refers only to issues of culture and identity in the narrow sense of those
words? That is, will the courts view this terminology as permitting the
Aboriginal government to legislate unilaterally only on matters associated
with the arts, language, and education? Clearly, this scope would be unacceptable to Aboriginal communities that wish to exercise jurisdiction over
not only these matters but also those tied to economics, criminal law, and
a host of civil law areas. It is not clear from the wording of the recommendation that these latter items would necessarily be viewed by the courts as
core matters. A court could take a very narrow view of the meanings of
these words that define the core area.[40]

Once again Canadian jurisprudence is not particularly helpful in penetrating the content of this phrase. Constitutional case law is of limited use
because the courts have never been asked to consider this degree of partic-
ularity when dealing with cases involving Aboriginal rights. However,
should the courts be asked to clarify this issue, they might consider the
positions taken by all the parties to the Charlottetown Accord. Such a
review could be very disquieting for Aboriginal people.

The Charlottetown Accord proposed a similar but more expansive jurisdiction than that recommended by RCAP. In Item 41, the accord states
that

> the exercise of the right of self-government includes the authority of the
> duly constituted *legislative bodies* of Aboriginal peoples, each within its own
> jurisdiction:
> (a) to safeguard and develop their languages, cultures, economies, iden-
>   tities, institutions, and traditions; and
> (b) to develop, maintain and strengthen their relationship with their
>   lands, waters and environment so as to determine and control their
>   development as peoples according to their own values and priorities
>   and ensure the integrity of their societies.[41]

It is significant that this wording includes the term "economies."[42] This
term, accorded its normal meaning, would include a host of issues not
ostensibly included by the RCAP phrase. A party wishing to limit the scope
of Aboriginal jurisdiction could therefore argue that the RCAP version is
intended to be more restrictive than the Charlottetown proposal. Notwithstanding the inclinations of the commission when drafting its proposal,

clearly a court would be at liberty to agree with such an inference and then impose a more restrictive interpretation on the RCAP proposal. Consequently, such a court may decide that an Aboriginal government possesses core jurisdiction only over the more artistic and educational matters within its community. Thus, only over these matters would an Aboriginal government be free to act unilaterally.

Adjacent Jurisdictions

Another dimension to the definition of core jurisdiction is the requirement that an Aboriginal government's unilateral authority "not have a major impact on adjacent jurisdictions."[43] Surely this limitation is too broad and unnecessary. This stipulation appears to address the concern that non-Aboriginal communities be protected from the decisions of nearby Aboriginal communities. The example provided by the RCAP report refers to pollution and the possible dangers of Aboriginal communities storing hazardous waste upstream from a non-Aboriginal community.[44] The fear is that the non-Aboriginal community might be injured due to the improper storage of these materials. As compelling as this health concern is, one must ask whether the remedy suggested is fair and balanced.

There are places in Canada where a river begins in one province and flows into another. No consideration has been given to the idea that the "downstream province" should have the ability to limit the jurisdictional authority of the "upstream province" to deal with issues of either river pollution or hazardous waste storage. Demanding this kind of authority would be an affront to provincial sovereignty. Furthermore, practical civil law remedies already exist to address situations that the commission seems to fear will inevitably arise. Currently, civil law actions may be brought before a court either to prevent or to compensate for an injury caused by the upriver province. If concern about pollution is so great, then the RCAP report could simply have recommended that in such instances Aboriginal governments be subject to civil liability for their actions. Surely this approach would address the commission's concerns yet not impinge unnecessarily on the jurisdictional authority of an Aboriginal government.

However, the implications of the RCAP recommendation are not limited to these scenarios. The wording of the recommendation appears to extend to matters not nearly as serious as storing hazardous wastes. For example, if an Aboriginal community such as the Anishnabek First Nation located partially within Sarnia, Ontario, were to permit the sale of alcohol two hours beyond the provincial regulation, then the city might argue that this authority is not within the unilateral jurisdiction of the Aboriginal government. The city could argue reasonably that the extended drinking hours contribute directly to the number of intoxicated drivers on roads in Sarnia. Or, should the community of Kahnawake in Quebec decide to open a casino, the City of Montreal might claim that it would draw patrons away from its own gaming institutions or add to the local problem of gambling addiction. In both scenarios, the cities could argue that the Aboriginal governments' unilateral exercise of authority will have a major impact on the adjacent jurisdictions. To be successful before the courts, the cities apparently would only need to demonstrate the seriousness of the impact.

This may not be a difficult hurdle to overcome. Unfortunately for Aboriginal people, neither Canadian law nor the RCAP report offers much assistance in determining precisely how difficult such a hurdle would be to overcome. Aboriginal people should be concerned that Canadian courts may not set such standards very high. Perhaps even more disturbing is the nature of the hurdle itself.

One should recall that an Aboriginal government can only act unilaterally when the concern is "vital" to the community. No incidental matter will meet this threshold. However, a similar standard is not required of the adjacent jurisdiction. The RCAP report requires not that the impact of any Aboriginal law on this jurisdiction affect a vital resource or even a very serious one but only that it have a significant impact. The courts may be loath to limit an Aboriginal government's jurisdiction when the impact on an adjacent non-Aboriginal community institution is of relatively minor significance to that community, but this is by no means assured. Clearly, there is no requirement that the area affected be "essential" to the adjacent jurisdiction. Thus, a matter of only moderate significance may be sufficient to constrain the authority of an Aboriginal government. The resulting scenario is that a matter "vital" to an Aboriginal community could be limited by an adjacent jurisdiction even though the impact of the Aboriginal law on the non-Aboriginal community affects an institution that is of only moderate significance to that community.

The RCAP recommendation regarding the potential impact of an Aboriginal law on an adjacent jurisdiction is seriously flawed. The concerns of the commission could more easily have been addressed simply by ensuring that Aboriginal governments be subject to civil suits. If an Aboriginal government in some way caused harm to others, then it could be brought before the courts just like any other level of government. There is no need to limit so thoroughly an Aboriginal government's jurisdiction if the concern is to simply ensure that these governments are held accountable for their actions.

Moreover, local towns and cities are free to contend that an Aboriginal government's authority should be limited even when the impact of any law on them has nothing to do with the life-threatening examples articulated by the commission. These jurisdictions might contend that simple economic impacts, which they would rather not endure, sustain the argument to restrain the unilateral exercise of Aboriginal authority.[45] Indeed, the courts may find that any major impact of an Aboriginal law on an adjacent community, no matter how minor the issue, will limit the Aboriginal government's ability to act.[46] There is certainly nothing in the RCAP recommendations to prevent this type of constraint. Hence, some matters clearly "vital" to an Aboriginal community will nevertheless be relegated to the classification of "peripheral." And of course they will have to be negotiated for before they can be acted on.

Vital versus Transcendent Federal or Provincial Concerns

Another limitation imposed on the definition of a core area of Aboriginal jurisdiction involves transcendent federal or provincial concerns. The RCAP report states that, even if an issue is vital to an Aboriginal community, it must "not rise to the level of overriding national or regional concerns."[47] Once again Aboriginal peoples should be concerned with the implications of this recommendation.

One of the most profound positions argued by Aboriginal communities over the years has been that they should have the right to address criminal law issues in their communities far more constructively than does the federal government. These communities have claimed that both perpetrators and victims[48] of offences would be better served by Aboriginal control over criminal law matters. This issue was reiterated by Aboriginal parties throughout the 1980s first ministers' conferences as well as at the subsequent Charlottetown discussions. Nonetheless, local control over criminal law matters would clearly not be available to Aboriginal communities under the limitation imposed by the RCAP report.

Evidence indicates that the federal government would argue that this area of jurisdiction does rise to the level of an overriding national concern. The federal government has already expressed its opinion that substantive criminal law authority is a national power.[49] Moreover, despite many assertions by Aboriginal people that the exercise of criminal law authority is integral to the protection and cultivation of harmony within the community, the federal government disagrees. It stated in its 1995 policy guide, entitled "Aboriginal Self-Government," that it "does not believe that these matters are integral to Aboriginal cultures or groups."[50] Surely, then, Aboriginal peoples can expect that any attempt by their own governments to exercise criminal law authority unilaterally will be challenged in the courts by the federal government as an infringement on a transcendent federal concern.[51]

What, then, should one surmise from the RCAP recommendation? Aboriginal people have continually asserted their interest in exercising criminal law jurisdiction. The federal government has also clearly stated its position, which opposes recognition of such authority. How did the commission itself respond to this specific conflict? With silence. The commissioners failed to engage the issue directly or to offer any halfway-house

or either party. This seems like an odd way to address an issue
tal importance to all Canadians.

so expect the federal government to challenge Aboriginal jurisdiction over taxation, fisheries, marriage, divorce, and health. Notwithstanding Aboriginal claims that all of these areas should fall within their
jurisdictional competence, the federal government would likely contest
most if not all of these areas as transcendent federal concerns.

Provincial governments may make similar claims against the jurisdictional authority of Aboriginal governments. One area of compelling jurisdictional interest to Aboriginal people is community policing. Policing falls
within the jurisdictional competence of a province in the administration of
justice.[52] Authority over policing is a natural complement to Aboriginal
people's desire to exercise criminal law authority. Thus, Aboriginal governments will likely claim that authority over policing in their communities is
vital to the safety of their members.

Today many Aboriginal communities exercise some local policing powers
pursuant to an arrangement (usually) with the respective provincial government.[53] Since Aboriginal police forces will exercise some authority over
non-Aboriginal persons in their communities, some provincial governments may argue that the present arrangements should be continued on a
negotiated basis. These governments will no doubt claim that any unilateral exercise of an Aboriginal policing authority will intrude on a transcendent provincial concern. A provincial government may make this claim
simply to ensure the integrity of its policing authority over non-Aboriginal
persons. Nevertheless, a core area of authority may be denied to Aboriginal
governments if the RCAP recommendation becomes law.

Provinces may make similar arguments concerning jurisdiction over marriages. Wedding ceremonies, who can perform them, and marriage licences
currently fall within provincial competence.[54] The wish of Aboriginal governments to exercise authority in this area may well be challenged in the
courts as an intrusion upon a matter of significant provincial interest.
Aboriginal people once again should be concerned that the courts will agree.

A similar scenario threatens Aboriginal jurisdiction over child welfare.
This issue is close to the hearts of many Aboriginal people and would no
doubt be considered vital to the welfare of a community. Yet it too may be
challenged by some provincial governments as an intrusion upon another
transcendent provincial concern. The success of such a claim would once
again diminish the scope of an Aboriginal government's ability to control
matters considered vital to its community.

Some Conclusions about Core Issues
The irresistible conclusion drawn from this analysis is that the scope of
core issues within which Aboriginal governments can act unilaterally is

alarmingly small. The Royal Commission on Aboriginal Peoples, however, would have one believe that this jurisdiction is much larger than common sense suggests. Figure 3.1 on page 218 of the RCAP report (see A in figure below) illustrates what seems to be a relationship among federal, provincial, and Aboriginal governments. This figure illustrates an Aboriginal jurisdiction approximately equal in size to those of the other two orders of Canadian government. Furthermore, the Aboriginal government's core area is decidedly larger than that of its peripheral area. It should be clear from the foregoing discussion that such a characterization is seriously mistaken.

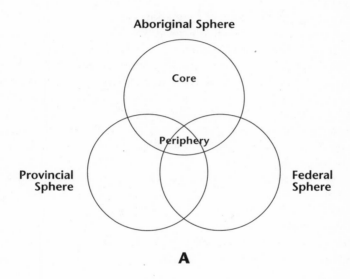

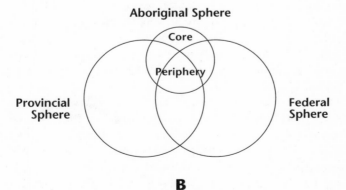

Aboriginal jurisdiction, as worded in the RCAP recommendations, would more accurately be about 90 percent peripheral matters and 10 percent core matters (see B above). Consequently, an Aboriginal government would be able to exercise very little of its total jurisdiction unilaterally.

However, this is not the most serious criticism of the report's recommendations in this area. Rather, it is the recommendation relating to the scope of Aboriginal authority that may present the greatest concern for Aboriginal people. The recommendations about core and peripheral matters do not describe the size of the sphere of Aboriginal authority; they only describe the ways in which the respective areas of competence must be treated if they are to be exercised. The report does provide, however, an opinion on the potential scope of a community's authority to exercise self-determination: "the Aboriginal sphere of authority under section 35(1), including both core and periphery, has roughly the same maximum scope as the federal head of power with respect to Indians, and lands reserved for Indians," recognized in subsection 91(24) of the Constitution Act, 1867.[55] The commission goes on: "This sphere includes all matters relating to the good government and welfare of Aboriginal peoples and their territories."[56] Attempting to elaborate this point, the commission lists matters that it believes fall within the boundaries of such a declaration:

- constitutional and governmental institutions
- citizenship and membership
- elections and referenda
- access to and residence in the territory
- lands, waters, seas (i.e. and natural resources)
- preservation, protection and management of the environment, including wild animals and fish
- economic life.[57]

Such assertions of the breadth of Aboriginal jurisdiction, particularly with such a broad list of subject areas, are unconvincing. Under the regime proposed by the commission,[58] Aboriginal people will never have the jurisdictional scope articulated. Rather, these assertions and this list appear to function more as a marketing tool than as a serious expression of actual Aboriginal authorities.

For example, the commission asserts that "the Aboriginal sphere of authority under section 35(1) ... has roughly the same maximum scope as the federal head of power with respect to ... [subsection] 91(24) of the Constitution Act, 1867."[59] The actual scope of the head of authority according to subsection 91(24) has not yet been clarified by the courts. Peter Hogg has argued that this "head of power" probably gives the federal government the authority to legislate outside the normal parameters of federal competence. However, subsection 91(24) does not permit the federal government to legislate indiscriminately. The legislation in question would have to aim at "particular Indian concerns."[60] Thus, according to this reasoning, if the proposed law lies outside the normal parameters of the area described as "Indians, and lands reserved for Indians," then the legislation will have to address a specific Indian matter. If it does not, then it will be subject to jurisdictional challenge.

Although such an interpretation may push at the boundaries of subsection 91(24), it would not render other rules of constitutional interpretation invalid. Thus, subsection 91(24) would not permit authority over other Section 91 powers unless the focus is uniquely on Indians. According to Hogg's view, federal areas of jurisdiction listed in Figure 3.1 would be available to Aboriginal governments only if the law relates particularly to Aboriginal people.

Hogg's position has thus far been unopposed, though the courts have yet to decide this point. Should they agree with Hogg, they may significantly restrict the scope of what he calls "particular Indian concerns." If the courts state that the legal issue must indeed be uniquely related to Aboriginal concerns, then the area in which Aboriginal governments can exercise authority will indeed be quite small. These governments can intrude into other Section 91 areas, such as criminal law, taxation, and marriage, only if these matters have a uniquely Indian flavour. If Aboriginal governments are not legislating particularly Indian expressions of such subjects, then they will fail to meet the Hogg test. Consequently, these matters will not fall under the authority of subsection 91(24) powers. The RCAP report does not even hint at such a limitation of Aboriginal authority, but surely such a restrictive view of Aboriginal jurisdiction is worth mentioning.

Equally important is the constitutional rule that prohibits the federal government from intruding upon provincial jurisdiction, which is outlined in Section 92.[61] Although Hogg's view of subsection 91(24) may permit Aboriginal governments to intrude into other areas of federal jurisdiction, there is no similar doctrine that would permit these governments to intrude into areas of provincial jurisdiction. Yet the list accompanying Figure 3.1 clearly includes areas of provincial authority.[62]

The history of Canadian constitutional jurisprudence is filled with cases attempting to resolve disputes between federal and provincial governments when both wish to exercise their respective authority over the same matter. As just mentioned, there is no case law that would directly support an Aboriginal government's right to act pursuant to a subsection 91(24) authority concerning provincial jurisdiction. Yet RCAP included provincial government heads of authority in its list. Since the courts have never expressed the possibility of such a unique legal perspective, the commission should have stated its basis for such an opinion. Unfortunately, no explanation for this curious assertion is offered.

The irresistible conclusion from such an analysis is clear. The RCAP articulation of the scope of Aboriginal authority is exaggerated. The commission lists areas of competence available to Aboriginal governments that not only exceed Hogg's liberal interpretation of subsection 91(24) but also intrude, without any substantiation, into the domain of provincial governments. Consequently, if the RCAP assertion were reviewed by the courts, then assuredly Aboriginal authority would be drastically diminished. Even where a subject area is determined to be vital to the interests of an Aboriginal community, its government would be denied jurisdiction because the matter lies much too far beyond the scope of subsection 91(24). Alternatively, it may be found to be an exercise of a subsection 91(12) or (27) power[63] but with no uniquely Indian dimension. Thus, the scope of Aboriginal government powers will certainly not be as large as that depicted in Figure 3.1 of the RCAP report.

The subsection 91(24) discussion reintroduces an issue worth noting. I suggested earlier that the RCAP term "vital" may be restricted to a very narrow definition – that is, the courts may interpret "vital to the life and welfare of a particular Aboriginal people" to include only issues that touch on "culture and identity" in the narrow senses of those terms. Some provinces may claim that this authority refers only to issues of language, the arts, and perhaps education – or at least to issues with a scope not much broader than this. The RCAP recommendation that Aboriginal governments have the jurisdiction that the federal government exercises under subsection 91(24) would actually support this argument.

The courts may agree with the commission's recommendation that an Aboriginal government's authority is equal to that of the federal government's subsection 91(24) authority. However, they may also agree with Hogg's characterization that the law must aim "at particular Indian concerns." If so, then in most instances broad areas of authority, such as criminal law and procedure, health, taxation, economics, and commerce (all federal areas of competence that fall outside this subsection), will be denied to Aboriginal governments – simply because they do not touch on unique Aboriginal concerns. The courts would then be free to find that the jurisdiction pertaining to "culture and identity" may limit an Aboriginal government to determining when, where, and how a pow wow will be held.[64] If this interpretation is supported by the courts, then all other areas of jurisdiction will be designated peripheral and therefore will need to be negotiated for before they can be exercised.

The Need to Negotiate

Based on its interpretation of the *Sparrow* decision, the Royal Commission on Aboriginal Peoples distinguishes between core and peripheral subject areas. In addition, it proposes that vital matters can be governed unilaterally by an Aboriginal government but that peripheral matters must first be negotiated with the appropriate federal or provincial government. It is unclear where such a paradigm is created in *Sparrow* (or in other case law for that matter). Nonetheless, the need to negotiate inherent rights is ill conceived.[65] Moreover, the motivation behind the RCAP recommendation must also be questioned.

The commission asserts that Aboriginal people represent a third order of government and that their authority to govern is an "inherent right."[66] However, in light of the "rules" set out by RCAP, such statements must be viewed as exaggerations.[67] The core-peripheral paradigm recognizes nothing more than the privilege to negotiate for the right to exercise sovereign authority. Given the arguments presented above, clearly most of an Aboriginal community's authority will be over peripheral matters only. The commission's recommendations therefore amount to: "come on down, let's make a deal!"

Why must Aboriginal governments negotiate for authority over so-called peripheral matters? This question assumes great urgency since so many areas of Aboriginal authority will inevitably fall within this designation. How can RCAP then claim that Aboriginal governments have an inherent right of self-determination? Since any Aboriginal authority will be so limited in scope, how can RCAP even suggest that Aboriginal governments constitute a third order of government?

Neither federal nor provincial governments must negotiate with each other before they can exercise their respective powers. One may argue that these authorities are clearly defined in the 1867 Constitution (particularly Sections 91 and 92) and that there is no need for such negotiations, whereas the nature and scope of Aboriginal authority is uncertain. Therefore, these negotiations would provide the requisite clarity with regard to understanding who can do precisely what. But such an assertion is very curious. Constitutional litigation in Canada has principally been a debate about what these heads of power actually mean. Even when a jurisdictional authority is clear, there has often been a significant dispute about which areas of jurisdiction should be shared. Clearly, to assert that some "clarity thesis" supports the need to negotiate Aboriginal jurisdiction is a less than satisfactory response. Canadian courts have provided this clarity for more than a century.

The RCAP recommendation that peripheral authority must first be negotiated is even less compelling given the clear doctrines of constitutional interpretation available to assist in penetrating the content of the authority recognized by subsection 35(1). There is no apparent reason why doctrines of paramountcy, pith and substance, double aspect, and so forth, which currently help to delineate federal and provincial authorities, would not also apply to disputes concerning Aboriginal governments. Surely the use of such mechanisms is more reasonable than the requirement that Aboriginal governments seek federal or provincial approval before they can exercise their "inherent" authority. RCAP might simply have recommended that these and other doctrines also apply to the exercise of the Aboriginal jurisdiction.[68]

The debate concerning Quebec as a "distinct society" is instructive. Many political leaders have taken the position that all provinces are equal in both the nature and the scope of jurisdiction that they exercise. They have argued that no exceptions should be made among the provinces, including Quebec. Those on the other side of the issue have enunciated that Quebec's unique heritage and cultural experience should be recognized. The exact form of this difference varies. When such compromise positions of "asymmetrical federalism" have been proposed, many of the parties have rejected them and maintained the position of "uniformity among provinces." Yet this is not the case when it comes to discussing the nature of the third order of government. Aboriginal governments must catch as catch can. According to the RCAP proposal, they must negotiate as best they can for whatever authority they will be permitted to exercise.

Obviously, the process of negotiating for fundamental authorities will necessarily vary from community to community across Canada. The result of these negotiations will be a patchwork of Aboriginal jurisdictions. Each community will possess only those authorities that it was successful in negotiating. Yet such an uneven jurisdictional scenario would never be contemplated for provincial governments. The RCAP proposal that Aboriginal governments must first negotiate for inherent rights and that doing so will produce a third order of government in this country strains credibility. Surely the idea of have and have-not Aboriginal jurisdictions offends any reasonable interpretation of a single third order of government.[69]

One is constrained to inquire what justifies the scenario of an Aboriginal nation in one part of the country having more "inherent" authority than an Aboriginal nation in another part of the country. Any approach based on principles would recognize that neither geography nor local political expediency should have any bearing on the scope of an Aboriginal nation's jurisdiction. Although the commission took pains to point to the various relationships, treaties, and pacts between Aboriginal and Canadian governments over the years, this alone does not explain its recommendation, particularly not when this authority is supposed to be an inherent right.

That one Aboriginal community may negotiate away an area of jurisdiction (e.g., one of the harvesting rights: hunting, fishing, or trapping) and therefore become jurisdictionally different from another Aboriginal community does not justify an entire process that will inevitably result in such inequalities across the country. If an Aboriginal community has already negotiated away certain areas of jurisdiction, perhaps pursuant to a treaty, then surely this fact could be recognized in any constitutional amendment entrenching self-government. That there has been a history of negotiations between Canada and Aboriginal nations does not justify imposing this system on communities that would be seriously disadvantaged in such negotiations. If an Aboriginal government exercises less jurisdiction than another, then it should be because it chooses to do so, not because negotiations prevented it from doing so.

RCAP has effectively said that the inherent authority of this third order of government depends on who has the best lawyers, the best negotiators, and the most financial resources. Aboriginal communities that possess these resources, or any other elements of political leverage, will thus fare better in negotiations than less well-off communities (these negotiations could include natural resource rights, harvesting rights, rights of way over roads, and so forth). Indeed, even when Aboriginal nations have such resources, they may be disadvantaged simply because their respective provincial governments have no interest in negotiating with them.[70] One can only wonder how the commission viewed such a process as a vehicle for recognizing a third order of government.

In addition, in proposing that Aboriginal communities negotiate the scope of this third order of government, the commission apparently did not understand Aboriginal culture. Aboriginal people across Canada have always expressed the belief that they share certain fundamental beliefs and obligations. These concepts are based on their unique heritage as original occupiers and stewards of the land. The various cultures are unified in the belief that they have been given sacred responsibilities from the Creator to care for the land and its inhabitants (Aboriginal creation stories commonly include all animals as inhabitants). Such responsibilities invoke rights as the indigenous occupiers of the land, with the resulting requirement to sustain their communities and cultures in order to meet these obligations. The right to self-government is one tool required to fulfil these commitments, which are not altered simply because a provincial government decides not to negotiate with Aboriginal leaders. Any process that requires negotiation for what Aboriginal people consider inherent rights and duties not only offends this philosophy but also proposes a wholly unfair result.

Nor do the commission's recommendations regarding negotiations ensure that all the jurisdictional rights of Aboriginal people will be recognized.

Indeed, there is no assurance that federal or provincial governments will even attend such negotiations. Nowhere does the report indicate that they can be compelled to do so. The absence of an enforcement mechanism points to a glaring weakness in the recommendations and reminds one of something that the commission stated in similar circumstances: "A right without a remedy is meaningless."[71] In the present circumstances, no statement could be more accurate.

Finally, a practical and potentially debilitating problem concerning process should not be ignored. Whatever the scope of peripheral jurisdiction may be, a significant political problem will almost certainly raise its unruly head. The commission indicated that these agreements will become constitutionalized through the legislative endorsement of the appropriate federal and provincial legislatures. However, what will happen if an agreement is concluded but a federal or provincial government refuses to endorse the deal? Surely this can occur when a government holds a majority mandate. Such a government may claim that the terms of the agreement are no longer acceptable or in the best interests of that government. Or a minority government may find it impossible to receive enough support for an agreement from an opposition party. Without this consent, the agreement cannot receive the necessary legislative endorsement. One need only remember the fate of the Meech Lake Accord.

Do the parties then return to the negotiating table and again begin a process that offers little certainty that its results will be implemented? How enthusiastic will the other two parties be to reengage in a process that will likely be as demanding as it was the first time around? And even if a second agreement is reached, what will prevent the federal or provincial governments from again refusing to endorse it? Surely Aboriginal negotiators might expect as much. If so, would they even consider engaging in a second set of negotiations? Could such a political dynamic ever produce consequences of any value for Aboriginal people? That the commission made such a recommendation without addressing these practical problems seems to fly in the face of common sense.

Misconception or Misdirection?

In light of the requirement for negotiations, the claim that Aboriginal governments are a "third order" of government possessing "inherent rights" that are "entrenched" within the Constitution is misleading in at least two respects. In the normal use of such terms (if one can ever use such constitutional terms normally), one might be forgiven for believing that such rights exist more fundamentally than most other rights.[72] However, as already illustrated, for the most part no tangible rights exist under the RCAP recommendations unless first negotiated. More significantly, even where they do exist,[73] they are not constitutionally protected in the way that Aboriginal people have been led to believe.

Before the Constitution was patriated in the early 1980s, Aboriginal peoples engaged in both an international and a domestic lobbying campaign. Aboriginal leaders spent almost two years prior to the enactment of the Canada Act in England educating the people and their parliamentary leaders about the various Aboriginal positions. Much of the campaign was directed at acquiring support for the recognition and entrenchment of an assortment of Aboriginal rights, including treaty, title, land claims, and so forth. Throughout roughly the same period in Canada, Aboriginal leaders, along with sympathetic non-Aboriginal organizations such as the Quakers, carried out a similar lobbying effort with federal and provincial governments. The issues discussed were much the same, though the need to educate people was somewhat less demanding. The present constitutional document is in no small measure the result of these lobbying efforts.

Later, throughout the 1980s, there were meetings of first ministers as required by the Constitution Act, 1982.[74] These conferences dealt exclusively with Aboriginal issues. The expectation, of the Aboriginal participants at least, was that constitutional amendments would flow from these discussions. Such was not the case. Nevertheless, Aboriginal leaders once again lobbied in the months and weeks prior to these meetings. Before each conference, issues concerning the entrenchment of Aboriginal title, self-government, and treaties received wide debate, most of which was driven by Aboriginal parties.

To carry out such lobbies, Aboriginal people had to familiarize themselves not only with the principal issues but also with the terminology common to the forum. Because Aboriginal interests are so often driven from the grassroots level, there was a need to educate the Aboriginal population on often complex ideas. Thus, Aboriginal people became familiar with both the issues and the meanings and implications of the legal terminology defining them. An appreciation of these facts makes the wording of the RCAP recommendations particularly distressing.

The understanding of Aboriginal people, gained throughout this period of lobbying, was that an entrenched right of self-determination was as secure as any other order of government pursuant to the Constitution Act, 1867. Moreover, such a right was viewed as being at least as immune to mitigation as the rights enumerated in the Canadian Charter of Rights and Freedoms. That the right to self-determination was articulated outside the Charter in subsection 35(1) reinforced in the minds of many the merit of this belief. Recognition of Charter rights is always subject to balancing through the use of Section 1. A right ostensibly protected by the Charter may nevertheless have to give way to a law if that law is justified in a free and democratic society. Because this interpretive section applies only to the Charter, it was assumed that Aboriginal rights, which lie outside the Charter in subsection 35(1), are more secure. It was thought that a law that conflicted with an Aboriginal right could not be similarly saved simply by showing that it is justified in a free and democratic society. Thus, Aboriginal rights were viewed by many as having stronger protection than Charter rights. However, as described earlier in this chapter, *Sparrow* indicated that such reasoning is unsound. But more importantly, the use of this terminology by RCAP clearly indicates that it no longer has the same meaning that it once had. The rules of the game appear to have changed. Unfortunately, the commission has not made this fact sufficiently clear to Aboriginal people.

An example of how the RCAP recommendations have generated new meanings for these terms may be found in the use of the phrase "inherent right." The RCAP report concludes that all rights, both core and peripheral, are inherent: "The Commission concludes that, generally speaking, the sphere of inherent Aboriginal jurisdiction under section 35(1) comprises all matters relating to the good government and welfare of Aboriginal peoples and their territories. This sphere of inherent jurisdiction is divided into two sectors; a core and a periphery."[75] However, given that these rights must first be negotiated before they can be exercised, such a statement amounts to the same thing as a union leader saying to a packed hall of auto workers: "Each and every one of you has an inherent right to make $100 per hour! All you have to do is go out and negotiate it." The political future of this union leader would be in serious jeopardy (as would his bridgework). For RCAP to assert that Aboriginal peoples have an "inherent right" to self-government is just as empty and misleading.

Similarly, the RCAP statement that Aboriginal governments constitute a "third order" of government is disquieting. In the past, it was understood that such a statement indicated that Aboriginal governments are partners in the Canadian federation. If the partnership is not entirely one of equals,[76] then one might be forgiven for assuming that the most junior partner possesses at least substantial powers, even if they are only somewhat akin to those of the more senior partners. The concept that each order of government is approximately equal, if not in nature, at least in terms of scope of authority, is never clearly explained. Indeed, the report reinforces the misconception that the third order of government is a substantial partner among equals.

As mentioned above, Figure 3.1 on page 218 of the report portrays Aboriginal governments as being of the same jurisdictional size as the federal and provincial governments. The earlier discussion clarifies that this is certainly not the case – nor can it ever be. If Aboriginal governments only have the authority exercised by the federal government pursuant to sub-section 91(24), then, as already reasoned, Aboriginal authority will be very limited. Moreover, the requirement that areas of peripheral jurisdiction must first be negotiated before being exercised further challenges the credibility of this diagram. The commission's insistence on using the term "third order of government," together with Figure 3.1, which charitably must be described as a misapprehension of the facts, is troublesome.

Principles Governing Conflicts

The RCAP recommendations regarding the rules governing conflicts between Aboriginal and non-Aboriginal governments are equally curious. The commission articulated a set of rules that clarifies what happens when federal and provincial laws conflict with assertions of Aboriginal authority:

13. When an Aboriginal government passes legislation dealing with a subject-matter falling within the core, any inconsistent federal or provincial legislation is automatically displaced. An Aboriginal government can thus expand, contract or vary its exclusive range of operations in an organic manner, in keeping with its needs and circumstances. Where there is no inconsistent Aboriginal legislation occupying the field in a core area of jurisdiction, federal and provincial laws continue to apply in accordance with standard constitutional rules.

14. By way of exception, in certain cases a federal law may take precedence over an Aboriginal law where they conflict. However, for this to happen, the federal law has to meet the strict standard laid down by the Supreme Court of Canada in Sparrow.[77]

An initial reading of these principles suggests that Aboriginal governments will retain a significant amount of authority when jurisdictional authorities collide. But this recommendation would appear to be more shadow than substance. A closer consideration indicates that its intent will never be realized. The commission surely knew this. The RCAP rules governing jurisdictional disputes will afford Aboriginal governments protection only in the case of conflicts over core jurisdictional matters. Although the report does not state this, the practical implications of its other recommendations ensure that this will be the only circumstance under which these principles will apply.

The report requires that all peripheral issues must be negotiated before being exercised. Any government negotiator will likely require that the rules regarding conflicts over jurisdiction be the subject of these negotiations. Indeed, these terms are likely to be critical to any jurisdictional negotiations. Since the Aboriginal parties have no way of excluding this element of conflict resolution from negotiations at the insistence[78] of the federal and provincial parties, principles regarding conflicts will certainly be determined by negotiations. Nothing in the RCAP report would preclude the inclusion of these matters in negotiations.[79]

This threat to the integrity of Aboriginal jurisdiction is only fully appreciated when one considers that the core jurisdiction of Aboriginal governments is so small. Over 90 percent of an Aboriginal government's authority will be subject to negotiation. Consequently, these negotiations, not the recommendations for conflict resolution set out in the report, will determine the rules to apply when jurisdictions conflict. Only matters found to be core elements of Aboriginal jurisdiction will escape such negotiations. In these cases, the RCAP rules for conflicts will apply. But since those instances will be so few, the general recommendation is both naïve and misleading.

Oversight or Marketing?

The Royal Commission on Aboriginal Peoples undertook an exercise vast in scope and complex in substance. Many areas of Aboriginal life and culture were addressed in its report. Perhaps, then, errors or oversights were bound to creep into the report. However, the foregoing recommendations constitute more than mere oversights.

The distinctive use of terms such as "entrenchment," "third order of government," and "inherent rights" is intriguing. Although one might argue that the new definitions are readily understood from a reading of the text, though perhaps not without a legal background, most Aboriginal people will never have such an opportunity (nor, for that matter, will most non-Aboriginal people). Neither the subtle distinctions nor the ramifications of complex constitutional reasoning, such as Hogg's analysis of subsection 91(24), will insinuate themselves into the understanding of most Aboriginal people. Instead, they will rely on the terms in the recommendations and apply their grasp of these terms as cultivated throughout the lobbying efforts of the 1980s and 1990s. Understandably, the new distinctions carried by the wording of the report will not make any impression. Importantly, the commission made no effort to clarify these new distinctions; indeed, some may even conclude that the commission tried to veil certain recommendations so that its report would be received more favourably by Aboriginal communities. One might argue that Figure 3.1 of the report reflects this kind of misinformation.

Other RCAP recommendations are just as bewildering. The commission must have realized that the principles of conflict resolution, which appear on the surface to be favourable to Aboriginal communities, would have little real application. While the non-lawyers who helped to develop this recommendation can perhaps be excused for not anticipating its practical implications, surely the lawyers cannot. Similarly, proposing rights without provisions for their enforcement should surprise both non-lawyers and lawyers alike. These inconsistencies may suggest that the commission was intent less on solving outstanding problems than on trying to make its report palatable to Aboriginal people. Whether or not this view is warranted, it is undeniable that clarity has been sacrificed in this report. Unfortunately it will be to the detriment of Aboriginal people clearly understanding the content of these recommendations.

Entrenching Agreements

The Royal Commission on Aboriginal Peoples proposed negotiations that would both recognize and implement Aboriginal self-government authority. Earlier analysis in this chapter suggested that these negotiations will address over 90 percent of the self-government subject areas in which Aboriginal nations have expressed interest. Consequently, what becomes of these agreements, and how they are to be treated by the courts, is very important. What is the purpose of these agreements? How are the parties to these accords assured that they will not be reopened or altered by another party? What ensures their political or legal durability? The commission provided an answer to these concerns, but it is less than satisfactory.

After discussing the need for treaties or agreements to resolve "matters on the periphery of Aboriginal jurisdiction,"[80] the RCAP report states that "a treaty dealing with the inherent right of self-government gives rise to treaty rights under section 35(1) of the Constitution Act, 1982 and thus becomes constitutionally entrenched."[81] Having jumped in with both feet, the commission then makes the following equally perplexing comment: "Even when a self-government agreement does not itself constitute a treaty, rights articulated in it may nevertheless become constitutionally entrenched."[82]

These are remarkable comments, and they are worth exploring for two reasons: first, they fly in the face of the plain reading of the relevant section of the act;[83] second, and more important, no foundation in Canadian law supports either allegation.

No case law is provided to support these bold assertions. Not even *Sparrow* dares to suggest that signed self-government agreements automatically become part of the Canadian constitutional rubric. Indeed, it is still not certain that *Sparrow* laid sufficient groundwork to ensure that Aboriginal self-government is a necessary consequence of its reasoning. *Sparrow* simply did not address this broad issue. Clearly, this case alone cannot stand behind the propositions of the commission. But no other cases or legal doctrines are offered in support of these assertions.

The commission was similarly reticent about providing rationales for its propositions. This point is particularly important since an obvious contrary argument does exist. This conflicting position is provided by the wording of the relevant section itself. Section 35 of the Constitution Act, 1982, states in subsection 1 that "the existing Aboriginal and treaty rights of the Aboriginal peoples of Canada are hereby recognized and affirmed" and in subsection 3 that, "for greater certainty, in subsection (1) 'treaty rights' includes rights that now exist by way of land claims agreements or may be so acquired."[84]

Subsection 35(1) certainly provides the basis for the contention that Aboriginal self-government is recognized as an Aboriginal right. It is much less clear how such an Aboriginal right, which requires a process of negotiation as proposed by the RCAP recommendations regarding peripheral matters, gets imported directly into the Constitution as entrenched and protected. Nothing in this section even suggests the existence of a process for the automatic adoption of self-government agreements into the Constitution.

However, subsection 35(3) does speak of a like-minded process. It anticipates that certain "land claims agreements" may be brought within the rubric of the Constitution. However, this subsection does not necessarily bring all such land claims agreements within constitutional parameters. To date, some land claims negotiations and agreements have specifically stated that they are not intended to be constitutionalized pursuant to this section (e.g., the outstanding Yukon Agreement). It appears that any "land claims" agreement that is to be constitutionally protected must have this intention specifically agreed to by all parties. Yet none of this explains how a "self-government" agreement finds its way into the Constitution.

Subsection 35(3) is intended to address the issue of what might be included in the future as a treaty right. The fact that it begins by stating "for greater certainty" and then speaks only to treaty rights seems to limit its scope. Furthermore, a plain reading indicates that these future treaty rights must be related to land claims. Presumably, such a future land claims process, once resolved, may be recognized as a modern treaty and thus have its terms constitutionally entrenched.

This is the plain reading of the section.[85] Nothing in subsection 35(3) mentions entrenching self-government agreements. However, if a land claims process includes self-government elements, then arguably such jurisdictional matters could be entrenched through the treaty process – but only if a land claims process is at the heart of the negotiations, as is apparently required by the subsection. The recently negotiated Nisga'a treaty would seem to be a good example of this.

RCAP might argue that self-government agreements are included as an element of the term "treaty rights" in subsection 35(1). But the commission can't have it both ways. It already argued that self-government exists as an Aboriginal right. The commission cannot then take the position that, in order to entrench these agreements, this entitlement also exists as a treaty right.[86]

There is little doubt that future land claims agreements will include a self-government component, which is currently contemplated by ongoing discussions. Moreover, some of these future agreements will no doubt eventually be constitutionalized under subsection 35(3). Thus, in those instances, matters of self-government resolved within these agreements will receive the same constitutional protection as other issues relating more specifically to land ownership and use. However, where there are no land claims issues, agreements resolving matters within the peripheral jurisdiction of an Aboriginal community will likely not constitute treaties within the plain reading of subsection 35(3).

The commission probably knew this. If it were confident in its initial position that all self-government agreements give rise to treaty rights protected under subsection 35(1), then why was there a need to clarify that, even though the agreements are not thus protected, the terms of the agreements are? Obviously, RCAP was not confident in just asserting that self-government rights, which it claimed existed as Aboriginal rights, are also protected as treaty rights. It seems that the commission was aware of the weakness of its initial declaration and therefore felt compelled to assert this alternative position.

As previously stated, the commission provided no constitutional doctrine, case law, or modicum of reasoning to explain how it came to its decision. However, a reasonable explanation for such an untenable position does exist. The Royal Commission on Aboriginal Peoples avoided making any recommendation that would necessitate amending the Constitution. The existence of the right to self-government and the rules concerning core and peripheral matters were expressed as flowing from the present wording of the Constitution Act, 1982. If the commission were to maintain this position when it comes to giving effect to the negotiated agreements, then it would have to find a way to bring them within the existing constitutional framework. The only section of the Constitution Act that even remotely addresses such an issue is subsection 35(3). However, as already explained, it was never intended to address self-government issues where no land claims are involved. This may explain why RCAP was forced to assert what it did devoid of any stated reasoning or law.

If agreements that flow from self-government negotiations are not entrenched through subsection 35(3), then how would they find their way into the Constitution? Moreover, how would the terms of such agreements later be protected from intrusion by federal or provincial governments? Simply put, they wouldn't. Aboriginal peoples have no reason to believe that self-government agreements, as RCAP proposed, will have any constitutional protection whatsoever. In light of the arguments against the commission's assertions, and until such an untenable position is clarified, it would be foolish for Aboriginal people to embrace this recommendation.

The inability of the commission to tie the knot concerning these negotiations is crucial. Whether or not one agrees with the various arguments in this chapter regarding the RCAP recommendations,[87] the shortcomings of this single position of the commission are critical. If the core area is indeed as small as has been argued, then it will only be through negotiation of the peripheral matters that any significant degree of Aboriginal self-government can be achieved. In light of historical difficulties between Aboriginal and non-Aboriginal governments, the prospects for the successful negotiation of a substantial degree of Aboriginal self-government are grim. But even if such negotiations are somewhat successful, unless a mechanism exists to bring these agreements within the protection of the Constitution, even their modest terms can be changed or simply ignored by non-Aboriginal governments. The commission's failure to provide a legally sound explanation that would ensure entrenchment of these agreements and their contents is one of its most critical failings.

More than a Passing Concern

If *Sparrow* stands for all that RCAP suggests, and even if Section 35 somehow adopts the terms of any agreement, then what ultimate value will this have? Since *Sparrow* recognizes the existence of both Aboriginal rights as entrenched and a process for extinguishing or deentrenching them, of what real value will these agreements be for Aboriginal people?

One cannot both inhale and exhale at the same time. Curiously, though, *Sparrow* seems to have done precisely this. On the one hand, it recognized Aboriginal rights and asserted their status as entrenched rights. On the other, it said that these rights could be regulated, even extinguished, provided that the government meets certain criteria.[88] If this is so, then how secure will any Aboriginal jurisdiction ever be? Seemingly, the peripheral agreements will entrench a process of both recognition and implementation. But should the federal government ever decide to limit or extinguish elements of Aboriginal jurisdiction, what is to prevent this from happening? Provided that the government meets the standards as prescribed in *Sparrow* for the elimination of those fishing rights, there appears to be no reason why the Aboriginal right of self-government cannot be similarly eliminated.[89] This will apparently hold true for the core jurisdictional subjects as well.

There are no recommendations in the final RCAP report that would prevent the courts from taking this position. Something should have been stated in the report to clarify that the courts cannot treat the entrenched right of Aboriginal self-government as cavalierly as they have treated Mr. Sparrow's fishing right. It is troublesome that RCAP did not even mention the issue. Surely this was a mistake.

The Charlottetown Accord

The obvious deficiencies in the RCAP recommendations regarding Aboriginal self-determination are exacerbated by the knowledge that they provide Aboriginal peoples with far less than they would have received under the terms of the Charlottetown Accord.

This accord was the most recent in a line of efforts by the federal and provincial governments to address changes to Confederation. In addition to proposals concerning Senate reform, Supreme Court appointments, and further decentralization of federal authorities, the accord included a wide-ranging series of proposals recognizing a new role for Aboriginal people in Canadian Confederation. The accord proposed amending the Constitution to clearly recognize the right of Aboriginal self-government. The agreement was eventually defeated in a national referendum for perhaps any number of reasons. Nevertheless, given that the Canadian governments reached consensus on matters that included a radical restructuring of the role of Aboriginal nations in Canada, RCAP could have chosen to build on this success. Instead, it took a large step backward from the point of success achieved by Aboriginal representatives at Charlottetown, and its recommendations will produce much less for Aboriginal people than what was agreed to in the Charlottetown Accord.

The accord not only proposed a clear recognition of the right of self-government but also would have amended the Constitution to unequivocally reflect this recognition. Item 41 states that "the Constitution should be amended to recognize that the Aboriginal peoples of Canada have the inherent right of self-government within Canada. This right should be placed in a new section of the *Constitution Act, 1982* Section 35.1(1)." Item 47 says that the inherent right of Aboriginal self-government should be entrenched within the Constitution. With this kind of amendment, there would be no need to rely on a *Sparrow* decision for this recognition. There would be no need, as there is with the RCAP recommendations, to infer from Canadian case law an uncertain recognition of this right. The Charlottetown approach was unambiguous.

The agreement dealt with the existence of a third order of government in a similarly straightforward manner. Item 41 clarified the status of Aboriginal governments as a third order of government and affirmed that this authority is an inherent capacity that was to be constitutionally recognized: "The recognition of the inherent right of self-government should be interpreted in light of the recognition of Aboriginal governments as one of three orders of government in Canada." On the other hand, the RCAP recommendations, though proposing this type of recognition of Aboriginal governments, relied on an implied understanding of this thesis from case law and recent policy statements of the federal government.[90] Clearly, an

Aboriginal nation would be in a stronger position in any legal dispute if its status were clearly articulated in a constitutional document, as the Charlottetown agreement proposed.

While the RCAP recommendations limited the scope of Aboriginal jurisdiction largely to cultural affairs, the Charlottetown Accord clearly enunciated a broader definition of an Aboriginal government's jurisdiction. Item 41 states that

> the exercise of the right of self-government includes the authority of the duly constituted legislative bodies of Aboriginal peoples, each within its own jurisdiction:
>
> (a) to safeguard and develop their languages, cultures, *economies,* identities, *institutions* and traditions, and
>
> (b) to develop, maintain and strengthen their relationship with their lands, waters, and environment so as to determine and control their development as peoples according to their own values and priorities and *ensure the integrity of their societies.*[91]

Compared with the RCAP recommendations, such statements more strongly assert the authority of Aboriginal nations to govern themselves.

It is important to recognize that, although RCAP may have believed that its recommendations regarding Aboriginal jurisdiction would apply to more than simply cultural matters, the wording in its report does not guarantee that this will occur. In fact, if a court were asked to clarify the scope of these recommendations, then it would have ample room in which to rationalize Aboriginal jurisdiction being limited to purely cultural matters (see the discussion earlier in this chapter). No court would have the latitude to reach such a finding pursuant to the Charlottetown text. The clearly enunciated scope of Aboriginal jurisdiction is, on the surface, much broader.

Furthermore, the Charlottetown proposal did not suggest artificial distinctions between core and peripheral jurisdictional matters. In all Aboriginal communities, efforts to resolve problems often overlap constitutional distinctions. In Canada over the past ten to fifteen years, notably, the creation of family courts reflects a similar effort to resolve a myriad of separate issues in a holistic fashion. It is clear that such a holistic effort has had a strong traditional presence in Aboriginal communities for centuries. Examples of American tribal justice, described earlier in this book, demonstrated how local criminal law activities were dealt with within a broader social context that sometimes included civil law issues. The proposed distinction between core and peripheral jurisdictional areas, with the requirement that the latter issues be negotiated prior to their exercise, surely prevents a balanced response to many problems. For the commission to assert these artificial distinctions would appear to fly in the face of Aboriginal history.

The Charlottetown Accord did not propose any such artificial distinction. All areas of Aboriginal jurisdiction were to be entrenched immediately; none was to be exempted or suspended until later negotiations approved its implementation. Surely the Charlottetown proposal represented a significantly stronger position for Aboriginal people than the RCAP recommendations.

Another concern closely associated with the RCAP core-periphery distinction raises the issue of "justiciability." RCAP recommends that, before peripheral matters can be implemented, other affected governments must come to some agreement about their nature, scope, and manner of implementation. However, the commission offered no recommendation as to how Aboriginal jurisdiction can be exercised if these other governments refuse to negotiate in good faith. The Charlottetown agreement addresses this problem directly. Item 45 requires that all parties commit to a process of negotiations: "There should be a constitutional commitment by the federal and provincial governments and the Indian, Inuit and Métis peoples in the various regions and communities of Canada to negotiate in good faith with the objective of concluding agreements elaborating the relationship between Aboriginal governments and the other order of government. The negotiations would focus on the *implementation* of the right of self-government, including issues of jurisdiction, lands and resources, and economic and fiscal arrangements." This item ensures negotiations on self-government matters. For reasons left unexplained, no similar recommendation was proposed by RCAP.

Item 41 refers to a court or tribunal taking certain matters into consideration "before making any final determination of an issue arising from the inherent right of self-government." The court is empowered to require that efforts be undertaken to "effect a negotiated resolution." The Charlottetown Accord therefore not only ensures that Aboriginal governments will have the power to have their rights adjudicated by the courts but also guarantees that the courts will have broad powers to ensure protection of these rights. This power includes the ability to enforce good-faith negotiations by non-Aboriginal governments.

Item 42 clarifies that, although the Aboriginal right to self-government can be enforced through the courts, "its justiciability should be delayed for a five-year period." However, "delaying the justiciability of the right will not make the right contingent and will not affect existing Aboriginal and treaty rights." Consequently, Aboriginal governments would be precluded from enforcing the right to self-government in the courts before this five-year period is up (presumably, this period would begin on the date that the constitutional amendment comes into effect). This limitation, however, would not prevent an Aboriginal government from immediately exercising a self-government jurisdiction if there is no opposition from a federal or provincial government. Only in the case of a conflict would the Aboriginal government be precluded from enforcing its rights through the courts during the five-year period.

In addition, the accord clarifies that, even though the right to self-government may not be enforceable in the courts during this period, this qualification does not affect the existence of this right. It is recognized that such Aboriginal rights continue to exist throughout this period. They simply lack the ability to be enforced, temporarily. The "non-derogation clause" in Item 46 states that "there should be an explicit statement in the Constitution that the commitment to negotiate does not make the right of self-government contingent on negotiations or in any way affect the justiciability of the right of self-government." If there was any doubt about an Aboriginal nation's absolute right to self-governing jurisdictional authority, then this item removed it. Aboriginal nations comprise a third order of government complete with an existing jurisdiction without any prior need to negotiate it. The exact nature and scope of this jurisdiction may still be undetermined, but it nevertheless exists. Under this accord, Aboriginal jurisdiction clearly exists independently of any negotiations. If parties cannot agree to its content or process of implementation, then the accord recognizes the right to have this authority elaborated through the courts.

Importantly, these items provide a basis on which to require that federal and provincial governments negotiate self-government issues in good faith. If they do not, then they can be brought before the courts and made to comply. Although this authority alone should provide significant impetus for the federal and provincial governments to negotiate in good faith, the knowledge that Aboriginal communities will eventually be able to enforce their jurisdictional rights in the courts should significantly motivate the actions of government parties. This fact alone would bring focus and urgency to the negotiations.

These "justiciability" items are alarmingly absent from the recommendations of the Royal Commission on Aboriginal Peoples. The commission apparently relied on the good will of the federal and provincial governments. In light of the historical animosities between federal and provincial governments and Aboriginal peoples,[92] one may conclude that such an absence is simply an oversight. Nonetheless, clearly the Charlottetown Accord's proposal to guarantee the justiciability of the right of Aboriginal self-government, as well as its requirement that governments negotiate in good faith, offer more advantages to Aboriginal people than do the RCAP recommendations.

The Charlottetown proposal stands in stark contrast to the RCAP recommendations, which recognize little more than a theoretical Aboriginal jurisdiction.[93] The RCAP recommendations make the exercise of jurisdiction contingent on the outcome of prior negotiations, with no assurances that government parties will even negotiate. The Charlottetown Accord's non-derogation and justiciability sections surely offer a stronger position for Aboriginal parties. In addition, the accord includes a process for resolving disputes between jurisdictions. Item 46 proposes the creation of a dispute-resolution mechanism that would use mediation and arbitration techniques to assist in negotiating the implementation of self-government measures. This mechanism was to be more fully explored in a subsequent political accord. Arguably, this recommendation reflects a mind-set lacking in the RCAP approach. The Charlottetown proposal provides a practical mechanism for dispute resolution, which is only the object of optimism in the RCAP recommendations. Multilateral negotiations are more probable where an official forum has been established for the respective parties. Furthermore, they will likely be more motivated to use such a forum if each has helped to contribute to its establishment. The RCAP recommendations offer no such similar motivation.

The Charlottetown Accord also provides stronger recommendations concerning conflicts between Aboriginal and non-Aboriginal governments' laws. Where an Aboriginal law conflicts with a federal or provincial law, which one will prevail? As already mentioned, RCAP recommended a series of conflict-resolution principles designed to reconcile such disputes. However, these rules will not apply as proposed. Negotiations of peripheral jurisdictional matters will surely also establish the preeminent rules to govern conflicts. There is nothing in the commission's report to prevent these newly negotiated rules from dominating the conflict-resolution principles. This scenario, however, would not apply in the few core areas of jurisdiction; in such instances, the principles recommended by RCAP would prevail.

The Charlottetown Accord, however, provides even stronger protection for Aboriginal jurisdictions. Item 47 addresses consistency of laws: "A constitutional provision should ensure that a law passed by a government of Aboriginal peoples, or an assertion of its authority based upon the inherent right provision may not be inconsistent with those laws which are essential to the preservation of peace, order and good government in Canada." Under the accord provision, the non-Aboriginal party would be required to show that the Aboriginal law has impinged on "laws which are *essential* to the preservation of peace, order and good government in Canada."[94] In such an instance, the non-Aboriginal government would have to prove to a court that the Aboriginal law is inconsistent with laws that are both "essential" and affect "peace, order and good government." Item 47 places the onus on the non-Aboriginal party to prove the essential nature of the law that ostensibly conflicts with the Aboriginal law.[95]

The Item 47 requirements are substantially higher tests than that proposed by RCAP. Its report argues that Aboriginal governments may not act unilaterally in areas where the subject matter is a transcendent federal or provincial concern. A transcendent concern may be of "serious" consequence to these levels of government, but it need not be "essential." Thus, the non-Aboriginal government under the commission's recommendations need not meet the higher standard as required by the Charlottetown text.

Furthermore, that text requires that the subject matter infringed on must be of "national" concern.[96] The courts have spent much time elaborating the constitutional subject matter referred to as "peace, order and good government," or POGG. They have said that the POGG authority is articulated within Section 91 of the Constitution Act, 1867. As such, this authority is one of the federal government's powers. The courts have also clarified that "the true test must be found in the real subject matter of the legislation: if it is such that it goes beyond local or provincial concern or interests and must from its inherent nature be the concern of the Dominion as a whole ... then it will fall within the competence of the Dominion Parliament as a matter affecting the peace, order and good government of Canada."[97] Since provincial governments do not possess any such national authority, they would be precluded from restraining an Aboriginal government's exercise of jurisdiction. The RCAP report, on the other hand, would permit a provincial government to challenge Aboriginal authority simply because it encroached upon some transcendent provincial concern.

In addition, the courts seem to indicate that POGG power extends to only two areas. Peter Hogg explains the dual-function theory as follows: "First it gives to the federal Parliament permanent jurisdiction over distinct subject matters which do not fall within any of the enumerated heads of S.92 and which by nature are of national concern. Secondly, the POGG power gives to the federal Parliament temporary jurisdiction over all subject matters needed to deal with an emergency."[98] He goes on to argue that in some cases the subject matter must only meet the test of national concern. If so, then even this requirement raises the standard beyond just a simple regional impact, a criterion that the RCAP recommendations permit. Clearly, if the POGG authority must address some degree of seriousness, and that seriousness must relate to an issue beyond a regional concern, as Hogg seems to imply, then the Charlottetown text requires that the federal government meet a higher standard than that required by the RCAP recommendations. The RCAP standard is that the issue only be of some seriousness to the federal authority, not necessarily a national concern.

In any event, the Charlottetown Accord requirement that Aboriginal laws must not be inconsistent with laws affecting POGG applies only to the federal government. The courts have never recognized the provincial governments as possessing any POGG authority, so provincial governments could not argue that an Aboriginal law threatens their POGG powers. On the other hand, the RCAP recommendations effectively provide provincial governments with a veto power that they do not possess under the Charlottetown proposal. The RCAP report states only that the matters over which Aboriginal governments seek to exercise jurisdiction must not be transcendent provincial concerns. The scope of what might constitute a serious provincial interest is almost limitless. Thus, a provincial government is provided with a broad basis on which to limit Aboriginal jurisdiction; such a basis is not available under the terms of the Charlottetown Accord.

An additional advantage for Aboriginal people, absent from the RCAP recommendations but present in the Charlottetown Accord, is the establishment of a new relationship with the Supreme Court of Canada. Item 20 of the accord states that

> The structure of the Supreme Court should not be modified in this round of constitutional discussions. The role of Aboriginal peoples in relating to the Supreme Court should be recorded in a political accord and should be on the agenda of a future First Ministers' Conference on Aboriginal issues.
>
> Provincial and territorial governments should develop a reasonable process for consulting representatives of the Aboriginal peoples of Canada in the preparation of lists of candidates to fill vacancies on the Supreme Court.
>
> Aboriginal groups should retain the right to make representations to the federal government respecting candidates to fill vacancies on the Supreme Court.
>
> The federal government should examine in consultation with Aboriginal groups, the proposal that an Aboriginal Council of Elders be entitled to make submissions to the Supreme Court when the court considers Aboriginal issues.

Item 43 expands the proposition that there is a need to consider additional alterations to the present structure of the judicial system: "The issue of special courts or tribunals should be on the agenda of the First Ministers' Conference on Aboriginal Constitutional matters referred to in item 53."

Both items suggest dramatic alterations to the present manner of resolving disputes affecting Aboriginal communities. Neither predetermines any specific alteration to existing methodologies or judicial processes, but both suggest that the door be opened to reasonable and creative possibilities. Consequently, suggestions may be made that alter the current jurisdiction and procedures of the Supreme Court.[99] Remarkably, no similar recommendations were proposed in the RCAP report. One can only surmise that the commissioners were satisfied with the status quo. Clearly, such an opinion is not shared by many Canadians, Aboriginal or otherwise, who believe that Aboriginal people's interests have not been adequately adjudicated.

RCAP and the Canadian Charter of Rights and Freedoms

Since repatriation of the Constitution in 1982, the Canadian Charter of Rights and Freedoms has played an increasingly important role in the lives of Canadians. It has had a significant impact on legislation as well as on individual attitudes toward government behaviour. Not surprisingly, then, the Royal Commission on Aboriginal Peoples chose to address its subject in relation to the Charter's role regarding Aboriginal self-government and its institutions.

Curiously, the commission did not spend much time discussing the potential impact of the Charter on Aboriginal culture. Rather, it premised its overall position on three simple assertions. First, "all people in Canada are entitled to enjoy the protection of the Charter's general provision in their relation with governments in Canada." Second, "Aboriginal governments occupy the same basic position relative to the Charter as the federal and provincial governments." And third, "the Charter should be interpreted in a manner that allows considerable scope for the distinctive Aboriginal philosophical outlooks, cultures and traditions. This interpretive rule is found in section 25 of the Charter."[100]

The commission recognized that the Constitution Act as drafted in 1982 did not expressly consider Aboriginal governments in the context of a third order of government. Therefore, there was no reference to them regarding application of the Charter.[101] However, RCAP reasoned that "the Charter should be read in a way that takes account of this recognition. Otherwise there would be a serious imbalance in the application of the Charter."[102] With simple assertions rather than detailed reasons, the commission stated that "the Canadian Charter of Rights and Freedoms applies to Aboriginal governments and regulates relations with individuals falling within their jurisdiction."[103] The commission went on to note, however, that "under section 25, the Charter must be given a flexible interpretation that takes into account the distinctive philosophies, traditions and cultural practices of Aboriginal peoples. Moreover, under Section 33, Aboriginal nations can pass notwithstanding clauses that suspend the operation of certain Charter sections for a period."[104]

Thus, the commission recommended that the Charter apply to governments of Aboriginal nations, which will have the same recourse to the notwithstanding clause as other orders of Canadian government. In addition, application of the Charter is to be interpreted through the prism of Section 25, thereby presumably providing a more culturally relevant application. Although initially the commission's recommendations appear to be reasonable, they pose troubling difficulties for any Aboriginal community.

One of the most serious concerns is the lack of substantive discussion about the problems created when Aboriginal communities' collective values conflict with the individualistic norms imposed by the Charter (as discussed in Chapter 6). The commission indicated that it had heard various Aboriginal leaders from across the country, many of whom had indicated a concern about the implications of the Charter for their collective rights. Seemingly, these concerns had little impact on the commissioners.

There is no discussion in the report about how Aboriginal values concerning clan mother elections are threatened by the democratic rights reflected in Section 3 of the Charter. No mention is made of the damage that threatens a community's values when an individual is insulated from having to speak on his or her own behalf in court.[105] Neither is an Aboriginal community protected from imposition of the Charter's double-jeopardy clause,[106] which would deny the community the ability to deal in a culturally significant way with an offender. Plainly, none of these issues appears to have been considered by the commission. If they were, the report itself is entirely silent on these matters.

In light of the commission's position, which clearly threatens these collective values of the Aboriginal community, it is important to understand the reasoning underlying it. Unfortunately, aside from stating initial principles, the RCAP report offers little insight into how the commissioners arrived at their position.

The need to establish gender equality within Aboriginal communities was apparent. The Native Women's Association of Canada (NWAC) had eloquently argued for this equality over the years. Prior to patriation of the Constitution, NWAC leaders such as Marlyn Kane had convinced Canadians that Aboriginal women had suffered too long from discrimination in their own communities. Kane and other Aboriginal women[107] had demonstrated that the Indian Act, which greatly influenced decisions of First Nations governments, had devastating effects on Aboriginal women, their children, and the very psyche of the community. Discussions with federal and provincial governments prior to 1981 had ensured that such discrimination would cease after patriation of the Constitution. The Indian Act was subsequently amended to eliminate the offensive sections, and the Constitution Act itself provides protection from gender discrimination. Section 28 states that, "notwithstanding anything in this Charter, the rights and freedoms referred to in it are guaranteed equally to male and female persons."[108] For further clarification of Aboriginal and treaty rights, subsection 35(4) states that, "notwithstanding any other provisions of this Act, the Aboriginal and treaty rights referred to in sub-section (1) are guaranteed equally to male and female persons."[109]

The case for gender equality had been forcefully articulated by Aboriginal women and clearly responded to, as evident in both of these sections.

However, some Aboriginal women's representatives argued that these efforts were insufficient. They asked that any further recognition of Aboriginal self-government ensure that any new form of Aboriginal government be incapable of gender discrimination. RCAP seems to have been persuaded by this argument. Consequently, it recommended that the Charter apply in its entirety to Aboriginal governments.

But the concern about gender equality does not support the broader RCAP recommendation that all Charter provisions apply to Aboriginal governments. In light of the damage that imposition of these provisions could do to critical cultural norms and values (see Chapter 6), one should inquire why the commission recommended application of the entire set of Charter rights. The interests of Aboriginal communities regarding collective rights are nowhere reflected in the RCAP recommendations. Surely alternative positions were available to the commission.

RCAP could have recommended that the Constitution be amended to ensure that the equality guarantees contained in Section 15 apply specifically to prohibit gender discrimination by Aboriginal governments. This would be the simplest and least intrusive way of addressing the problem. But the commissioners did not recommend such a course of action. Instead, they chose to impose all of the individualistic guarantees of democratic, legal, and fundamental freedoms on Aboriginal nations. Given the serious implications that these non-gender guarantees could have for Aboriginal communities, one is struck by the lack of sensitivity to Aboriginal concerns.

The RCAP assertion that the Charter should apply to Aboriginal governments' actions, as it does to those of federal and provincial governments, is also surprising in light of the wording of Section 32 of the Constitution Act, 1982:

32.(1) This Charter applies
    (a) to the Parliament and government of Canada in respect of all matters within the authority of Parliament including all matters relating to the Yukon Territory and Northwest Territories; and
    (b) to the legislature and government of each province in respect of all matters within the authority of the legislature of each province.[110]

A plain reading of this section suggests that the Charter does not and was never intended to apply to the actions of a third order of Aboriginal government. The commission made the surprising claim that its interpretation of the law led it to believe that the courts would find the Charter applicable to Aboriginal governments. The report offers no clarification of why the courts would reach this conclusion. However, the commissioners state that "in reaching this conclusion we have been assisted by the analysis of Peter Hogg and Mary Ellen Turpel. These authors suggest that despite the silence of section 32 of the Charter with reference to Aboriginal governments, it is probable that a court would hold that Aboriginal governments are bound by the Charter."[111] The problem here is that the article by Hogg and Turpel does not provide any substantive legal reasoning why the Charter should apply to Aboriginal governments. In fact, the authors actually provide a case statement from the Supreme Court of Canada that suggests the opposite opinion.[112] The Hogg-Turpel "analysis" consists simply of the assertion that "Section 32 does not contemplate the existence of an Aboriginal order of government."[113] However, "despite the silence of Section 32 on Aboriginal governments, it is probable that a court would hold that Aboriginal governments are bound by the Charter."[114]

This is the extent of the reasoning that so influenced the commission. No constitutional doctrine, case law, or simple legal analysis was provided to dispel the plain reading of Section 32 of the Constitution Act, 1982. Instead, the bare assumption in the Hogg and Turpel article seems to have been enough for the commission to justify its recommendation that the entire Charter should apply to Aboriginal governments. Granted, the Hogg-Turpel assumption may be reflected in a future decision of the Supreme Court. Should an Aboriginal third order of government eventually be recognized in the Constitution, absent a clear indication of whether the Charter applies to this new order, the Supreme Court will be called upon to provide an opinion. The rule of law and the intention of the equality sections of the Constitution, among a host of other issues, may be used to support the Hogg-Turpel position. And perhaps they will prevail, though similar constitutional guarantees do not bind American tribal governments (see Chapter 2). What is distressing about the RCAP position is that none of these arguments appears in the report. Perhaps the commissioners were not even aware of them. In light of the potentially debilitating effects of the Charter on an Aboriginal community, this seems like a curious oversight.

What makes this puzzle even more perplexing is that the commission possessed a contrary opinion provided by a noted Aboriginal and constitutional scholar, Kent McNeil.[115] He was contracted by the commission to address, among other matters, the question of the Charter's application to Aboriginal governments. Interestingly, his opinion was that the Charter would not apply.[116] Consequently, one wonders what motivated the commission to ignore the reasoning in Professor McNeil's study in favour of the stark statements offered by Hogg and Turpel. Since the commission provided no discussion of this matter, there are no obvious indicators of what motivated its choice.

In fairness, I should note that Hogg and Turpel do argue that any agreement between federal, provincial, and Aboriginal parties that required "implementation legislation" would be subject to the Charter guarantees due to the application of Section 32 to the legislative actions of the first two orders of government.[117] As accurate as this may be, though, it does not sustain the argument that the Charter applies to the independent actions of Aboriginal governments. If the Charter were to apply, then it would only be to the extent that Section 32 applies to the specific actions of the federal and provincial governments. Clearly, these governments would not be able to enact valid legislation that offends the Charter. However, an Aboriginal government's actions exercised pursuant to the agreement would not be directly affected because the government would be exercising not delegated but rather inherent authority.[118]

The *Canadian Bar Review* article fails to provide a compelling argument that the Charter applies to Aboriginal governments; moreover, ironically, it provides a contrary opinion of the Supreme Court of Canada. The authors refer to the case of *R.W.D.S.U.* v. *Dolphin Delivery*.[119] In this case, the court asserted that Section 32 applies to the government of Canada and to the legislature and government of each province. Hogg and Turpel conclude that "the Supreme Court of Canada has held that this is *an exhaustive* statement of the bodies that are bound by the Charter. Section 32 does not contemplate the existence of an Aboriginal order of government."[120] If this is an exhaustive statement of the application of Section 32, then Aboriginal governments will not be bound by the Charter rules – despite the bold assertion of the Royal Commission on Aboriginal Peoples.

If Aboriginal communities are eventually recognized as possessing the right to self-government, it is safe to say that the Supreme Court of Canada will probably expand on its opinion in *Dolphin Delivery*. Some will no doubt argue that this case was decided at a time when the idea of an Aboriginal third order of government was not seriously contemplated by the Supreme Court. Others may argue that the Constitution should not be shuffled like a deck of cards every time one is dealt an unfavourable hand. Consequently, this latter group may argue, opinions expressed in this case should apply notwithstanding changing times.

In which direction the court will decide the issue is, for present purposes, unimportant. What is relevant here is why RCAP ignored *Dolphin Delivery* and its implications, and instead asserted a contrary recommendation that the Charter apply unequivocally to Aboriginal governments. In light of the potential significance of this recommendation for Aboriginal cultures, the decision not to point out this case or discuss its implications was to turn a blind eye to issues of clarity and balance.

Notwithstanding Clause

The RCAP recommendations seem to ignore conflicts between traditional Aboriginal communities and Charter values. The report provides no compelling reason why the courts would find the Charter applicable to Aboriginal governments. Moreover, the recommendations present additional difficulties in this area. The report recommends that the notwithstanding clause of Section 33 should be available to Aboriginal governments. They could then enact legislation that offends the Charter (except for the equality guarantee) provided they expressly state in the legislation that it intends to do so. The federal and provincial governments currently possess this authority.[121]

However, the RCAP report stipulates that this clause can only be exercised unilaterally in core jurisdictional areas. Otherwise, opting out of the Charter in other subject areas must first be agreed to by both federal and provincial parties. Once such an agreement is reached, it would be included as a term in the agreements on peripheral jurisdiction.[122] Federal and provincial governments, on the other hand, can choose unilaterally to exempt any of their laws from the impact of the Charter.[123] Curiously, the RCAP recommendation permits Aboriginal governments to exercise this exemption only with the federal and provincial governments' consent.[124]

This section of the report is disturbing for a number of reasons. The recommendation clearly does not reflect any respect for Aboriginal governments as a truly independent third order of government. Whereas federal and provincial governments do not require the consent of any other order of government before they can exercise the notwithstanding clause, Aboriginal governments would have much less independent discretion. The report treats this third order of constitutional government very differently than the other two. In fact, Aboriginal governments would be treated much like wards in need of the advice and consent of one who knows better. They would not be treated like equal partners in the Canadian Confederation.

In addition, the recommendation imposes an unrealistic rigidity on use of the notwithstanding clause. Aboriginal governments would be required to know at the time of signing self-government agreements precisely when and how they intend to exercise the notwithstanding clause. If such instances are not accurately anticipated, then years later, when an Aboriginal government wishes to invoke the notwithstanding clause concerning one of the Charter guarantees, no such exemption could be exercised – at least not without first reopening negotiations with the federal and provincial parties to the agreement and obtaining their consent. And such consent might only come at a further negotiated price.

Requiring that the notwithstanding exemptions be part of the peripheral jurisdictional agreements challenges the credibility of the recommendation. The notwithstanding clause was not intended to be used liberally by a Canadian government. Indeed, it has not been used much since adoption of the Charter as a fundamental element of the Constitution.[125] Hence, there is no reason to expect that federal and provincial governments, already lacking a strong appreciation of Aboriginal cultures and values, would agree to any intention by an Aboriginal government to suspend application of Charter rights in its community in favour of unfamiliar Aboriginal cultural practices. Inevitably, consent to the use of this clause by an Aboriginal government becomes simply another negotiating tool for the non-Aboriginal governments. Clearly, this is inappropriate. The issues balanced in anticipation of use of the clause are too serious to be treated as little more than chips in a high-stakes poker game. The RCAP proposal regarding the notwithstanding clause seems to challenge both common sense and respect for Aboriginal culture.

Finally, perhaps the most perplexing question that Aboriginal people have about the Charter issue is why RCAP chose an all-or-nothing approach. As previously mentioned, if the commission wished to guarantee gender equality, then a simple amendment to Section 15 could have been proposed. Other alternatives, though much less comprehensive but much more culturally sensitive, were also available. Yet none was adopted. In light of the financial and professional resources available to the commission to address the role of the Charter in Aboriginal cultures, one might reasonably have anticipated more from its recommendations. The commission could have struck a special committee to review a range of options. It could have inquired into mechanisms such as an Aboriginal charter of rights, how it would work, as well as which rights and responsibilities it would protect. Indeed, it might even have drafted a sample charter in consultation with Aboriginal people. Surely RCAP had the resources for such an endeavour.

If the commission seriously considered situations of cultural conflict, which is not apparent in the report, then it declined to offer measures to address any of these conflicts. Instead, it chose to recommend that the Charter apply to Aboriginal governments without exception. Aboriginal peoples and their customs deserved more contemplation of the issues than the RCAP recommendations reflect.

Comment

Many Aboriginal people are understandably disappointed by the commission's recommendations. Unfortunately there are many reasons to justify this disappointment. The commission was in a position to build on the Charlottetown Accord and to correct the weaknesses so apparent in the *Sparrow* decision. Remarkably, the commission chose to ignore both of these opportunities.

The most straightforward approach to resolving the self-government issue would have been to recommend that the Constitution be amended to clearly recognize this Aboriginal authority, perhaps clarify certain elements of its content, and even offer a method for its implementation. These items had already been endorsed at Charlottetown. The practical and political difficulties associated with entrenchment would remain, but they would be little different from problems currently presented by the RCAP recom-mendations.[126]

Recognizing that a constitutional amendment would clarify the meaning of Aboriginal self-government, RCAP proposed that the Constitution be revised to include "six essential elements":

1. explicit recognition that section 35 includes the inherent right of self-government as an Aboriginal right;
2. an agreed process for honouring and implementing treaty obligations;
3. a veto for Aboriginal peoples on amendments to sections of the consti-tution that directly affects their rights, that is section 25, 35 and 35.1 of the Constitution Act, 1982 and 91(24) of the Constitution Act 1867;
4. recognition that section 91(24) includes Métis people along with First Nations and Inuit;
5. constitutional protection for the Alberta Métis Settlements Act; and
6. alteration to section 91(24) to reflect the broad self-governing jurisdic-tion Aboriginal Nations can exercise as an inherent right and to limit federal powers accordingly.[127]

Each item has merit and should be encouraged, but none addresses the critical issue of the content and scope of Aboriginal jurisdiction. For instance, will Aboriginal governments in Canada wield more or less power than that exercised by tribal governments in the United States, as outlined in Chapter 2? Seemingly, RCAP preferred to leave this task in the hands of negotiators.

Consequently, the report proposes a bewildering series of recommenda-tions that have more to do with a theoretical view of Aboriginal societies than a pragmatic understanding of their needs. These recommendations seem to be wholly impractical and to be guided by a naïve optimism in the relationships between Aboriginal societies and Canadian governments. Where the reasoning behind a recommendation is evident, it is often laboured and raises doubts about its sincerity.

The agreement reached at Charlottetown included an amendment to the Constitution to entrench self-government, recognized Aboriginal authority as a third order of government, ensured enforcement of Aboriginal juris-diction through the courts, offered favourable methods of resolving juris-dictional conflicts between Aboriginal and other Canadian governments, and provided an implementation process and a dispute-resolution mecha-nism. These are all superior substantive terms to those proposed by RCAP because they are to be recognized through a constitutional amendment. RCAP argued that its recommendations will also be entrenched, but only as a consequence of dubious case law inferences. Moreover, this case law includes the *Sparrow* decision, which, as Justice Ian Binnie has stated, permits the Canadian government to marginalize Aboriginal rights at its pleasure, even to the point of extinguishment.[128] Thus, even if a Canadian court recognizes as an Aboriginal right some expression of self-government emanating from Section 35 of the Constitution, there is no guarantee that this right will last any longer than the federal government permits. The Charlottetown Accord guaranteed much more.

Another product of *Sparrow* is the *Van der Peet* decision reviewed in Chapter 4. That analysis was intended to illustrate the conservative tendencies of the Supreme Court when interpreting Aboriginal rights in Section 35 of the Constitution. The additional significance of *Van der Peet* to self-government is twofold. First, it builds directly upon the earlier *Sparrow* decision. Thus, anyone championing the merits of *Sparrow* must recognize its implications as reflected in *Van der Peet*. Second, since *Van der Peet* specifically addresses the topic of Aboriginal rights, self-government, as an expression of such rights, will be directly affected.

It remains uncertain how the *Van der Peet* reasoning will affect the issue of self-government. The case suggested that an Aboriginal right is protected by Section 35 only in the form in which it existed prior to contact with Europeans. Moreover, the case indicated that an Aboriginal practice must be distinctive to a particular community if that practice is to be protected. Both requirements impose severe limitations on any attempt to exercise an Aboriginal right.

One difficulty confronting any analysis of *Van der Peet* in the context of self-government is the nature of the Aboriginal right to fish, the subject of the case. Perhaps in such an instance the limited interpretation imposed on Section 35 can be justified. But it would apparently be less applicable to the Aboriginal right to self-government. It is doubtful that the Supreme Court would respect this right only if it were practised as at contact. It would be worse if the court imposed the requirement that only elements of self-government that are distinctive to a community will receive Section 35 recognition. Such standards would give Aboriginal communities both a very dated and a very limited ability to exercise self-government.

The decision of the Supreme Court in *Delgamuukw* does not clarify the problem.[129] Although *Delgamuukw* was argued in part as an Aboriginal rights and self-government case, it was ultimately resolved as an Aboriginal title case. Arguably, it is the most significant Aboriginal title decision ever rendered by this court, and, though the decision clarified issues relevant to the sources of Aboriginal title, rules of evidence and proof, as well as the nature of social practices that can be exercised on lands under Aboriginal title,[130] the court did not directly address the issue of Aboriginal self-government. Due to procedural defects, the issue was returned to the trial-level court perhaps to be argued at a later date. Nor did the court offer new principles for the development of Aboriginal rights, particularly that of self-government. References to Aboriginal rights were confined to principles already established in *Van der Peet*. Since this was in essence an Aboriginal title decision, any such comments would have no binding implications for future cases. However, as an indicator of the direction in which the court may be heading on this issue, any comment would have been helpful.

Statements by the Supreme Court in *Sparrow* do not clearly indicate that Section 35 will recognize self-government as an Aboriginal right. The matter has yet to be clarified. However, even if *Sparrow* can be used to justify recognition of self-government, the thrust of *Van der Peet* suggests that considerable limitations will be imposed by the court on any such recognition. Given *Van der Peet*'s conservative interpretation of the *Sparrow* doctrine, one should inquire why RCAP insisted on basing many of its recommendations on *Sparrow*. The court's views in both *Sparrow* and *Van der Peet* indicate that the recognition that it might ultimately extend to an Aboriginal right of self-government will be quite unremarkable. A simple recommendation to amend the Constitution would have avoided most of these uncertainties,[131] and it is troubling that the commission did not choose this path.

The commission's reliance on existing case law, in particular *Sparrow*, to justify its conviction that Aboriginal self-government is currently protected by Section 35 as an Aboriginal right is undermined by admissions of the commission itself: "We conclude that the Aboriginal and Treaty Rights recognized and affirmed in the section include the right of self-government. [However,] it is impossible to predict whether the Supreme Court would reach the same conclusion, but it is a major premise upon which much of our report is based."[132] Such an admission must be disconcerting for Aboriginal people. The commission seems to be saying that, even though it was confident that Aboriginal self-government flows from existing case law, it was not entirely confident that the Supreme Court of Canada would agree with this assumption. In fact, after asserting that Section 35 supports an Aboriginal claim for self-government, that the Charter will apply to these governments, and that they will have the benefit of the notwithstanding clause, the RCAP report also states that "these conclusions may be challenged, and the Supreme Court may find our interpretation incorrect."[133] Perhaps because of this realization, RCAP chose to recommend one of the few constitutional amendments that it proposed.

As mentioned earlier in this chapter, the commission did offer a number of proposals for eventual constitutional change. Perhaps out of concern that the Supreme Court may not find a basis for Aboriginal self-government in Section 35 (and in case law such as *Sparrow*), RCAP recommended that the Constitution Act, 1982, be amended to provide "explicit recognition that section 35 includes the inherent right of self-government as an Aboriginal right."[134] All of the commission's suggested amendments seem to be designed to achieve "greater certainty."[135] Nevertheless, RCAP seemed to be confident of its findings.

But why not propose a constitutional amendment to clarify everything? RCAP need not give Aboriginal people everything that they ask for or resolve that Aboriginal people should simply move to the cities and be "Canadians like everyone else." The commission could have chosen to paint in detail a picture of self-government that, from its point of view, would be appropriate in Canada. RCAP consulted with many people, Aboriginal and non-Aboriginal alike. It also had the benefit of scholarly opinions from every facet of Canadian society. Upon this foundation it might have fashioned a cogent response to the issues raised by Aboriginal self-government. Instead, it chose a more enigmatic path, one fraught with ambiguity and uncertainty.

The commission recognized the advantages of amending the Constitution to achieve its goals. After expressing doubt about the Supreme Court's endorsing its viewpoint, it states that "the way to resolve this uncertainty is with a constitutional amendment – a negotiated amendment with Aboriginal peoples at the table to assure that their position is protected."[136] However, "the level of political consensus required for constitutional amendment is not easy to achieve."[137] Hence, a non-amending approach to resolving these issues may have value. RCAP asserts that at some future time others will be free to argue the merits of a constitutional amendment. At this point, it seems to envisage inclusion of its six recommendations in such an amendment – particularly a clear recognition of Aboriginal self-government as a Section 35 Aboriginal right.

Is it not strange that a royal commission with enormous amounts of time, money, and expertise would tender recommendations that it acknowledges may not receive support from the courts? Moreover, it offered such proposals despite awareness of an alternative methodology that does not suffer from the same disadvantages. This might suggest to some observers that RCAP was playing fast and loose with the aspirations of Aboriginal people. Worse still, the commission may have turned its back on an invaluable opportunity.

If case law inferences established a strong basis for the RCAP conclusions, then perhaps they could be recommended. However, as this chapter illustrates, the commission's recommendations are fraught with ambiguities and lack clear reasoning that might serve to resolve these uncertainties. The commission seemed to be aware of these weaknesses, acknowledging that the Supreme Court might not see things the same way, so it recommended an amendment to Section 35 of the Constitution to resolve at least recognition of Aboriginal self-government. However, if the Supreme Court does not locate a source for self-government in Section 35, and if a constitutional amendment is as difficult to achieve as RCAP suggests, then Aboriginal self-government has a dubious future.

The commission may have reconsidered its position for another reason. Although it provides a creative view of how a self-government paradigm might unfold, it lacks a description of the content of self-governing authority. It suggests a wide array of jurisdictions that may be negotiated (far more than I think are available), but it stops short of stating which ones should be exercisable by Aboriginal governments. Chapter 2 described the scope of authority of tribal governments in the United States. RCAP might have considered the US model and then provided its own view on the pros and cons of this approach. It might have further suggested the most appropriate alternative for the Canadian environment. With this alternative in hand, the RCAP recommendation to entrench Aboriginal self-government in the Constitution would have provided all Canadians with some expectation of how such a government might crystallize in Canada. Even if this approach were not subsequently endorsed by all Canadians and their governments, it would surely have formed the basis for eventual consensus.

Perhaps it would have been better for RCAP to argue things the other way around. Since RCAP believed that a constitutional amendment would be difficult to achieve, it suggested a line of thinking that would provide the same results without reopening the Constitution. Should the Supreme Court subsequently reject its arguments, others would still be free to engender support for a first ministers' conference and an amendment recognizing self-government. But wouldn't the reasoning be more effective if it were reversed?

A recommendation to amend the Constitution, together with all the bells and whistles that RCAP considered appropriate, would entrench the right along with a clear indication of its content. The present proposal suggests little more than a methodology of jurisdictional negotiation, which, as the RCAP report says, might not survive judicial scrutiny. Any future proposal to amend the Constitution would once again start from scratch.[138] On the other hand, a proposal recommending entrenchment of the right along with some content would still – if rejected – provide others with an opportunity to argue the utility of this position in the courts. And, importantly, the courts would have the benefit of being persuaded by the reasoning of a royal commission. This seems to be a stronger position than that suggested by RCAP.

By not recommending a constitutional amendment, RCAP may also have inadvertently undermined its own intentions. Any amendment to the Constitution will present a challenge to the diplomacy and patience of everyone involved, as is discussed in the next chapter. Yet that is as it should be. Constitutional documents are not intended to be opened and closed like an accordion. Arguably, only after a considered debate and perhaps a good deal of gnashing of teeth should constitutional changes be made. However, in this instance, the RCAP decision not to recommend entrenchment may well have made this option even more difficult to achieve.

Had the commission recommended a series of constitutional amendments to recognize Aboriginal self-government, then this proposal would assuredly have a serious and perhaps positive impact on the attitudes of Canadians toward self-government. In turn, Canadian governments would not easily be able to ignore the political implications of this sentiment, which would be of assistance in galvanizing support for any subsequent amendment. However, by not recommending the amendment option, the commission did not really take a neutral stand. The pragmatic implication will no doubt be that those opposed to the amendment option will point to the findings of the commission. Unlike in the months and years preceding the Charlottetown discussions, self-government opponents can now rely on the RCAP conclusions to claim that there is no need to amend the Constitution to achieve Aboriginal self-government. After all, the RCAP report asserts that it already exists and encourages the appropriate parties simply to go about negotiating some expression of it. This opinion may be used to deflect attention away from a more effective treatment of the issue. This reasoning could well be effective in blunting any efforts to entrench self-government through constitutional amendment. If so, then it appears that the RCAP proposal will make constitutional recognition even more difficult to achieve.

The recommendations of the Royal Commission on Aboriginal Peoples concerning application of the Charter fail to consider seriously the implications of an individual rights-based charter for the collective rights and values of Aboriginal communities. Indeed, the absence of any discussion of situations in which the Charter will collide with collective rights and values suggests that the commission was simply not aware of these issues. How this could have been possible, given the time and financial resources enjoyed by the commission, is perplexing and even disturbing. The need to guarantee that Aboriginal governments will ensure gender equality is insufficient to explain why the entire Charter should apply simply to provide this egalitarian treatment. The commission might have recommended alternatively that the Constitution be reopened by an amendment to ensure gender equality. In light of the serious implications of the Charter for the collective rights of Aboriginal communities, surely this would have been a more reasonable approach.

The RCAP recommendations also suffer from an absence of sound judicial reasoning. Indeed, too often there is little evidence of the underlying reasoning that one would normally expect to support such bare declarations. Instead, personal commitments to an ideal appear to have been substituted for any consideration of Aboriginal concerns. The report itself offers no constitutional doctrine, case law, or legal rationale why the Charter should apply to Aboriginal communities. The commission simply deferred to the opinions of others and then summarily concluded that Aboriginal governments should be bound by the Charter. Surely more than this cursory review is demanded of such a significant issue. Again, ironically, the only article on which the commission relied provides a Supreme Court opinion indicating that the Charter will not likely apply to Aboriginal governments. Moreover, in light of a contrary opinion provided by Kent McNeil, the commission might have engaged the debate more vigorously. Unfortunately, it declined to do so.

If the Charter does not apply to Aboriginal governments, then the issue of whether the notwithstanding clause is available to them is moot. However, the RCAP recommendations on this issue should not go unnoticed. The report recommends that Aboriginal governments, as a third order of government in Canada, should have the option of suspending application of certain elements of the Charter. However, unlike these other two orders of government, which may act unilaterally to invoke the notwithstanding clause, Aboriginal governments may not. They must obtain the consent of both federal and provincial governments before they can use this authority.[139] The RCAP recommendations require that the self-government agreement resolve the use of the notwithstanding clause years in advance. This requirement is of little practical use. The clause would become simply another matter to be bargained for among the many other issues included in negotiations of self-government agreements. Reopening these agreements at a later date, for the sole purpose of employing the notwithstanding provision, is problematic. Such a recommendation clearly offends the idea that Aboriginal nations are third orders of government similar to the other two. This recommendation reflects an inequitable and paternalistic view of Aboriginal peoples. Even more distressing, from a practical point of view, is that the recommendation is naïve and unworkable.

Finally, the commission's recommendation concerning the Charter is surprisingly dull and uninventive. The commission simply offered an all-or-nothing approach to the issue. One would have expected a more balanced and imaginative response to a highly important topic. Yet the commission apparently lacked the time or the interest to seriously engage the issue on its merits. Given how long the commission took in deliberations before releasing its final report, clearly time was not the confining element.[140] Before these issues can be resolved to the satisfaction of all Canadians, they will have to be addressed by those with more conviction and a clearer sense of balance and fairness.

9

The Future of Self-Government: Building Trust and Confidence

The future of Aboriginal self-government in Canada is uncertain. Gone are the heady days following the patriation of the Constitution in 1982. This document, describing in Section 35 the three Aboriginal peoples and recognizing and affirming their Aboriginal and treaty rights, sparked a great deal of optimism in Aboriginal communities. Section 25 appeared to further insulate these entitlements from intrusion by the individual rights guarantees of the Canadian Charter of Rights and Freedoms, while Section 27, as it then was, called for a first ministers' conference to elaborate these Aboriginal entitlements. All this seemed to indicate that the rights of Aboriginal peoples were finally assured. But this optimism appears to have been premature.

The four first ministers' conferences held during the 1980s failed to produce significant alterations to the Constitution.[1] The failure of the federal and provincial governments to agree on any of the issues discussed was disheartening. Although Aboriginal people themselves may have emerged from these conferences more sharply focused on issues such as self-government, the anticipated constitutional clarification of their rights remained unstated and perhaps even more uncertain.

Moreover, Aboriginal people were dismayed to discover that the federal and provincial governments were introducing an "empty box" interpretation of the term "existing" in Section 35 (see Chapter 1 for discussion of the theory). This assessment could surely limit the scope of any Aboriginal entitlement under this section. Aboriginal people were heartened by the Supreme Court of Canada's significantly broader interpretation of this term in the *Sparrow* decision, but this too has proven to be a misplaced sigh of relief. Other elements of *Sparrow* have been devastating for Aboriginal aspirations. The severely limited constitutional protection afforded to Aboriginal and treaty rights by this case is significantly weaker than that provided by individual Charter rights, and it is now clear that the entitlements ostensibly protected by Section 35 can be entirely extinguished provided that this is done in the appropriate manner. Even the arguably less than substantial mobility rights protected by the Charter cannot entirely be extinguished in the same manner as Aboriginal entitlements.

The Supreme Court's approach in *Sparrow* was maintained in *Van der Peet*. Whereas the *Sparrow* decision seemed implicitly to minimize the value of Aboriginal and treaty rights through limited protection by the Constitution, *Van der Peet* further narrowed the implications of these rights. The Supreme Court now restricted the manner in which Aboriginal rights could be expressed (see Chapter 6). It only recognized rights practised "at the time of contact" with Europeans, and then only if those practices were somehow integral to the particular Aboriginal community. Although the Supreme Court has yet to rule on whether Aboriginal self-government is an expression of a collective Aboriginal right, if its reasoning follows that in *Sparrow* and *Van der Peet*, then the restrictions imposed on self-government may be profound.

The results of the Charlottetown Accord referendum proved to be just as disappointing as the failed promises of the new Constitution Act, 1982. Ten years after proclamation of the act, the federal and provincial governments agreed to a host of changes to the Constitution that would clearly entrench the Aboriginal right of self-government. With the unequivocal recognition of this right as being inherent and entrenched, and with a clear statement of Aboriginal authority as constituting a third order of government, once again Aboriginal people were given the hope that their place in the Canadian mosaic was now secured. Failure of the accord to survive the referendum held on 26 October 1992 once again disappointed many Aboriginal communities.

Before proceeding further, I should note two points about this referendum. First, to suggest that it failed simply because the Canadian public rejected the proposed Aboriginal amendments to the Constitution would be overreaching. The Charlottetown Accord contained amendments that affected much more than recognition of the Aboriginal right of self-government. The agreement proposed amendments to significant elements of the Constitution, including a reformed Senate, a revised process of appointments to the Supreme Court of Canada, and an amended Charter that would include protection of property rights. Although some Canadians who rejected the accord were no doubt expressing their dissatisfaction with its Aboriginal content, clearly these were not the only elements that provoked controversy and dissent.[2]

There is no reliable evidence that the accord was rejected by a majority of Aboriginal Canadians, even though there is anecdotal evidence about dissension over certain terms of the agreement.[3] No doubt some Aboriginal voters were critical of the final agreement, but there is simply no way of knowing precisely how many or for what reasons. Thus, there is little reason to believe that another amendment package will fail to be supported by an Aboriginal electorate, assuming that credible proposals for self-government are included.

The final report of the Royal Commission on Aboriginal Peoples also held great promise for Aboriginal aspirations of self-government. While the discussions of the 1980s first ministers' conferences were fruitless, the *Sparrow* decision disarming, and the results of the Charlottetown referendum disheartening, these disappointments all could have been mitigated by the commission with unequivocal recommendations regarding self-government. Although RCAP itself could not alter the constitutional status of self-government, clear recommendations to entrench this authority would have constituted a major step forward in revitalizing Aboriginal aspirations. Both Aboriginal communities and a sympathetic Canadian public might galvanize around such recommendations to spur their politicians toward constitutional revision. But this too was not to be.

Although the commission's final report offered valuable recommendations regarding issues such as health care, education, and other social problems, its recommendations regarding Aboriginal self-government were less than helpful. In addition to pragmatic difficulties associated with implementing these recommendations, the proposals themselves fall far short of the successes achieved during the Charlottetown negotiations. Perhaps this was inevitable once the commission chose to reject the one course of action that would have reconciled the most significant and difficult issues: amendment of the Constitution. The resulting efforts to fit square pegs into round holes led to a patchwork of principles (see Chapter 8, which describes this laboured process). The RCAP recommendations will never generate the kind of self-government authority to which Aboriginal communities aspire.

The inability of governments, courts, and the Royal Commission to remove any of the impediments to a truly community-driven form of self-governing authority has generated only greater mistrust and a lack of confidence that Canadian governments are truly interested in including Aboriginal people as active partners in Confederation.

An Obvious Step
Perhaps the most effective way to resolve the many issues regarding Aboriginal self-government is to amend the Constitution appropriately. This option, the same as that proposed at Charlottetown, would provide the opportunity to state in clear terms the nature and scope of Aboriginal self-government. Whether it is recognized as a third order of government, and whether it would possess full criminal law and civil law jurisdiction, could be clearly characterized by such an amendment. Recent decisions by the Supreme Court of Canada, particularly *Sparrow* and *Van der Peet,* might indicate how the courts will approach interpretation of the self-government

amendments. This awareness should provide governments with some guidance in structuring any amendment so that it will reflect the intentions of the parties. This perspective was unavailable to the signatories to the Charlottetown agreement, but it should provide useful insights for future discussions. In particular, having the *Sparrow* and *Van der Peet* decisions to draw on, Aboriginal people may justifiably heed the observations of Ronald Dworkin (see Chapter 4). Hence, they may wish to include in the amendment package some of the suggestions offered in earlier chapters. In particular, amendments to the Canadian judicial structure would ensure both a fuller understanding of and better sensitivity to Aboriginal interests. The recommendation in the Charlottetown Accord regarding a review of the Supreme Court is particularly relevant here.

It is not just Aboriginal communities that would benefit from a constitutional amendment. Although they may be the obvious benefactors, both federal and provincial governments could also gain from such an amendment. Both levels of government would derive a greater sense of certainty from a precise definition of Aboriginal self-government. Although the recent decisions of the Supreme Court of Canada have arguably favoured the federal and provincial positions, there is no guarantee that this tendency will continue. Before the judicial pendulum swings the other way, these governments may also wish to have the situation clarified by an amendment to the Constitution.

One might be cautioned against viewing the federal and provincial governments as villains in this piece. Blame is seldom a very constructive instinct. These governments are aware that opinion polls indicate that the majority of Canadians favour greater recognition of Aboriginal entitlements, including self-governing authority. Cognizance of this fact no doubt helped to motivate these governments to agree to the Aboriginal elements of the Charlottetown package. Moreover, the "Aboriginal issue" has been a thorn in the sides of federal and provincial governments for years. Canada's international image has suffered over the years because of its treatment of Aboriginal Canadians. Third World living conditions, staggering unemployment rates, and odious health conditions with which Aboriginal people must contend have all taken their toll on Canada's image worldwide. Domestically, recent confrontations between provincial governments and Aboriginal people at Oka, Ipperwash, and Gustafson Lake have usually resulted in violence and ultimately in embarrassment for the respective provincial governments. Surely these governments have an interest in finally resolving the persistent conflicts with Aboriginal communities that have occasioned so much tragedy and misfortune. All of these factors militate in favour of a nationally supported reconciliation of Aboriginal issues. An amendment to the Constitution clearly recognizing Aboriginal self-government would be an immense step forward in achieving this goal.

Once again US tribal experience offers some insights. In Canada, physical confrontations between Aboriginal communities and federal and provincial governments seem to be never-ending. These confrontations usually take the form of Aboriginal people occupying land, blockading roadways, and undertaking marches and demonstrations. Too often violence has been the only product of these efforts. In the United States, such confrontations are far less frequent, largely because the motivating factors behind such conflicts have already been addressed. Self-government authority together with reasonable resource accommodations by both state and federal governments seems to avoid Canadian-like conflicts. Canadian governments should take note of this relationship.

Although the amendment option seems to be the most appropriate course of action, politically it is not without difficulties. Recent attempts to amend the Constitution have been arduous and painful for Canadians. Attempts to find a balanced resolution through the Meech Lake and Charlottetown agreements reflect the difficulty of such an enterprise. There is no reason to believe that future attempts regarding self-government would be any less difficult.

In addition, it is unlikely that future first ministers' conferences held on the issue of Aboriginal self-government would begin where the Charlottetown Accord left off. Although the federal and provincial governments ostensibly found common ground on many Aboriginal issues, one must bear in mind the nature of the final agreement. Aboriginal concerns comprised a central feature in the final accord, but they were by no means the only element. As already mentioned, the package included agreements to amend the Senate, to include property rights protection within the Charter, and to decentralize federal authority in areas such as workplace training, tourism, and mining. Hence, one should appreciate that some parties accepted the final agreement regarding Aboriginal issues only because of their own gains on non-Aboriginal matters.

This fact presents Aboriginal leaders with a dilemma. Although the non-Aboriginal components of the Charlottetown package helped to galvanize an agreement with some parties to the accord, Aboriginal leaders should be concerned that any similar inclusion of non-Aboriginal issues in a future first ministers' conference on self-government will unnecessarily complicate the discussions. Moreover, the failure of the Charlottetown Accord to pass the referendum hurdle resulted in a setback for the Aboriginal elements of the agreement. Aboriginal leaders should ponder the merits of again engaging in a process in which the Aboriginal elements may be rejected only because the non-Aboriginal proposals are rejected by Canadians in a second referendum. It may be difficult, though, to avoid such a referendum, since the Charlottetown Accord seems to have established a process. To avoid these difficulties, Aboriginal leaders might insist on a first ministers' conference to deal exclusively with Aboriginal self-government (concomitant issues such as financing would no doubt be included). But therein lies the rub. Without non-Aboriginal issues also on the table, what would compel governments that were not supporters of the Aboriginal issues at Charlottetown to come to any agreement this time around? The federal and provincial governments may have found common ground on Aboriginal issues at Charlottetown; however, without non-Aboriginal issues on the agenda, it is doubtful that the Charlottetown successes constitute a starting point for new discussions.[4]

There is a similar problem on the Aboriginal side of the table. Past first ministers' conferences have illustrated the difficulty for Aboriginal people in finding agreement on what they believe to be their most pressing concern. Among the Métis, Inuit, and First Nations peoples, there have often been differences of opinion about their respective priorities. Even within a group such as First Nations people, there have been differing opinions about which issue is the most important or about whether compromises should be made. Thus, like their federal and provincial counterparts, Aboriginal parties to any first ministers' conference must find the motivation to overcome their differences if such a conference is to produce a satisfactory amendment about self-government.

The Next Step

At this point, there are a number of steps that Aboriginal communities might consider taking to further the chances of success for the amendment option. To begin with, they should officially abandon the recommendations on self-government contained in the report of the Royal Commission on Aboriginal Peoples. Clearly, the commission was not given a mandate to accede to every wish of Aboriginal communities on the issue of self-government. Rather, its goal was to balance a multitude of Aboriginal and non-Aboriginal interests. But surely Aboriginal communities deserve more than the meagre recommendations in the RCAP report. As Chapter 8 illustrated, if the report's recommendations are implemented, then Aboriginal people will never realize their aspiration of self-government.

The threat posed by the RCAP report is plain. If its recommendations were to be implemented tomorrow, then both the Canadian governments and, perhaps more importantly, the general public will close the door on the "Aboriginal issue." Although there are other matters to deal with, such as treaties and land claims, in the minds of many the principal issue will have finally been resolved. However, once Aboriginal communities have discovered the emptiness of the RCAP recommendations (perhaps after ten years), it will probably be too late to argue that the Constitution should once again be changed. After having endorsed a multimillion-dollar report and then spending further millions implementing it, Aboriginal people will be in a precarious position if they claim that these measures are not enough. One can go to the same well only so many times.

A further complicating factor is the present policy of the federal government regarding Aboriginal self-government. Although the 1995 federal statement endorses negotiations for self-government, such negotiations only recognize a limited form of self-governance. Indeed, the authority currently being negotiated under such agreements is far less than that described as a third order of government in the Charlottetown Accord. With limited law-making authority, the resulting governments will resemble little more than municipal operations.[5]

Moreover, this policy excludes from such negotiations Aboriginal people such as the Métis (though the Inuit seem to be doing very well without such negotiations). It leaves the "Aboriginal problem" to the respective provinces.[6] Consequently, the policy has driven a wedge between Aboriginal communities that can opt into these negotiations and those that are excluded from any discussion of self-governing authority.

However, this policy poses perhaps an even more serious dilemma. If Aboriginal communities that now opt into these negotiations believe that they can take the temporary benefits of municipal-like powers until a constitutional amendment recognizes their broader jurisdictional authority, then they may find themselves dancing with the devil. If many agreements are negotiated, then the Canadian public may assume that such an approach represents the best way to resolve the self-government issue. Hence, in the same way as the RCAP recommendations may be wrongly viewed as the answer to the "Aboriginal problem," the municipal-like agreements under the federal policy may ultimately deflect a more comprehensive answer to self-government questions. Although a cynical observer may believe that this federal policy represents a strategy of divide and conquer, I am not suggesting that here. Nevertheless, the impact of this policy may produce the same results.

The federal policy of negotiating with individual First Nations communities illustrates a problem that continually threatens to undermine the Aboriginal position.[7] Throughout the first ministers' conferences of the 1980s and during the subsequent Charlottetown meetings, Aboriginal delegates were anything but united in their quest for greater constitutional recognition. The failure to present a united front throughout the first ministers' conferences partly permitted the meetings to end without resolution of any Aboriginal issue. If the Aboriginal parties cannot agree on the issues, then is there any reason to believe that the federal and provincial governments should be any more productive? Charlottetown did produce consensus, but only after a number of exceptions were included to accommodate differences between the First Nations and Métis situations. The preparatory meetings between Aboriginal delegates and their federal and provincial counterparts clearly indicated, however, that Aboriginal parties could work cooperatively in such discussions. The success of any future first ministers' conference will be achieved only if the Aboriginal parties themselves can build bridges between their respective positions.

This observation is critical for Métis communities in Canada. Philosophical differences have already created a division within this group. The Congress of Aboriginal Peoples (formerly the Native Council of Canada) and the Métis National Council represent the Métis communities of Canada at first ministers' conferences. They do not, however, always bring the same issue or perspective to the negotiating table. This division alone has presented difficulties for the perception of Métis claims.[8] But these Métis communities may have an even more pressing reason to consolidate their efforts. The present law setting forth the criteria required to establish successful Aboriginal title and to settle Aboriginal rights claims refers to time-specific occupancy of the land. The *Baker Lake* case, a seminal reference in cases involving claims of Aboriginal title to land, required the claimant to demonstrate that its "occupation" was established when England first asserted sovereignty.[9] Similarly, in *Van der Peet*, which established criteria regarding Aboriginal rights, the Supreme Court of Canada required that a particular custom or tradition existed "prior to contact with Europeans."[10] Consequently, any Métis community wishing to assert a claim of self-government through the courts may have to show that such a practice existed in a community before contact with European governments. Obviously, this will be a daunting task for a people who are partly of European ancestry. If they are required to prove the existence of established societies at or near European settlement, then many present-day communities will surely be disqualified. And, should Métis and First Nations make apparently valid overlapping claims, surely the Métis position will be at an ostensible disadvantage.[11] Therefore, Métis communities would likely welcome the opportunity to have their self-government authority recognized through an amendment option rather than be faced with the uphill battle of establishing it through the courts. Accordingly, they might aggressively build bridges between themselves and other Aboriginal groups.

Importantly, Métis communities would not be the only beneficiaries of a united Aboriginal position. All Aboriginal parties would benefit from a common position on self-government issues (on all issues, for that matter). First Nations communities could more forcefully and without distraction present their positions with the combined support of Métis and Inuit partners. Division of the northern territories into Nunavut and Denedah will provide the Inuit with de facto control over most of their communities. Nevertheless, they could receive additional authorities (e.g., criminal law) through the amendment option, authorities that they would not otherwise possess under the present territorial arrangements.

Should Aboriginal parties overcome the political and personal animosities that have divided their communities, they face a further challenge. Aboriginal people must find an effective way to communicate their self-government aspirations to both the Canadian governments and the general public. It is not enough to roll out generalizations about never having surrendered their sovereignty or their lands. Doing so will not generate the support required to promote a constitutional amendment. Nor, perhaps, should it be. Aboriginal representatives must be prepared to respond with specificity to reasonable questions about some of the practical problems associated with self-government. For example, how and by whom will self-governing communities be financed? Will social services be maintained at national levels? By whom? These are reasonable inquiries and they do not challenge the integrity of self-government itself. More importantly, they are questions to which much of the Canadian public is seeking answers. This is a public that largely supports Aboriginal inclinations, and its support will be required if constitutional amendments are to be achieved. Thus, Aboriginal parties must be prepared to provide clear answers to reasonable inquiries.

If responses to these inquiries require further research, then this exercise should be undertaken sooner rather than later. What is not widely appreciated, perhaps, is that Aboriginal peoples have already offered tangible opinions on many of these issues. During the Charlottetown discussions, Aboriginal delegates introduced a number of proposals intended to deal with some of the more contentious issues. For example, they discussed the subject of financing self-governing communities through equalization payments similar to those used between federal and provincial governments. However, the content of this suggestion has not been effectively conveyed to the Canadian public. Consequently, the feasibility of the self-government proposal remains problematic in the minds of many Canadians. It seems unwise for Aboriginal leaders to permit this misconception to continue.

Aboriginal people are not the only party to the constitutional debate who have challenges to overcome. If the federal and provincial governments truly wish to resolve Aboriginal claims, then they must be prepared to recommit themselves to a process of compromise. The recent decisions of the Supreme Court of Canada suggest that perhaps the easiest course of action is to let the courts resolve constitutional issues. This would require another twenty years of highly contentious litigation, but present judicial trends suggest that this is what will occur. Such a strategy seems to be both cynical and naïve.

The threat of Quebec's unilateral separation from Canada was not finally resolved by the Supreme Court of Canada's decision that the province has no constitutional authority to do so.[12] Simply put, this was the wrong forum in which to decide such an issue, and the court suggested as much. The "Quebec separation issue" raised questions about democracy, popular will, national reconstruction, and Canadian identity. In its decision, arguably, the court was urging the federal government and other provinces simply to do the right thing.[13] This is no different than the need to reconcile a place for Aboriginal people in Confederation.

Moreover, if resolving the Quebec dispute is to be viewed as an expression of nation building, the courts have never indicated any capacity to fulfil such a role. Rather, court decisions have played a purely supplementary role in constructing the Canadian federation. This nation-building exercise has only been achieved through legislative and constitutional amendments.[14] The role of the courts has been to clarify and balance federal and provincial interests.

Should Aboriginal people be unsuccessful in achieving their goals through the courts, this will change little. They will not go away. Their problems will not dissipate, nor will the moral claims to their entitlements disappear. Even in the face of contrary legal opinions, Aboriginal communities will assert what they believe to be historical rights. Must they and other Canadians endure further Oka crises or perhaps worse before the political will is found to respond to their claims equitably?

The choice of Canadian governments to wait out the inevitable court challenges to resolve Aboriginal issues also seems to be an antidemocratic strategy. Many Canadian politicians seem to have taken the view that democracy means "rule by the majority." Thus, they write off the concerns of minorities as only the desires of "interest groups." This suggests that the concerns of such interest groups warrant neither notice nor representation. Yet the Greek origin of this word actually means "rule by the people."[15] This implies that all people must be represented, even those with minority interests. Given this definition of the term, it is difficult for many Canadian governments to claim that they have heard appeals from their Aboriginal constituents and taken steps to accommodate them. If, as Chapter 2 illustrates, non-Aboriginal American communities can amicably coexist with their tribal neighbours, one wonders what fears resonate in the hearts of reluctant Canadian politicians.

Democratic urges also express themselves in an entirely different fashion. Time and again, as the polls suggest, most Canadians indicate that they are in favour of Aboriginal people exercising greater control over their lives. Even when *Maclean's* asked voters who rejected the Charlottetown Accord why they did so, only 4 percent indicated that they had been motivated by the Aboriginal terms of the agreement.[16] Clearly, most Canadians support the existence of Aboriginal self-governing communities. Surely a fundamental concept of democracy requires that Canadian governments respond to this expression of public will.

Politicians may counter that the average Canadian has little real understanding of what self-government will mean. Thus, these leaders, perhaps
thinking that they are more informed, believe that they must act in the best
interests of all Canadians. They are partly right; most Canadians have little
appreciation of the content of Aboriginal self-government, but few Canadian politicians have any greater sense of what it will mean. Few politicians
and bureaucrats illustrated much understanding of Aboriginal issues during
the first ministers' conferences of the 1980s. Self-governing Aboriginal communities in the United States were largely unknown to almost all non-
Aboriginal representatives. None exhibited more than a rudimentary
appreciation of the basic tribal political and legal realities in that country.
Yet these political leaders resist recognition of Aboriginal entitlements with
a vigour seldom seen in Canada. What explains such reluctance? If there is
to be any movement toward a constitutional amendment recognizing
Aboriginal self-government, then these attitudes must change. If Canadian
governments are truly interested in resolving the serious problems presented
by Aboriginal people, then they must have an equally serious commitment.
Canadian politicians must come to understand, as does the Canadian public, that resolution of Aboriginal entitlements is in the national interest.

A reasonable step for Canadian governments would be to actively court
the opinions of Aboriginal people. Most provincial governments have what
may charitably be described as a cool relationship with their Aboriginal
counterparts. Some of these relationships may even be described as hostile.
Prior to the election of a new national leader of the Assembly of First
Nations in the summer of 1997, when Ovide Mercredi was replaced by Phil
Fontaine, Mercredi could not even arrange a meeting with the minister of
Indian affairs. These differences must be overcome. Canadian governments
must gain a greater understanding of the issues before more serious discus-
sions can occur regarding constitutional revision.

These governments must not only fully understand Aboriginal proposals
but also clearly express their own concerns. These governments have often
either rejected out of hand many Aboriginal suggestions[17] or asked meaningless questions such as "What would self-government look like?" But this
is a mug's game in which Aboriginal leaders would refuse to become
involved. Governments that sympathetically entertain Aboriginal suggestions and then attempt to overcome the difficulties inherent in any proposal would certainly produce a highly constructive atmosphere (perhaps
the lawyers should be escorted out of the room). Federal and provincial
governments must come to appreciate that this is an exercise not of protecting turf but of national reconciliation.

Other inquiries should also be absent from these discussions. Questions
such as "Who is to be a community member?" are of dubious merit (see
Chapter 2). First Nations already possess the ability, under Section 10 of the

Indian Act, to determine community membership. There are no lineups to get in. Does anyone truly believe that there will be great financial or other benefits from becoming a community member? There is no evidence of such an interest among the US tribal communities, who may define their own membership. Such a question is also of little practical value in Canada.

Protests that the existence of Aboriginal communities with the authority to legislate their own criminal laws will result in hundreds of such codes across the country are equally dubious. Is it plausible that Aboriginal people do not wish to protect themselves from fraud, assault, or kidnapping? As described in Chapter 5, the principal differences will be in how trials are held and in resulting forms of punishment. The many criminal codes used by state governments across the United States, as well as those enacted by tribal governments, suggest that the fear regarding multiple criminal codes is misplaced.

One effort that would greatly assist in resolving many Aboriginal issues is the establishment of an arm's-length federal agency to research and generate policy suggestions regarding Aboriginal matters. Currently, much of this work is undertaken by federal government departments (e.g., Indian affairs, justice, and secretary of state). However, most of the research that emanates from these departments is highly partisan and decidedly lacking in creativity. Not surprisingly, the resulting opinions have been of limited value.

Yet there are many areas of concern that still need to be probed. This book has addressed only the "subject matter" jurisdiction of Aboriginal governments. Observations have been largely limited to the kinds of matters over which these new governments will exercise authority. Will they have authority over both criminal and civil law? To what extent will these jurisdictions be shared, and which order of government should prevail in instances of conflicting laws? Similarly, discussions of application of the Canadian Charter of Rights and Freedoms have largely been limited to subject matter.

But the area of personal jurisdiction must also be reviewed. Should the laws of self-governing Aboriginal communities apply to outsiders? If so, then under which circumstances? Would certain circumstances exempt some individuals? What reasoning would support such an exemption? Does such an exemption constitute a distinction based on race? Or is it based on cultural or political distinctions? Would any basis be contrary to the equality provisions of the Charter? Legal issues aside, what is in the best interests of preserving and protecting the integrity of Aboriginal communities?

Questions of physical or geographical jurisdiction have also gone unaddressed in this book.[18] For example, are all Aboriginal laws to be "land-locked"? That is, will they apply only within the physical parameters of the community, or should some areas of Aboriginal authority extend beyond these boundaries? In the United States, the Indian Child Welfare Act clearly recognizes decisions of tribal governments outside Indian country.[19] Should there be similar recognition in Canada? If so, then under what circumstances?[20]

The general issue of Aboriginal self-government may be viewed discretely from land claims, treaties, and Aboriginal title. However, it may be difficult to undertake such a discussion without some sense of how Aboriginal governments will be financed. The issue of financing arose at Charlottetown and will no doubt reassert itself in future discussions. Who would be responsible for financing these governments? Would the communities themselves be required to generate self-sustaining income? Would a federal or provincial government also be required to finance them? Under what formula? Would federal transfer payments be adequate? For which elements of governance? Would social service delivery be part of the commitment to such Aboriginal governments? Some American tribal governments contract out services that they cannot adequately provide to county and state governments. Is this approach tenable in Canada? These and a host of other questions could be considered by an arm's-length agency before the next round of constitutional discussions.

In the United States, organizations such as the National Indian Justice Center at Petaluma, California, undertake research, policy development, and personnel training for tribal justice matters. University research centres such as those at the University of New Mexico and the University of Oklahoma engage in similar efforts. Many tribal developments in the United States evolve from the work accomplished by such institutes. Nongovernmental Aboriginal organizations such as the Ontario Native Council on Justice, located in Toronto, attempt to perform the same function in Canada. However, too often they lack sufficient funds to perform this role adequately. Such organizations, relying almost exclusively on government funds, are limited in their work when governments severely restrict grants. Constructive research on pressing judicial and related matters is effectively undermined when this occurs.

Before self-government is achieved, a number of tasks need to be completed. It would be helpful to know the sorts of constitutional arrangements that Aboriginal communities might propose. It has been said that the significance of a written or unwritten constitution lies in its relationship to the society that produced it.[21] What type of constitution might Aboriginal communities choose? It would be useful to see a variety of sample constitutions that these communities might employ. A research institute could draft sample constitutions to be used by groups such as the Iroquois people of eastern Canada, the Prairie Métis, or the Montagnais of Quebec. This exercise would be useful to an Aboriginal community that wishes to explore culturally relevant options before it chooses its own. In accordance with the cultural norms of the communities considered, the sample constitutions could illustrate how the legislative, judicial, and administrative elements of government might function. Such a constitution might suggest how the democratic will of the people is to be expressed. It might also indicate whether certain institutions are to be comprised of elected or appointed officers, whether principles such as the rule of law will be employed, and/or which ethical guidelines are to be used in conflict resolution.

It has been asserted that the preamble to the Constitution Act, 1867, implies a bill of rights. This bill would include principles articulated in the Magna Carta, the British Bill of Rights, the Petition of Rights, doctrines of parliamentary sovereignty, responsible government, and the rule of law.[22] Would Aboriginal communities want to adopt any of these values into their constitutions? If so, then which ones and in what manner? Are there other principles, perhaps reflected by certain beliefs or practices as described earlier in this text, that should be included in an Aboriginal constitution? What might they be? Such questions might be asked during the development of sample constitutions.

A metaphorical charter of rights was suggested earlier in this text as a tool for balancing collective and individual rights. Research could be undertaken to determine with greater clarity how this or any other Aboriginal charter might function. A description of the specific cultural concerns of various Aboriginal communities might be included in such a charter, from which other Aboriginal communities might then generate their own charters.

When Aboriginal peoples discuss issues of justice, the focus inevitably seems to fall on criminal justice matters. It is therefore reasonable that research be undertaken to explain the content of an Aboriginal code of justice. As discussed earlier in this book, the crimes listed in such a code will mimic, for the most part, those articulated by the Canadian Criminal Code. Aboriginal communities do not look any more favourably on kidnapping and murder, for instance, than do other Western cultures. However, since criminal codes perform two other functions, one might examine these areas. A research group could draft sample codes describing how different Aboriginal cultures might enact criminal law procedures for dealing with an accused. Similarly, a sample code might describe which punishment or sanctions are to be imposed by Aboriginal criminal law. Presumably, the analysis in each instance would explain the unique cultural values involved.

Although civil law jurisdiction is seldom the basis of discussion in judicial debates, it is at the core of day-to-day life in each Aboriginal community. Since the report of the Royal Commission on Aboriginal Peoples makes only a single footnote reference to this area of law,[23] its intricacies remain to be explored.[24] A research facility could draft sample civil codes addressing family law, business and commercial law, landlord and tenant law, estate law, and an assortment of other subject areas. Presumably, like the criminal code exercise, these codes would reflect the cultural concerns of designated communities (e.g., Micmac, Cree, or Métis). Once again two goals would be achieved by this exercise. Non-aboriginal people would better understand the intentions of Aboriginal communities, and these codes might be borrowed by other Aboriginal communities in developing their own codes.[25]

The development of sample constitutions and legal codes strongly suggests the next step to be taken: that of training. Few Aboriginal communities are currently prepared to implement any form of self-government. Besides the development of substantive codes of laws, including constitutions and charters, there is a need to develop "how to" codes. That is, one could develop procedural codes that would perform two principal functions. First, they would explain how to develop substantive law and order codes that each community will require for its own governance. Second, they would describe how to implement these law and order codes. Such codes might explain how to implement civil laws and criminal laws, how to establish membership rules, or how to develop institutions to address human rights issues or legislative conflicts.

Once sample procedural codes have been created, the next step is to promote education. Aboriginal communities will require training manuals for persons working in their governments. These manuals will assist persons working at every level of government, from court personnel to judges and legislators. Every newly elected government in Canada commonly distributes to the new members of Parliament a manual to assist them in understanding their new roles. Similar but much more involved manuals might be developed for the new forms of Aboriginal government. Even more important, perhaps, manuals should also be developed for their citizens. Such teaching tools would explain the nature of their new government, its jurisdiction, its underlying values, the roles of its personnel, rules for resolving disputes, and so forth. This may be the most important manual developed. Besides such manuals, audiotapes and videotapes or DVDs might be developed to assist community education.

Once the various constitutions, law and order codes, procedural manuals, and supplementary teaching tools have been developed, members of the Aboriginal governments will have to be trained. As in baseball, simply knowing the rules of the game will not ensure that one can actually hit the ball. Training of government personnel will be required to ensure that the rules of the new game are properly executed. This is another task that might best be undertaken by a research institute.

More abstract questions might also be examined by a qualified Aboriginal research institute. Political theorists might wish to take advantage of this unique opportunity to examine matters related to social contract theory. Philosophers such as Hume, Rousseau, Mill, and Rawls have developed theories within purely hypothetical contexts, but Aboriginal self-government presents a unique opportunity to examine such matters in a more pragmatic setting. An examination of the fundamental ideas of governance would benefit both Aboriginal and non-Aboriginal communities.

Establishment of an agency independent of political influence and devoted to exploring Aboriginal concerns would be welcome. Organizations that perform similar roles in the areas of human rights and multiculturalism are the International Centre for Human Rights and Democratic Development and the Canadian Race Relations Foundation, located, respectively, in Montreal and Toronto. Given the magnitude and implication of Aboriginal issues, such an agency is long overdue. Research undertaken by the Royal Commission on Aboriginal Peoples provides a useful starting point. Establishment of such an agency could contribute profoundly to national reconstruction and avoid the chilling effect resulting from the failure of governments to finance Aboriginal organizations.

Not the Road to Camelot

Self-government presents many possibilities for both Aboriginal and non-Aboriginal Canadians. However, for different reasons, both must guard against unreasonable expectations. The likelihood of achieving self-government is undermined by federal and provincial authorities that anticipate more from Aboriginal governments than is reasonable. The inquiries made of Aboriginal leaders justifiably have been rigorous – perhaps too rigorous at times. Often these inquiries have resonated with an uncommon degree of scepticism. Similarly, doubts about the credibility of Aboriginal leadership or collective rights claims hint at unusual intransigence. Does this degree of scrutiny arise only in the context of Aboriginal claims? It does not occur, for instance, in the context of Quebec separation. One senses at times that these doubts emanate from the fundamental Canadian perception of Aboriginal people.

Too often when the term "Aboriginal people" is used, it implies a culture of dependency and welfare or, alternatively, the noble savage. Brian Maracle offers a vivid picture of how Aboriginal people are often portrayed: "Indian reserves are hopeless puddles of poverty. People there live in shacks surrounded by garbage and wrecked cars. Everyone's on welfare. The men drink and beat their wives. The women play bingo and neglect their kids. The boys sniff gasoline and the girls have babies."[26] Either perception of Aboriginal people, as welfare bums or noble savages, is bound to generate only ideological mischief. In such instances, perhaps there is too much emphasis on the first word of this phrase, "Aboriginal"; a more appropriate emphasis should be on the second word, "people."

Like any other Canadian society, an Aboriginal community is comprised of people. They enjoy the same pleasures as other Canadians, have the same strengths, and struggle to overcome the same weaknesses. But most Canadians seldom seem to understand this. Over the years, criticism has occasionally been directed at Aboriginal leaders regarding political or financial improprieties alleged to have occurred in their communities. For example, the media have sometimes reported stories of government mismanagement in First Nations communities.[27] These stories have usually dealt with political leaders accused of exercising personal bias or mismanaging funds. And they may in fact be guilty. But is it any surprise that people who have been forced to endure Third World living conditions all of their lives occasionally succumb to these temptations? Perhaps the real surprise is that more such incidents haven't occurred. More importantly, are these actions any different than the kinds of favouritism reflected in the political appointments made by Canadian governments or the kinds of financial improprieties that occasionally threaten the integrity of these governments?

In January of 2000, Jane Stewart, the federal human resources minister, admitted that her department had mismanaged a job creation program that controlled as much as one billion dollars in operating funds.[28] Does this mean that democracy has failed in Canada? BC premier Glen Clark was forced to step down by the disclosure that a neighbour who had performed thousands of dollars worth of work on his home subsequently received approval for a gaming licence. In March 1999, the premier's home was raided by the RCMP in an investigation of this matter. Concerns about conflict of interest were subsequently raised in the provincial legislature.[29] In another case, on 16 March 1999, Senator Eric Bernston was sentenced to one year in jail for his involvement in a corruption scandal that rocked the Saskatchewan Tory government of Grant Devine. Bernston, at one time Devine's deputy premier, was found guilty of defrauding Saskatchewan taxpayers by making false claims regarding government allowances. His conviction brought to fifteen the number of Tory members of the Devine government convicted for improprieties during the scandal.[30] It also brought to two the number of sitting members of the Senate convicted of financial mismanagement or influence peddling.[31]

Two months earlier, the Ontario government of Premier Mike Harris was hit by a similar scandal. The president of the Ontario Trillium Foundation, an independent, non-profit financial granting agency ostensibly at arm's length from the provincial government, was dismissed from her position. Despite apparent agreement by most observers that she had performed her role eminently well for six years, she lost her job. Since the Harris government took office, twenty-two of the twenty-four board members have been Tory appointees, often with past Tory associations.[32] Many observers expressed the fear that this foundation, with an annual budget of more than $10 million, would become little more than a slush fund for the Tory faithful.

How different are the federal, British Columbia, Saskatchewan, and Ontario scandals from the claims made by those either inside or outside Aboriginal communities? Certainly, the influence that Aboriginal leaders exert both politically and financially is decidedly less than that of their provincial and federal counterparts.

A further response to the claims of "mismanagement on reserves" may be better appreciated through an understanding of political pluralism in a democracy. The American form[33] of the participatory pluralism theory, most often associated with theorists such as R.A. Dall, Talcott Parsons, and David Truman, takes issue with Rousseau's view that it is through the participation of individual citizens that the democratic will of the people best expresses itself. These more recent theorists agree that this conception of democracy is naïve. To maintain Rousseau's position would make it very difficult to explain how Canada can impose a goods and services tax in the face of so much clear public opposition. Recent theorists argue that Western democracies actually express the will of a variety of competing interest groups. These groups may reflect opinions regarding health care, human rights, business, or environmental matters. Often these interests conflict and compete not only for government policy attention but also for available funding or tax benefits. For example, sawmill operators and loggers often find themselves at odds with environmentalists disputing tree-harvesting practices. Pluralist theorists argue that most often the laws that emanate from government as a consequence of the clash between these competing sets of values reflect a balancing of the opposing interests – not the will of the majority on one side or the other of an issue. Pluralists assert that, as long as no particular interest group captures a monopoly over the government's attention, the dynamic represents a fair interpretation of the democratic will. Moreover, in light of the complexities of modern life, only through this balancing of competing interests can a democratic society function.

Like other expressions of Western democracies, Aboriginal communities today express a multitude of competing interests. Groups in these communities also compete for the attention of local governments, such as band councils. Should financing be expended on sewers, education, health, or roads? Who will receive the next homes built, homes that are always in such demand? Which local entrepreneur should receive the next contract for clearing waste or constructing a school? Inevitably, there are competing opinions about how best to resolve these issues. Perhaps the greatest distinction, then, between how Aboriginal and non-Aboriginal governments resolve such matters is in the availability of mechanisms for resolution.

These mechanisms may sometimes be quite legalistic (e.g., relying on principles of due process). Or they may take the form of protocols to be followed when conflicts of interest arise. Ombudsman offices commonly provide this form of review for the actions of Canadian governments. The recent land claims settlement by the Nisga'a people of British Columbia included conflict-resolution guidelines that may be applied when conflicting interests collide in the administration of their government. This element of the treaty hints at a problem that may loom for Aboriginal communities about to implement broad self-governing authority.

Traditionally, Aboriginal communities had their own forms of conflict resolution. However, since these communities have not been permitted to practise their respective expressions of self-government, many of these traditional mechanisms for resolving or avoiding disputes have fallen into disuse. Nor has legislation such as the Indian Act provided adequate measures for responding to the natural conflicts that arise in First Nations communities. Consequently, there may now be a lack of adequate procedural guarantees of government evenhandedness. Perhaps the obvious response would be either to reinvigorate the old customs or to initiate new ones appropriate for these communities. Perhaps both. But prohibiting outright the democratic expression of self-government as a way of responding to claims of kickbacks and favouritism is surely too harsh a response. It certainly would be for the citizens of British Columbia, Saskatchewan, and Ontario.[34]

The chief difference between these two societies is found in cultural expression (see Chapter 6 for discussion of traditional Aboriginal values). It is believed that the traditional values underlying Aboriginal societies will help these communities to recover from the infirmities that have befallen them. In particular, many community members trust that their cultural values will prevent the kinds of mismanagement and personal indiscretion that have occasionally occurred in the past. Thus, to a large extent, confidence in these cultural expressions inspires self-government ambitions.

It is therefore important to keep present circumstances in perspective. The indiscretions of Aboriginal governments should not automatically disqualify them from exercising self-governing authority. Similar mistakes have certainly not disqualified Canadian governments from exercising their powers. Canadian governments should be mindful of the fact that many Canadians have argued that the cod fishery on the east coast was destroyed by government mismanagement. A similar complaint is heard in British Columbia regarding salmon stocks. And many Canadians have been dismayed by the failure of their governments to resolve the threat of

Quebec separation. For more than twenty years, this problem has threatened to divide Canada both physically and culturally. Meanwhile, first ministers' meetings are like an annual gnashing of teeth as the provinces continually attempt to gain greater political authority while the federal government insists on retaining its powers.

Moreover, Canada's record regarding civil liberties is also not without blemish. For years, the Duplessis government of Quebec unlawfully persecuted both communists and Jehovah's Witnesses. The Liberal government of Pierre Trudeau suspended the civil liberties of every Canadian when it invoked the War Measures Act in October 1970 to address the kidnapping and murder of two people. And the incarceration of innocent Canadians of Japanese ancestry during the Second World War will never be seen as Canada's finest hour. More recently, the unlawful incarceration of Canadians indicates that the judicial arm of government is also not without defect. Guy Paul Morin, David Milgaard, and Donald Marshall were unjustly imprisoned for the capital crime of murder (both federal and provincial jurisdictions were involved in these prosecutions). Each man spent considerable time in prison for a crime that he didn't commit.

The appropriate response to the aforementioned problems is not to close up shop and go home. Rather, Canadians should rededicate themselves to ensuring that these mistakes do not happen again. Aboriginal people are seeking the same opportunity. They wish to confront past problems and commit themselves to improving their communities. A misapprehension of who Aboriginal people are should not prevent them from achieving this goal.

Aboriginal people, too, must guard against unreasonable expectations. Many have expressed the belief that "if we had self-government, then our problems would be solved." There is little evidence that this would be the case. The experience of American tribal governments illustrates that, even when Indian communities exercise self-governing authority, a host of difficulties may persist. Unemployment remains chronic in many of these communities. A community without a source of income on which to base its economy will not suddenly develop one simply because it now possesses self-governing authority. Similarly, substance dependency, child and elder abuse, and a myriad of other health-related afflictions will not magically disappear. In recent years, though, many of these communities have begun to engage these problems with greater success.

Broader education among the population, as well as increasing awareness of marrying new technologies to natural resources, have improved the conditions of many tribal societies. Rediscovery and reimplementation of customary cultural practices, which impart traditional values, have given new hope to Aboriginal people in addressing some of the current social problems, which were never present in traditional communities. In particular in recent years, use of more culturally sensitive ways of resolving legal disputes has produced judicial structures arguably more effective and relevant for these societies. However, finding a balance between old and new ideas remains a challenge.

When Aboriginal people finally regain their self-governing authority, they will still be faced with many problems. Both common sense and American tribal government experience suggest that the path to self-government is not the road to Camelot. Nevertheless, it will be the first significant step toward reacquiring the integrity and dignity that once epitomized Aboriginal societies. It will be upon these strengths that Aboriginal people can confront the remaining challenges. And perhaps, like Jumping Mouse, they will rediscover who they are and all that they can become.

Notes

Introduction

1 This point was made clear by the Royal Commission on Aboriginal Peoples, *Report of the Royal Commission on Aboriginal Peoples*, vol. 2 (Ottawa: Supply and Services Canada, 1996), 1, 139, 184.

Chapter 1: The Self-Government Ideal

1 These divisions often grew out of the distinctions created by Canadian laws, in particular the Indian Act. Distinctions such as non-status Indians, treaty Indians, Eskimos, and certain Métis groups evolved only as a result of the wedges driven between them and their natural Aboriginal communities by legal enactments. However, in some instances, there were natural sociopolitical divisions. Donald Purich explains some of these naturally evolving distinctions. See Donald Purich, *The Métis* (Toronto: James Lorimer, 1988).

2 The British Parliament had already renounced the right to legislate for the Dominion of Canada in the 1931 Statute of Westminster.

3 Not just legislative enactments but also any activity or expression of government, such as an administrative activity, are bound by the Charter. The concept of entrenchment and how Section 52 provides this function is explained in Chapter 8.

4 Constitution Act, 1982, being Schedule B to the Canada Act 1982 (U.K.), 1982, c. 11, as amended in 1984.

5 Ibid. at subsection 35(2).

6 Ibid. at subsection 35(1).

7 Ibid. at subsection 35(4), as amended in 1983.

8 Ibid. at subsection 35(2), as amended in 1983.

9 As we will see in Chapter 8, until the decision in *R. v. Sparrow*, 1 S.C.R. 1075 (1990) [hereinafter *Sparrow*], not even federal and provincial governments quite understood its implications.

10 This is the terminology used in the original subsection and thought by Aboriginal people to suggest that these meetings were to be a forum for changes to the Constitution.

11 Within the Assembly of First Nations there existed many issues, all of which were championed by different factions at different times. The result was often a mass of sometimes conflicting positions that could never reasonably be expected to generate agreement at the first ministers' conferences. One such sweeping AFN proposal presented at the second conference was referred to as the "composite amendment."

12 If each Aboriginal party to the first ministers' conferences was in some disarray, then among the four Aboriginal organizations there was little more than chaos.

13 Some proposals dealt with treaty rights interpretation and implementation. Others addressed issues of Métis and First Nations land claims, while still others expressed legal concerns regarding recognition and expression of Aboriginal title and rights.

14 The Inuit shared only a minor role in such conflicts. More commonly, these disputes arose between Métis and First Nations claims. A commentary by Neil Sterritt regarding the

Nisga'a Treaty lucidly illustrates the difficulties that arose in that instance regarding competing land claims. See Neil Sterritt, "The Nisga'a Treaty: Competing Claims Ignored!" *BC Studies* 120 (1998-9): 73.

15 This topic is discussed in Chapter 6.

16 *Special Committee on Indian Self-Government in Canada* (Ottawa: Supply and Services Canada, 1983).

17 Ibid. at 39-68.

18 Ibid. at 64, recommendation 21.

19 This was a principal concern for Métis people at the first ministers' conferences.

20 Some Aboriginal people whose communities are structured along matrilineal lines have traditional practices dictating that all the family property belongs to the woman's side of the family. Such practices are clearly at odds with the more common presumption of fifty-fifty sharing of family assets upon marital breakdown.

21 Commonly known as a "third order of government." This is explored in Chapter 8 within the context of the recommendations of the Charlottetown Accord and the Royal Commission on Aboriginal Peoples.

22 The implications of international law principles for Aboriginal claims in Canada are brought into sharp relief by Sharon Helen Venne, *Our Elders Understand Our Rights: Evolving International Law Regarding Indigenous Rights* (Penticton, BC: Theytus, 1998). See also P. Hutchins and C. Hilling, "International Law and Aboriginal Disputes," in Stephen B. Smart and Michael Coyle, eds., *Aboriginal Issues Today: A Legal and Business Guide* (North Vancouver: Self-Counsel, 1997), 257.

23 Such as the standards of proof necessary if one were to successfully establish a case for Aboriginal rights to hunt or trap. An example is the requirement in *Sparrow,* supra note 9, that a successful claimant prove occupation and exercise of such rights prior to settlement by Europeans.

24 Not at any appellate level. The Supreme Court of Canada in the recent *Delgamuukw* v. *British Columbia,* [1997] 3 S.C.R. 1010 [hereinafter *Delgamuukw*] case declined to comment on the issue.

25 P. Chartrand made this point in his Opening Address to a Conference on Implementing the Recommendations of the Royal Commission on Aboriginal Peoples, Toronto, 22-4 April 1999.

26 For a fuller appreciation of the significance of being able to define the rules of the game by controlling the use of language, see: Michel Foucault, *The Archaeology of Knowledge* (New York: Harper and Row, 1976); and *Power/Knowledge: Selected Interviews and Other Writings, 1972-1977* (New York: Pantheon, 1980).

27 Government of Canada, *Aboriginal Self-Government: The Government of Canada's Approach to Implementation of the Inherent Right and the Negotiation of Aboriginal Self-Government* (Ottawa: Department of Indian Affairs and Northern Development, 1995).

28 Comments from the final afternoon session, February 1998.

29 *Sparrow,* supra note 9, may have opened the door to the assertion that Aboriginal self-government currently exists in Canadian law as a consequence of Section 35. This is the opinion of RCAP as reviewed in Chapter 8. However, this position is only notional. Neither the Supreme Court of Canada nor any provincial appeal court has recognized this point of law. The courts have simply not been asked to settle this issue. (Although the issue arose in *Delgamuukw,* supra note 24, the court chose not to consider the issue due to a defect in the pleadings.)

30 For a broad outline of some of the relevant issues within an international context, see J.W. Littlechild and D. Calihoo, "International Law and Indigenous Self-Determination," paper prepared for the Conference on Implementing the Recommendations of the Royal Commission on Aboriginal Peoples, Toronto, 22-4 April 1999.

31 Since black holes cannot be seen, they are usually detected by observing their strong gravitational forces on a neighbouring star. For an excellent explanation of this general phenomenon, see Igor Novikov, *Black Holes and the Universe* (Cambridge: Cambridge University Press, 1990).

32 There are differences of opinion among Aboriginal peoples as to which forms self-government will take. They agree, however, about their fundamental right to self-government.

33 Canadian governments suffered significant international embarrassment by disclosure of issues such as gender discrimination (see the Sandra Lovelace case in Chapter 5) and the Third World conditions with which Aboriginal people are forced to contend. These issues have been made known by Aboriginal organizations, which would disappear along with the demise of Aboriginal communities, as proposed by the White Paper.

34 Of course, other leaders were involved in this process, without whose support this goal would never have been achieved.

35 For an enlightening response to the White Paper, see Harold Cardinal's insightful observations in *The Unjust Society: The Tragedy of Canada's Indians* (Edmonton: Hurtig, 1969).

Chapter 2: The American Tribal Government Experience

1 Canadian First Nations and Métis communities typically occupy a much smaller land base than do their American cousins.

2 21 U.S. (8 Wheat.) 543 (1823) [hereinafter *Johnson*].

3 Unless the federal government had extinguished title in some other fashion, such as through legislation or treaty.

4 *Johnson*, supra note 2 at 574.

5 Ibid.

6 30 U.S. (5 Pet.) 1 (1831) [hereinafter *Cherokee Nation*].

7 Article III, Section 2.

8 *Cherokee Nation*, supra note 6 at 16.

9 Ibid. at 17; emphasis added.

10 31 U.S. (6 Pet.) 515 (1832) [hereinafter *Worcester*].

11 Ibid. at 557.

12 Ibid. at 556; emphasis added.

13 *Worcester*, supra note 10.

14 *Cherokee Nation*, supra note 6.

15 Ibid.

16 *Worcester*, supra note 10. This point would be modified later in *McBratney, Draper, Williams v. Lee* and in *McClanahan*, as described and cited later in this chapter.

17 *Ex parte Crow Dog*, 109 U.S. 556 (1883).

18 All references to the Supreme Court in this chapter are to the Supreme Court of the United States.

19 18 U.S.C. s. 1153 (1885) [hereinafter Major Crimes Act].

20 (a) Any Indian who commits against the person or property of another Indian or other person any of the following offences, namely murder, manslaughter, kidnapping, maiming, a felony under chapter 190A [18 U.S.C. ss. 2241 et seq., that is, certain sexual offences, including rape and sexual abuse], incest, assault with intent to commit murder, assault with a dangerous weapon, assault resulting in serious bodily injury, arson, burglary, robbery, and a felony under section 661 of this title [18 U.S.C. s. 661, that is, theft] within the Indian country, shall be subject to the same law and penalties as all other persons committing any of the above offences, within the exclusive jurisdiction of the United States.

21 Current terms of the Major Crimes Act, subsection (a). There is a debate over whether the act extinguishes jurisdiction of the tribe in these areas or simply preempts it until the federal legislation is withdrawn.

22 At least it was thought to be at that time. *Oliphant* v. *Suquamish Indian Tribal*, 435 U.S. 1912 (1978) [hereinafter *Oliphant*]; and *Duro* v. *Reina*, 110 S. Ct. 2053 (1990) [hereinafter *Duro*], altered this perception.

23 18 U.S.C. s. 1152 [hereinafter General Crimes Act], described later in this chapter.

24 The terms "Indian country" and "Indian reservation" are used interchangeably for the sake of simplicity. For a clearer distinction between these two terms, see 18 U.S.C. s. 1151 and *De Couteau* v. *District County Court*, 420 U.S. 425 (1975).

25 104 U.S. 621 (1881).

26 164 U.S. 240 (1896).

27 Federal law could preempt state jurisdiction provided that this intention was expressly stated through legislation.

28 General Crimes Act, supra note 23.
29 Ibid.
30 18 U.S.C.A. s. 13.
31 Ibid.
32 *Oliphant,* supra note 22.
33 *Duro,* supra note 22.
34 The tribe had wanted him prosecuted for the murder of a young boy pursuant to the Major Crimes Act. However, since the FBI failed to prosecute him, the tribe laid a firearms charge.
35 The reasoning of the Supreme Court in both *Oliphant,* supra note 22, and *Duro,* supra note 22, is highly suspect and is discussed more fully in Chapter 8.
36 Pub. L. No. 102-37, 105 Stat. 646 (1990).
37 Major Crimes Act, supra note 21.
38 Restated in *Sigana* v. *Bailey,* 282 Minn. 367, 164 N.W.2d 886 (1969); and *Gourneau* v. *Smith,* 207 N.W.2d 256.
39 480 U.S. 9 (1987).
40 Ibid. at 17.
41 *New Mexico* v. *Mescalaro Apache Tribe,* 462 U.S. 324 (1983).
42 *Confederated Salish and Kootenai Tribes* v. *Namen,* 665 (8th Cir. 1982), *appeal denied* 459 U.S. 977 (1982).
43 *California* v. *Cabazon Band of Mission Indians,* 480 U.S. 202 (1987).
44 *United States* v. *Mazurie,* 419 U.S. 54 (1975).
45 *Milbank Mutual Insurance Co.* v. *Eagleman,* 705 P.2d 1117 (Mont. 1985); *Wyoming ex rel. Peterson* v. *District Court,* 617 P.2d 1056 (1980) [hereinafter *Wyoming ex rel. Peterson*].
46 *Cardin* v. *De La Cruz,* 671 F.2d 363 (9th Cir. 1982), *appeal denied* 459 U.S. (1982).
47 *Morris* v. *Hitchcock,* 194 U.S. 384 (1904).
48 *Washington* v. *Confederated Tribes of the Colville Indian Reservation,* 447 U.S. 134 (1980).
49 *Ashcroft* v. *United States,* 679 F.2d 196 (9th Cir. 1982), *appeal denied* 459 U.S. 1201 (1983).
50 *Hunt* v. *Hunt,* 16 Indian Law Reporter 6039 (Fort McDermitt Tribal Court 1988); *Sanders* v. *Robinson,* 894 F.2d 630 (9th Cir. 1988), *appeal denied* 109 S. Ct. 3165 (1989).
51 See *Federal Indian Child Welfare Act,* 25 U.S.C.A. s. 1901-63 (1978).
52 Ibid.
53 358 U.S. 217 (1959).
54 Ibid. at 219-20.
55 Ibid. at 223; emphasis added.
56 455 U.S. 130 (1982).
57 *Fisher* v. *District Court,* 424 U.S. 382 (1976).
58 Infra. at note 83.
59 *Bryan* v. *Itasca County,* 426 U.S. 373 (1976).
60 *Ramah Navajo School Board Inc.* v. *Bureau of Revenue,* 458 U.S. 832 (1982); *Central Machinery Co.* v. *Arizona Tax Commission,* 411 U.S. 164 (1973).
61 *Washington Dept. of Ecology* v. *EPA,* 752 F. Id. 1465 (9th Cir. 1985).
62 *Wyoming ex rel. Peterson* v. *District Court,* 617 P.2d 1056 (Wyo. 1980).
63 *Wyoming ex rel. Peterson,* supra note 45.
64 *Barta* v. *Oglala Sioux Tribe,* 259 F. 2nd 553 (8th Cir. 1958).
65 *Bundale* v. *Confederated Yakima Tribes,* 492 U.S. 408 (1989).
66 *Moe* v. *Confederated Salish and Kootenai Tribes,* 425 U.S. 463 (1976); *Fort Mojave Tribe* v. *County of San Bernadino,* 543 F.2d 1253 (9th Cir. 1976), 430 U.S. 983 (1977).
67 380 U.S. 685 (1965).
68 41 U.S. 164 (1973).
69 Ibid. at 172.
70 462 U.S. 324 (1983).
71 Ibid. at 334.
72 490 U.S. 163 (1989).
73 107 S. Ct. 971 (1987).
74 480 U.S. 202 (1987).
75 455 U.S. 130 (1982).

76 Notable exceptions are gaming, the Indian Civil Rights Act, and off-reservation laws regarding children. See note 51.
77 For the seminal treatise on tribal governance in the United States, see Felix Cohen, *Handbook of Indian Law* (Washington, DC: United States Government Printing Office, 1984), in particular Chapter 7, 122.
78 18 U.S.C. s. 1151.
79 Pub. L. No. 83-280 (codified at 18 U.S.C. s. 1162 and at 28 U.S.C. s. 1360).
80 *Washington* v. *Confederated Yakima Tribes,* 439 U.S. 463 (1979) at 488.
81 Originally, California, Minnesota, Oregon, Nebraska, Wisconsin, and, later, Alaska. These states had no choice in exercising this authority. Hence, they have become known as the "mandatory" states.
82 "Option" states could choose whether to assume this jurisdiction and to what degree.
83 Montana exercised authority only over the Flathead Reservation among all the reservations within its borders.
84 Arizona chose to assert jurisdiction only over issues concerned with clean air and water.
85 Minnesota disclaimed its authority over the Nett Lake Reservation in 1975. Washington did likewise with the Quinault Reservation (1969), Suquamish Port Madison Reservation (1972), and Colville Reservation (1987).
86 25 U.S.C. s. 1321-26.
87 A special vote has to be held for this purpose. In practice, this means that state governments would never be permitted to usurp tribal authority.
88 25 U.S.C. s. 1521.
89 Ibid. at s. 1451.
90 42 U.S.C. s. 2991.
91 Pub. L. No. 93-638 (1975).
92 25 U.S.C. s. 461.
93 Laguna Pueblo, Law and Order Code, s. 3.
94 Ibid. at s. 8.
95 Southwest Inter-Tribal Court of Appeal, Rules of Procedure, Rule 1.
96 Ibid. at Rule 3.
97 Not litigants. Lawyers (mercifully) are also excluded from these forums.
98 Mission statement of the Northwest Inter-Tribal Court System.
99 This is the issue of comity, whereby courts from different jurisdictions enforce one another's decisions. Tribal courts have found some state courts reluctant to enforce their decisions.
100 See Constitution Act, 1982, being Schedule B to the Canada Act 1982 (U.K.), 1982, c. 11, s. 35.
101 For further discussion of the need to self-identify, see P. Chartrand, "Opening Address," Conference on Implementing the Recommendations of the Royal Commission on Aboriginal Peoples, Toronto, 22-4 April 1999, 9-11. See also J.W. Littlechild and D. Callihoo, "International Law and Indigenous Self-Determination," paper presented at the Conference on Implementing the Recommendations of the Royal Commission on Aboriginal Peoples, Toronto, 22-4 April 1999, 3.
102 For a general view of social contract theory that rationalizes the values of voluntariness, individualism, rationality, and consensuality, see Michael Lessnoff, *Social Contract* (London: Macmillan, 1986). John Rawls uses contract theory to build a modern approach to judicial theory in *A Theory of Justice* (Cambridge, MA: Harvard University Press, 1971), while Robert Nozick establishes his brand of libertarian theory based on his contractarian views in *Anarchy, State, and Utopia* (New York: HarperCollins, 1974).
103 For a discussion of the importance of this test of pedigree, at least for legal positivists, see John Austin, *The Province of Jurisprudence Determined* (1832). For a more recent exploration of this idea, see H.L.A. Hart's views on "secondary laws" and "rules of recognition" in *The Concept of Law* (New York: Oxford University Press, 1961).
104 Arguably, this prior point itself is founded on pragmatic concerns.
105 See Brian Maracle, *Back on the Rez: Finding the Way Home* (Toronto: Penguin, 1997).
106 The commission recommended that Aboriginal communities self-identify. However, the

RCAP recommendations gave the federal and provincial governments the final decision regarding with whom they would negotiate self-governing authority. Aboriginal people find this unacceptable. It provides federal and provincial parties with de facto control over how Aboriginal communities can associate themselves, at least if they hope to participate in negotiations with the respective Canadian governments. See *Report of the Royal Commission on Aboriginal Peoples* (Ottawa: Supply and Services Canada, 1996), conclusion 6, 184.

107 For example, the Assembly of First Nations, Métis National Council, Congress of Aboriginal Peoples, Inuit Tapirisat of Canada, and Native Women's Association of Canada.

108 Some of these include the Union of Nova Scotia Indians, Confederacy of Mainland Micmacs, Union of New Brunswick Indians, Association des Métis et Indiens Hors-Réserve du Québec, Grand Council of the Crees of Quebec, Association of Iroquois and Allied Indians, Nishnawbe-Aski Nations Confederacy, Federation of Saskatchewan Indian Nations, Métis Nation of Alberta, Indian Association of Alberta, Confederacy of Treaty Six First Nations, United Native Nations, Union of British Columbia Chiefs, Gwich'in Tribal Council, and Council of Yukon First Nations.

109 Also, currently, three locals have a role to play; see Chapter 11, Section 13 and subsection 14(c).

110 In September 1999, NASA miscalculated and fired its "Orbiter" directly into Mars. In December of that year, it similarly lost its "Polar Lander" for reasons unknown.

Chapter 3: Entrenching Self-Government: The Treaty Option

1 Consensus Report on the Constitution, Charlottetown, 28 August 1992, final text, Item 41.

2 The Royal Commission on Aboriginal Peoples (RCAP) maintains in its final report (1996) that this right currently exists in law. However, no appeals court has yet recognized this proposition.

3 International documents have clearly recognized the right of a "people" to protection of their "culture." Aboriginal people assert self-government as an expression of their culture. This perspective in international law is elaborated in Chapter 6.

4 Constitution Act, 1867 (U.K.), 30 and 31 Vict., c. 3, subsection 92(14) [hereinafter Constitution Act, 1867].

5 Any fundamental alteration to the present constitutional order will require provincial consent pursuant to the amending elements of Part V of the Constitution Act, 1982, being Schedule B to the Canada Act 1982 (U.K.), 1982, c. 11 [hereinafter Constitution Act, 1982].

6 There would be a need to understand how potential conflicts of jurisdiction will be resolved. Similarly, issues such as comity would require serious discussion.

7 Both the Saskatchewan Office of the Treaty Commissioner and the British Columbia Treaty Commission predate the release of the RCAP report and constitute forums for treaty negotiation and facilitation. Both attempt to resolve issues concerned, for instance, with education, health, and harvesting practices, though not all the issues bear directly on self-government. The BC Treaty Commission recently facilitated a Draft Agreement in Principle regarding the Sechelt First Nation (26 January 1999).

8 For an excellent account, see Sharon Helen Venne, "Treaty Making and Its Potential for Conflict Resolution between Indigenous Nations and the Canadian State," paper presented at the Conference on Implementing the Recommendations of the Royal Commission on Aboriginal Peoples, Toronto, 22-4 April 1999.

9 There are hundreds of treaties and surrenders signed between Aboriginal people and Canadian governments. The numbered treaties were signed with the British queen (or king) and did not include provinces as signatories.

10 Constitution Act, 1867, *supra* note 4.

11 Labour Conventions case, *A.G. Can.* v. *A.G. Ont.* (1937), A.G. 326.

12 Although the reasoning of the Privy Council has since been criticized, and although the "peace, order and good government" authority of Section 132 of the Constitution Act, 1867, supra note 4, is thought to prevail for different reasons, this is the current state of the law. For a discussion of this issue, see W.R. Lederman, *Continuing Canadian Constitutional Dilemmas* (Toronto: Butterworths, 1980), Chapter 19.

13 To date, the discussion has centred on whether the federal authority can enact the terms

of a treaty unilaterally. The debate has never recognized the authority of provinces to be signatories.

14 Perhaps the most influential statement of this proposition and the history of the "nation-state" was articulated by Emmerich de Vattel, see *The Law of Nations* (London: G.G. and J. Robinson, 1797).

15 The plain reading, otherwise known as the "literal" or "dictionary rule," is not the only such rule of statutory interpretation. However, the "golden rule" (which requires one to consider the law prior to the new legislation to determine what mischief is intended to be corrected) is not obviously applicable. In addition, the "purposive rule" wouldn't appear to work either. It would seem to be a fanciful and laboured bit of reasoning to argue that this section was intended to fulfil this function in the face of the requirements under the Constitution Act, 1982, supra note 5, which seemed to require that this be done by constitutional conference. Only a contrived analysis would suggest that these other interpretive tools would be of much use. For a discussion of constitutional judicial review, see Barry Strayer, *The Canadian Constitution and the Courts: Function and Scope of Judicial Review* (Toronto: Butterworths, 1988). A good introduction to statutory interpretation is provided by Ruth Sullivan in *Statutory Construction: Essentials of Canadian Law Series* (Toronto: Irwin Law Books, 1997).

16 It is critical to understand that the distinction here concerns the recognition or creation of this authority. This is quite dissimilar from a negotiating forum that debates how these rights will be "implemented." The Charlottetown Accord proposed this latter approach – but only once the right of self-government had been entrenched. This proposal is elaborated in the final chapter.

17 Many international agreements, such as the North American Free Trade Agreement, as well as the proposed Multilateral Agreement on Investments, include terms that address such issues.

18 Constitution Act, 1982, supra note 5, Part I.

19 Ibid. at Part VI.

20 The initial memorandum of agreement was signed on 4 August.

21 Chapter 2, Section 1, of the agreement, unreported at the time of writing.

22 Ibid. at Chapter 11, s. 3.

23 Ibid. at ss. 8 and 9.

24 Ibid. at s. 13.

25 Ibid. at s. 14.

26 Ibid. at s. 9.

27 Ibid. at s. 11.

28 Ibid. at ss. 19-23.

29 Ibid. at s. 39.

30 Ibid. It appears that this would not permit active participation in either Nisga'a village government or Nisga'a Lisims Government. See Chapter 1, Definitions, "Nisga'a Institution"; see also "Nisga'a Public Institution."

31 Supra note 21, at ss. 1 and 4.

32 See Chapter 11.

33 Ibid. at s. 108. The Criminal Code, R.S.C., c. 46, s. 207, prohibits operation of a permanent full-time casino unless it is regulated by provincial law.

34 Supra note 21, at s. 61.

35 Ibid. at ss. 59 and 60.

36 Ibid. at s. 62.

37 Ibid. at s. 9.

38 Ibid. at ss. 64 and 65.

39 Ibid. at s. 67.

40 Ibid. at s. 76.

41 Ibid. at s. 111.

42 Ibid. at s. 79.

43 Ibid. at s. 83.

44 Ibid. at s. 72.

45   $165.7 million in cash.

46   See Sections 89, 96(a), 100(a), and 104.

47   Section 86, medicinal substances.

48   I recognize that it doesn't work quite like this. The issues are often more complex and blended. However, setting the scene this way helps to illustrate my point.

49   Chapter 6, Section 100(a).

50   For a further critical view of this agreement, see John Borrows, "Domesticating Doctrines: Aboriginal and Treaty Rights, and the Response to the Royal Commission on Aboriginal Peoples," paper presented at the Conference on Implementing the Recommendations of the Royal Commission on Aboriginal Peoples, Toronto, 22-4 April 1999, 14-17.

51   However, as Neil Sterritt points out, apparently neither the BC government nor the federal government held the Nisga'a negotiations up to the standard of proof that should have been required. See Neil Sterritt, "The Nisga'a Treaty: Competing Claims Ignored!" *BC Studies* 120 (1998-9): 73.

52   Sterritt clearly outlines the competing claims of the Tahltan, Gitksan, and Gitanyow to the Nass watershed, which, he argues, the Nisga'a bargained away. He also illustrates how the *Delgamuukw* v. *British Columbia*, [1997] 3 S.C.R. 1010, decision of the Supreme Court of Canada determined how such overlapping claims should be addressed. Ibid.

53   *Toronto Star,* 5 December 1998: 3, 4.

54   Both Neil Sterritt and Gordon Gibson have argued that, at least in British Columbia, this treaty will become a template for other negotiations. See Neil Sterritt, supra note 51, 74; and Gordon Gibson, "Comments on the Draft Nisga'a Treaty," *BC Studies* 120 (1998-9): 64.

55   In the case of the Nisga'a agreement, reportedly, there are large divisions within the community concerning the merits of ceding away claims to traditional lands.

56   Although there have been disputes between First Nations and Métis communities regarding land claims in which First Nations have argued a superior claim, there have been no such hierarchical claims between one First Nation and another.

Chapter 4: Entrenching Self-Government: The "Principled Approach"

1   See Alan Borovoy, *When Freedoms Collide: The Case for Our Civil Liberties* (Toronto: Lester and Orpen Dennys, 1988), for a vivid description of such developments.

2   Although *R.* v. *Sparrow,* 1 S.C.R. 1075 (1990) [hereinafter *Sparrow*], has been described as an immense step forward for Aboriginal interests, even it is not without serious limitations, which are elaborated in Chapter 8.

3   William Pentney, "The Rights of Aboriginal Peoples of Canada in the Constitution Act, 1982, Part II – Section 35, the Substantive Guarantee," *UBC Law Review* 22 (1988): 207.

4   I am suggesting not that this bias is conscious but that there appears to be a tendency, however unintentional, that has never benefited Aboriginal interests.

5   This exercise is not a matter of making minor adjustments to the Constitution. Any significant recognition of Aboriginal self-government as proposed in this book would result in radical alterations to the present dynamic of the federation. Thus, if such major changes are intended to be implemented, then one must be prepared to alter constitutional documents as needed. This should not become a paper-saving exercise.

6   For an excellent introduction to the strain of Legal Realism known as the Critical Legal Studies movement, see *The Politics of Law,* ed. David Kairys, 3rd ed. (New York: Basic, 1998).

7   Arguably, the absence of such insights in *Duro* v. *Reina,* 110 S. Ct. 2053 (1990), resulted in wholly unjust consequences (see Chapter 8). See also Constitutional Law, Patrick J. Monahan, *Essentials of Canadian Law Series* (Toronto: Irwin, 1997).

8   The "rule of law" has received a great deal of scholarly attention over the centuries. Here it may generally be described as a rule or methodology intended to prevent arbitrary behaviour by governments. For a discussion of this principle at work in a Canadian context, see R. Van Loon and M. Whittington, *The Canadian Political System* (Toronto: McGraw-Hill Ryerson, 1987), 166-70.

9   For example, the federal Indian Claims Commission (ICC) undertakes research for all of its claims and prepares these documents for the benefit of the parties at the subsequent hearings before the ICC tribunal. The parties then plead their respective cases, making whatever use of the material they wish.

10 See Chapter 2, in particular the cases of *Duro, Oliphant,* and *Indian Civil Rights Act.*

11 The Southwest Inter-Tribal Court of Appeal, described in Chapter 2, offers this function for a number of different tribal communities.

12 That is, whether an exclusive federal or provincial area of jurisdiction is being impinged on by the Aboriginal law or by an error in law.

13 Notwithstanding the opinion of legal positivists, and those such as H.L.A. Hart, who might argue that law is best understood as a system of social rules that can be objectively studied and identified without recourse to contextual or non-normative considerations. See H.L.A. Hart, *The Concept of Law* (New York: Oxford University Press, 1961). Legal realists such as Justice Oliver Wendell Holmes have persuasively argued that the role of the judge is much more discretionary. For a defence of legal realism, see John Chipman Grah, *The Nature and Source of the Law* (New York: Macmillan, 1921).

14 *Ex parte Crow Dog,* 109 U.S. 556 (1883) [hereinafter *Crow Dog*], discussed in Chapter 2.

15 *Williams* v. *Lee,* 358 U.S. 217 (1959), discussed in Chapter 2.

16 In recent years, presentations have been made to segments of the United Nations such as UNESCO's Working Group on Indigenous Populations. Nonetheless, such international activity is rare, and it is not premised on nation-state theory. In particular, the Working Group on Indigenous Populations is developing a "Draft Declaration on the Rights of Indigenous Peoples." However, this instrument is apparently intended to recognize and preserve the rights of Indigenous populations within domestic borders, not to create nation-to-nation relationships between Indigenous peoples. For a review of these developments, see Sharon Helen Venne, *Our Elders Understand Our Rights: Evolving International Law Regarding Indigenous Peoples* (Penticton, BC: Theytus, 1998), S. James Anaya, *Indigenous Peoples in International Law* (New York: Oxford University Press, 1996).

17 *U.S.* v. *McBratney,* 104 U.S. 621 (1881).

18 *Crow Dog,* supra note 14.

19 *McClanahan* v. *Arizona Tax Commission,* 411 U.S. 164 (1973).

20 *Washington* v. *Confederated Tribes of the Colville Indian Reservation,* 447 U.S. 134 (1980).

21 The federal Indian Gaming Regulatory Act, Pub. L. No. 100-497, 102 Stat. 2374 (1988) (codified at 25 U.S.C. s. 2701), is a notable exception.

22 Part 1 of the Constitution Act, 1982, being Schedule B to the Canada Act 1982 (U.K.), 1982, c. 11, subsection 32(2).

23 See Oliver Wendell Holmes, *The Path of the Law* (New York, 1897).

24 However, it is in the use of principles that Aboriginal people should have cause for concern.

25 Ronald Dworkin, *Taking Rights Seriously* (Cambridge, MA: Harvard University Press, 1977), 40; emphasis added.

26 Ibid. at 160.

27 Ibid. at 67.

28 Ibid. at 79.

29 For an example of a modern approach using strict construction or originalism, see Robert Bork, *The Tempting of America: The Political Seduction of the Law* (New York: Free Press; London: Collier Macmillan, 1990).

30 Ronald Dworkin, *Freedom's Law: The Moral Reading of the American Constitution* (Cambridge, MA: Harvard University Press, 1996). Widely accepted in American jurisprudential thought are two general approaches to constitutional interpretation. Dworkin expounds what is referred to as the attitudinal model. The alternative, the legal model, focuses on the plain meanings of statutes, the intentions of the framers, precedents, and a modicum of balancing of societal interests. For a discussion of the respective merits of these models, see Jeffrey Segal and Harold Spaeth, *The Supreme Court and the Attitudinal Model* (Cambridge, UK: Cambridge University Press, 1993).

31 Dworkin, supra note 30 at 7.

32 Ibid. at 4; emphasis added.

33 Ibid. at 10; emphasis added.

34 For a discussion of this concept, see Gerald L. Gall, *The Canadian Legal System,* 3rd ed. (Toronto: Carswell, 1990), 274.

35 *Sparrow,* supra note 2.

36 Ibid. at 1109.

37   Ibid.
38   Ibid. at 1113.
39   Ibid. at 1119.
40   Unreported at time of publication. Decision released 19 January 1999.
41   Criminal Code of Canada, R.S.C. 1985, c. C-46, ss. 278.1-278.91.
42   Supra note 40, at para. 61 of the decision.
43   *Sparrow,* supra note 2 at para. 61; emphasis added.
44   *Van der Peet* v. *R.* (1996), 2 S.C.R. 507 [hereinafter *Van der Peet*].
45   Ibid. at 556.
46   *R.* v. *Sundown,* [1999] 1 S.C.R. 393.
47   Ibid. at paras. 29-33.
48   *Pamajewon* v. *R.* (1996), 2 S.C.R. 821.
49   For a discussion of the court's approach to rights "frozen in time," see Brian Slattery, "Understanding Aboriginal Rights," *Canadian Bar Review* 66 (1987): 727.
50   *R.* v. *Badger,* [1996] 1 S.C.R. 771.
51   Unreported as of date of publishing, released 17 September 1999.
52   Dworkin, supra note 30 at 10.
53   *Van der Peet,* supra note 43 at 535.
54   As we will see in Chapter 8, the Supreme Court of Canada introduced in *Sparrow* a novel and highly restricted interpretation of entrenchment regarding Section 35 rights.
55   In *Taking Rights Seriously,* Dworkin pursues an analysis of the judicial philosophy of "deference" and its implications for recognizing constitutional rights.
56   *Delgamuukw* v. *B.C.,* [1997] 3 S.C.R. 1010.
57   Ibid. at 1065-66.
58   The original Multilateral Agreement on Investment has been described as blending Canadian constitutional law with similar American precepts. See Tony Clarke and Maude Barlow, *MAI: The Multilateral Agreement on Investment and the Threat to Canadian Sovereignty* (Toronto: Stoddart, 1997), Chapter 2.
59   For an explanation of how the entrenchment doctrine works, see Monahan, supra note 7 at 5-15.
60   Dworkin, supra note 30.

Chapter 5: Historical Aboriginal Collective Rights

1   An association of First Nations in the province providing research, policy advice, lobbying, and a multitude of other services.
2   Some community leaders claim that limited resources prevent some of the women and their families from being reintegrated. Others, however, argue that their continued exclusion is motivated by lingering prejudice.
3   For example, many have presented a utilitarian theory in support of such rights, while others, such as Aquinas, have supported their approaches with a religious foundation, emphasizing a strain of natural rights theory.
4   *Jackson* v. *City of Joliet,* 715 F.2d 1200 (7th Cir. 1983) at 1203.
5   For a discussion of these promises, see C.R. Sunstein, "Constitutionalism after the New Deal," *Harvard Law Review* 101 (1987): 421.
6   Swedish Instrument of Government, The Basic Principles of the Constitution, Article 2.
7   Ibid. at Article 22.
8   Ibid. at Article 25.
9   Constitution Act, 1982, s. 52, being Schedule B to the Canada Act, 1982 (U.K.), 1982, c. 11, s. 35.
10   Ibid. at s. 23.
11   *C.H.R.C.* v. *Taylor,* [1990] 3 S.C.R. 892, and *R.* v. *Andrews,* [1990] 3 S.C.R. 870, set out this analysis.
12   *R.* v. *Tran,* [1994] 2 S.C.R. 951.
13   See, though, *Zylberg* v. *Sudbury Board of Education* (1988), 34 C.R.R. 1, 65 O.R. (2d) 641.
14   See *Peacemaker Court Manual,* Navajo Nation Judicial Code.
15   For a discussion of Navajo peacemaking philosophy, see James Zion, "The Navajo Peacemaker Court: Deference to the Old and Accommodation to the New," *American Law Review* 11 (1983): 89.

16 In 1794, Benjamin Franklin attended a meeting in Albany, New York, of the Hodonoshonee Confederacy and left inspired by its use of democratic ideals.
17 Robert J. Miller, "American Indian Influence on the United States Constitution and Its Framers," *American Indian Law Review* 18 (1994): 147-8.
18 Ibid. at 148-9; emphasis added.
19 The fathers of the American Constitution were also familiar with the recent writings of John Locke. Writing under a pseudonym, Locke argued for a balancing of governing authority in *Two Treatises of Government* (notably, the second treatise). However, for these authors of American government, the people of Six Nations provided a working model of exactly what Locke theorized.
20 Manitoba was the first province to recognize the right of women to vote (1916). Federal recognition was extended two years later.
21 Mark Dockstador, "Justice in Traditional Aboriginal Communities" (PhD diss., Osgoode Hall, York University).

Chapter 6: Aboriginal Values versus Charter Rights
1 Other than harvesting practices and the exercise of self-government. See Thomas Isaac, "Individual versus Collective Rights: Aboriginal People and the Significance of *Thomas* v. *Norris*," *Manitoba Law Journal* 21,3 (1992): 618-30.
2 Will Kymlicka provides a useful overview of this conflict in "Individual and Community Rights," in Judith Baker, ed., *Group Rights* (Toronto: University of Toronto Press, 1994).
3 Canadian Charter of Rights and Freedoms, Part I of the Constitution Act, 1982, being Schedule B to the Canada Act 1982 (U.K.), 1982, c. 11, s. 3 [hereinafter Charter].
4 Ibid. at subsection 11(e).
5 In Hopi culture, when an individual is found responsible (criminally or civilly) for an injury, the clan of the accused's uncles may be responsible for compensating the victim or his or her clan.
6 Charter, supra note 3.
7 For a discussion of traditional forms of justice, see Michael Coyle, "Traditional Indian Justice in Ontario: A Role for the Present?" *Osgoode Hall Law Review* 24, 3 (1986): 605.
8 If the accused was motivated by a dysfunctional family life, then perhaps other siblings or the parents should be involved in the process of reconciliation, particularly if there is concern that the siblings may also offend.
9 *U.S.* v. *Wheeler*, 435 U.S. 313, 328 (1978) [hereinafter *Wheeler*].
10 Although the more commonly used term may now be "natural justice," the term "due process" has a significant Canadian usage, particularly in the context of the Canadian Bill of Rights.
11 This constitutional guarantee in the US context does not always require an attorney.
12 Lansdowne House First Nation in Ontario is accessible only by air. This remoteness is not uncommon for many Aboriginal communities across Canada.
13 *Wheeler*, supra note 9.
14 This option has been exercised by courts wishing to avoid the rigorous requirements of the Indian Civil Rights Act (Pub. L. No. 90-284, s. 201, title 11 (1968). This approach is more common among the more traditional communities (e.g., the Pueblo).
15 See Revised Constitution of the Pueblo of Laguna, enacted 10 November 1958.
16 Members of a community are not always from an Aboriginal blood line.
17 See *R.* v. *Big M Drug Mart Ltd,* [1985] 1 S.C.R. 295 (note Justice Dickson's comments at 347). See also *Andrews* v. *Law Society of British Columbia,* [1989] 1 S.C.R. 143 (note Justice McIntyre's comments at 164-5). See also *R.* v. *Turpin,* [1989] 1 S.C.R. 1296 and *McKinney* v. *University of Guelph* [1990] 76 D.L.R. (4th) 545.
18 Ibid.
19 Andrews was not a Canadian citizen, and therefore by law was not permitted membership in the BC law society, notwithstanding his successful completion of his courses. His abilities were never in question, only his citizenship.
20 For an elaboration of this viewpoint, see Lenore Keeshing-Tobias, "Stop Stealing Native Stories," *Globe and Mail,* 26 January 1990, A6.
21 This prohibition is also intended to apply to other Aboriginal people who are not members of this specific community.

22 Although not all of the above examples may fit within the strict definition of defamation, the point is moot. Since these governments will articulate their own laws, they may well choose to introduce a broader definition of this concept. The term does suggest, however, the serious nature of the problem.

23 A tribal judge of the Hopi Nation first shared this idea with me, and it was reiterated by a tribal judge of the Acoma Pueblo in the summer of 1994.

24 Many Aboriginal practices in both Canada and the United States have been criminalized over the years.

25 Until recently, the ambit of such rights was limited largely to defamation and freedom of information legislation. In a decision involving the Quebec Charter, which recognizes a greater breadth of privacy rights, an individual's privacy rights were sustained in the face of media claims of free expression. No citation is currently available, but for discussion see David Vienncau, "Ruling Restricts Photographers," *Toronto Star* 10 April 1998, 3.

26 Section 25 of the Constitution Act, 1982, s. 52, being Schedule B to the Canada Act 1982 (U.K.), 1982, c. 11, ostensibly provides a shield between Aboriginal and treaty rights and Charter intrusions. However, there is neither case law nor government indication that this section would provide adequate insulation. Moreover, given the recommendation that the Charter should apply to future Aboriginal governments, surely some of the aforementioned practices must give way. The discussions in Chapters 4 and 5 suggest that how this is effected is crucial.

27 *Rebrin* v. *Minister of Citizenship and Immigration et al.* (1961), S.C.R. 376.

28 *Mapp* v. *Ohio,* 367 U.S. 643 (1961).

29 *Robinson* v. *California,* 370 U.S. 660 (1962).

30 *Mally* v. *Hogan,* 378 U.S. 1 (1964); *Murphy* v. *Waterfront Commissioners,* 78 U.S. 52 (1964).

31 *Pointer* v. *Texas,* 380 U.S. 400 (1965).

32 *Miranda* v. *Arizona,* 384 U.S. 436 (1967).

33 *Klopfer* v. *North Carolina,* 386 U.S. 213 (1967); *Duncan* v. *Louisiana,* 391 U.S. 145 (1968); *Benton* v. *Maryland,* 395 U.S. 784 (1969), respectively.

34 See Canadian Bill of Rights, S.C. 1960, c. 44, subsections 1(c) to (f).

35 [1972] S.C.R. 889.

36 Ibid.

37 As opposed to the American belief that it can have a substantive content. Indeed, the procedural rules have taken on an even more demanding standard sometimes referred to as "super due process." For a discussion of this subject, see Margaret Radin, "Cruel Punishment and Respect: Super Due Process," *Southern California Law Review* 53,4 (1980).

38 See *Limiting Rights: The Dilemma of Judicial Review,* Janet L. Hiebert (Montreal: McGill-Queen's University Press, 1996).

39 The Critical Legal Studies (CLS) movement in the United States challenges the objectivity and independence of similar ideas, such as the rule of law. See discussion by David Kairys, *Politics of Law: A Progressive Critique* (New York: Basic, 1990).

40 See John Locke's *Second Treatise of Government* (1690) and John Stuart Mill's *On Liberty (1959).* A more recent expression of this philosophy may be found in John Rawls' *A Theory of Justice* (Cambridge: Harvard University Press, 1971).

41 The term "equity" in this context approaches the sense of justice that has often been expressed by Aboriginal peoples. The term is perhaps most closely associated with general notions of fairness. For a brief review of the common law development of equity in a Canadian jurisprudential context, see Ralph Newman, *Equity and the Law: A Comparative Study* (Toronto: Oceana, 1990), Chapter 1.

42 Kachinas have a long and complex history of involvement in Hopi life. They are "spirits" that carry messages and provide guidance for the tribe. Even today, many tribal members believe that they exact punishment for particularly offensive actions.

43 The failure to recognize Aboriginal self-government in Canada has provided too few examples of how these communities can express this preference. Rupert Ross, *Returning to the Teachings: Exploring Aboriginal Justice* (Toronto: Penguin, 1996), provides some examples of this idea. Ross Gordon Green undertakes a similar challenge in *Justice in Aboriginal Communities: Sentencing Alternatives* (Saskatoon: Purich, 1998). However, American tribal courts remain the clearest and most developed examples of Aboriginal equity.

44 This denied both mother and children access to funding for education or health care as well as other programs.

45 Throughout the 1970s and 1980s, the issue was often introduced from "the floor" at national and regional meetings of the Assembly of First Nations.

46 Although some may argue that the Aboriginal philosophy of care eventually motivated a change in attitude in accepting these people back into their communities. However, one could assert with equal validity that "rights"-based principles eventually decided the issue.

47 Advisory Opinion, 1935, P.C.I.J. (Ser. A/B No. 64).

48 Ibid.

49 Convention on the Prevention and Punishment of the Crime of Genocide, 9 December 1948 (entered into force on 3 September 1953).

50 E.A. Res. 47/135, 18 December 1992.

51 Proclaimed in the fourteenth session, 4 November 1966, Article 1.

52 Ibid.

53 This is a revision of an earlier convention (No. 107) entered into force in 1957. Convention No. 169 was entered into force on 5 September 1991.

54 This draft declaration was submitted by the UNESCO working group to the UN Commission on Human Rights in 1994.

55 Such a claim would only be made, of course, if this state was a signatory to the relevant instrument. Importantly, not all nations have signed these accords. However, for purposes of this chapter, recognition and evolution of these ideas in international law is of the greatest significance. The concepts are relatively new but are evolving and reflect the conceptual basis of many of the assertions in this chapter.

56 Not all communities place the same importance on values such as honesty and responsibility. A community that does not enshrine such values in clearly defined practices would have a much less compelling argument that they are fundamental to its culture.

57 Charter, supra note 3, s. 1, those limits that can be justified in a "free and democratic society." The notwithstanding clause found in Section 33 suggests that these limitations may be much broader than even those enunciated in Section 1.

58 435 U.S. 191, 98 S. Ct. 1011 (1978).

59 110 S. Ct. 2053 (1990).

60 More recent theories of democracy move beyond just counting votes. These approaches argue that democratic theory must include some fundamental content, and principles such as the rule of law and due process commonly receive attention. Such views of democracy would then include natural limits to democratic choice, taking it beyond the status of simply "mob rule."

61 Although they may indeed be activities, such as those reflected by the term "cultural defamation" or related to the environment, that will be prohibited by some communities.

62 Although the early liberal theorists barely recognized this view, more recent theorists like Robert Nozick and John Rawls have each accepted the idea of the individual considered within a societal context. Nevertheless it has amounted to little more than a nod and a wink.

63 It should be understood that far more is at stake here than simply the side effects of some moral decay. Much larger issues concerning beliefs about institutions of justice, politics, and leadership lie at the core of this discussion. These issues are addressed at length in my forthcoming book.

64 Georg Wilhelm Friedrich Hegel (1770-1830), see *The Philosophy of Right* (1821).

65 For a sampling of communitarian ideas, see *Liberalism and Its Critics*, ed. Michael J. Sandel (New York: New York University Press, 1989); *What's the Matter with Liberalism*, Ronald Beiner (Berkeley: University of California Press, 1992); *Liberalism and the Limits of Justice*, Michael J. Sandel (Cambridge: Cambridge University Press, 1998); and *Spheres of Justice*, Michael J. Sandel (Cambridge: Cambridge University Press, 1983).

Chapter 7: A Metaphorical Charter

1 Although Mill arguably laid the theoretical groundwork for today's liberal feminism in his seminal essay "The Subjection of Women," this was never a major thrust in his work.

2 See *Andrews* v. *Law Society of British Columbia* (1989), 1 S.C.R. 143 (decision of McIntyre J.)

[hereinafter *Andrews*]; *R.* v. *Turpin* (1989), 1 S.C.R. 1296 (decision of Wilson J.); *McKinney* v. *University of Guelph* (1990), 76 D.L.R. (4th) 545 (decision of Wilson J.); and *R.* v. *Swain* (1991), 1 S.C.R. 933 (decision of Lamer J.).

3   See Justice Dickson's comments in *R.* v. *Big M Drug Mart* (1985), 18 D.L.R. (4th) 321 at 362. See also the remarks of Justice McIntyre in *Andrews, supra* note 2 at 164: "identical treatment may frequently produce serious inequality."

4   Part I Constitution Act, 1982, being Schedule B to the Canada Act 1982 (U.K.), 1982, c. 11; emphasis added [hereinafter Charter].

5   This distinction includes more than just legislative enactments. Any expression of government will is intended to be included (for example, administrative decisions).

6   Section 1 of the 1982 Constitution Act currently does this through its ideological references to democracy. Moreover, this reference is given an even larger context by the Constitution's preamble, which clearly refers to "the rule of law." The recent reference to the Supreme Court of Canada regarding the possibility of Quebec's unilateral separation repeated these two terms from both sides of the issue.

7   Although unions and class actions are good examples of the recognition of collective rights by the courts, at a constitutional level few such rights have been recognized.

8   Navajo Judicial Code, 1982, Code of Judicial Conduct of the Judicial Branch of the Navajo Nation.

9   Ibid., Administrative Order No. 96 (1991).

10 Phrases such as "free and democratic society" and "rule of law" have little functional relevance outside a purely legal context – and receive only limited appreciation from the average Canadian.

11 A reference to a number of current Charter rights.

12 See the discussion in Chapter 6.

13 In this instance, this statement is intended to relate only to individuals who are defendants in a criminal law proceeding. The subsection 11(c) protection is available in other circumstances and to non-criminal law matters. In such circumstances, Charter protection would not be so absolute.

14 The rule of law and due process are closely tied to the term "democracy" found in Section 1.

15 See Alan Borovoy, *When Freedoms Collide: The Case for Our Civil Liberties* (Toronto: Lester and Orpen Dennys, 1988).

16 For example, democratic rights are expressed in Sections 3-5 and legal rights in Sections 7-11.

17 Charter, *supra* note 4 at subsection 32(2), as it then was. "Notwithstanding subsection (1), section 15 shall not have effect until three years after this section comes into force."

18 The American case of *Duro* v. *Reina,* 110 S. Ct. 2053 (1990), which enlightens this point, was discussed earlier and will be reviewed in Chapter 8.

Chapter 8: The Royal Commission on Aboriginal Peoples and Self-Government

1   Royal Commission on Aboriginal Peoples [hereinafter RCAP], *Report of the Royal Commission on Aboriginal Peoples,* vol. 5 (Ottawa: Supply and Services Canada, 1996), 2.

2   *R.* v. *Sparrow* (1990), 1 S.C.R. 1075 [hereinafter *Sparrow*].

3   It also had an earlier appeal from the trial-level court to a provincial appeal panel.

4   Constitution Act, 1982, s. 52, being Schedule B to the Canada Act 1982 (U.K.), 1982, c. 11, Part II [hereinafter Constitution Act, 1982].

5   *Sparrow, supra* note 2, at 1093.

6   Part I Constitution Act, 1982, being Schedule B to the Canada Act 1982 (U.K.), 1982, c. 11 [hereinafter Charter].

7   Ibid. at Part VII.

8   See Constitutional Law, Patrick J. Monahan, *Essentials of Canadian Law Series* (Toronto: Irwin, 1997) at 5.

9   Ibid. at page 6.

10 Subsection 24(1) of the Charter, *supra* note 6, provides an enforcement mechanism for anyone whose rights, as protected by the Charter, have been impinged.

11 *Sparrow, supra* note 2 at 1110.

12 Ibid. at 1109.

13 Ibid. at 1113-16.

14 Since few reasons were offered to explain these comments, perhaps these observations would be better characterized as assertions.

15 *Sparrow,* supra note 2 at 1116; emphasis added.

16 Although *Sparrow,* ibid., recognizes that certain hurdles must be overcome by federal regulators, the Aboriginal right must give way once this is achieved. Importantly, this giving way may be to the point of extinguishment. Thus, there is no absolute protection of the Aboriginal right – only a procedural hurdle to overcome, one that does not seem to be set very high.

17 Ibid.

18 Charter, supra note 6.

19 Although the court perceived that the term "recognizing and affirming" entails different language than do the terms used in the Charter Sections (supra note 6), it never explained why such a distinction makes any difference. It offered no discussion why this wording was intended by the framers of the Constitution to provide significantly less protection to Aboriginal and treaty rights than to any other rights in the act.

20 Throughout its report, the commission prefers to use this term rather than the term "self-government." It explains that, conceivably, an Aboriginal community may choose to have a federal or provincial authority govern it rather than to govern itself. This is an early indication that the commission's approach was grounded more in theoretical possibilities than in realistic and practical considerations. I will use the more familiar term "Aboriginal self-government" throughout this chapter rather than this purely theoretical and unrealistic term.

21 RCAP, supra note 1 at 173.

22 *Connolly* v. *Woolrich,* (1867) IRLOS 253, ICNLC 151 (Q.B.).

23 RCAP, supra note 1 at 193.

24 Ibid. at 213.

25 As will be described, this entrenchment is novel and far weaker than what has been recognized in Canadian jurisprudence.

26 RCAP, supra note 1 at 167.

27 Ibid.

28 Ibid. at 223.

29 Ibid.; emphasis added.

30 Ibid. at 223-4.

31 The First Nation Lansdowne House in Ontario is so isolated that it has few roads. Many Aboriginal communities exist in similar circumstances. How, then, could such communities argue that traffic laws are "vital" to their existence? If, on the other hand, a community has roads intersecting provincial highways and can therefore successfully assert such a claim, then the problem of patchwork jurisdictions will result as per the RCAP recommendations. This point will be discussed more fully later in this chapter.

32 Family law matters regarding separation, support, child custody, and divorce are examples of this approach. These various matters are commonly decided in unified provincial family courts.

33 Sections 91 and 92 of the Constitution Act, 1867, (U.K.), 30 and 31 Vict., c. 3 [hereinafter Constitution Act, 1867], provide straightforward indications of exactly who possesses what authority. On the other hand, constitutional law is filled with cases that reflect the disputes between federal and provincial governments regarding just how straightforward such sections are in delineating jurisdiction. Nonetheless, these sections offer more advantages than do the vague terms offered by the commission.

34 For example, principles of law such as the doctrine of paramountcy, pith and substance test, effect test, and so forth. The RCAP report does not comment about whether any of these principles should apply to the Aboriginal order of government.

35 *Williams* v. *Lee,* 358 U.S. 217 (1959).

36 Ibid. at 219-20; emphasis added.

37 State jurisdiction appears to have been enlarged somewhat by decisions in *United States* v. *Wheeler,* 435 U.S. 313 (1978); *Washington* v. *Confederated Tribes of Colville Indian Reservation,*

447 U.S. 134 (1980); *Iowa Mutual Insurance Co.* v. *LaPlante,* 197 S. Ct. 971 (1987).
38 Also known as the "frozen rights" theory.
39 RCAP, supra note 1; emphasis added.
40 Chapter 4 discusses the potential for the Supreme Court of Canada to take a very conservative approach to interpreting any Aboriginal entitlement. See "Dworkin's Caution."
41 Consensus Report on the Constitution, Charlottetown, 28 August 1992, final text.
42 Other references to identities, institutions, and traditions – in the subsection as well as in environmental references in subsection (b) – also appear to be more expansive.
43 RCAP, supra note 1 at Chapter 3.
44 Ibid. at 219.
45 A prime example would be gaming institutions such as high-stakes bingos or casinos, which are becoming popular as sources of revenue on many US reservations. Such institutions could have a significant impact on gambling profits in Winnipeg, Montreal, and Windsor, all of which are close to Aboriginal communities.
46 One can have a "major" impact on an activity that is of only minor concern.
47 This point is elaborated in the commission's interim report regarding justice issues. See RCAP, *Bridging the Cultural Divide* (Ottawa: Supply and Services Canada, 1996), 246.
48 Aboriginal people include more than just the immediate victim within this term. Commonly, family and clan members are also included. Traditionally, anyone – no matter how remote – who suffers injury is considered a victim.
49 RCAP, supra note 1 at 222-23.
50 Ibid.
51 This will be in addition, of course, to the earlier arguments regarding how the term "vital" should receive a very restrictive meaning.
52 Constitution Act, 1867, supra note 33 at subsection 92(14).
53 This is sometimes done in conjunction with the Royal Canadian Mounted Police.
54 Constitution Act, 1867, supra note 33 at s. 92.
55 RCAP, supra note 1 at 216.
56 Ibid.
57 Ibid. at 216-17.
58 Which include limitations regarding the core jurisdiction having to relate to "vital" matters only, having to be of a non-transcendent nature, and having a minimal impact on adjacent jurisdictions.
59 RCAP, supra note 1.
60 Peter Hogg, *Constitutional Law of Canada,* 2nd ed. (Toronto: Carswell, 1985), 544.
61 Professor Monahan explains that the defining lines between exclusive federal and provincial governments may not be quite as clear as the originators of Confederation might have guessed they would become. He asserts that the courts have allowed the federal and provincial governments to occasionally wander into the others domain. Monahan, *supra* note 8 at Chapter 1.
62 RCAP, supra note 1.
63 Supra note 52.
64 Obviously, an Aboriginal government would have a broader jurisdiction. Matters regarding language and education, but perhaps little more than them, would likely also fall within this classification. The point is that Hogg's interpretation of subsection 9(24) could be used to support a claim that the unilateral core jurisdiction of a government is limited to little more than cultural matters.
65 Wilton J. Littlechild and Dennis Calihoo are similarly critical of any negotiations that would recognize less than what is recognized by emerging international norms. See Wilton J. Littlechild and Dennis Calihoo, "International Law and Indigenous Self-Determination," paper presented at the Conference on Implementing the Recommendations of the Royal Commission on Aboriginal Peoples, Toronto, 22-4 April 1999, 20.
66 The RCAP report never clearly takes on the issue of personal jurisdiction. The findings in the interim justice issues report create racial distinctions that would give non-Aboriginal persons the opportunity to opt out of the jurisdiction of an Aboriginal court. See RCAP, *Bridging the Cultural Divide,* Recommendation 5 at 256. Although the final report suggests

that race should play no role in matters of governance, it does not specifically tackle justice issues but seems to leave this matter to the earlier findings in the interim report.

67 Mark Dockstador refers to this characterization as "nations and not quite nations." See Mark Dockstador, "Understanding Concepts and Implications of Aboriginal Nationhood," paper presented to the Conference on Implementing the Recommendations of the Royal Commission on Aboriginal Peoples, Toronto, 22-4 April 1999, 15.

68 Although the discussion in earlier chapters suggests that Aboriginal interests may not be enthusiastically endorsed by Canadian courts, that avenue might be more profitable than having to bargain with federal or provincial parties, which may have no inclination to negotiate at all.

69 Taiaiake Alfred asserts that such treaties or agreements are no more than paths to assimilation. See Taiaiake Alfred, *Peace, Power, and Righteousness: An Indigenous Manifesto* (Don Mills, ON: Oxford University Press, 1999), 119.

70 Provincial governments will not be equally motivated to negotiate with Aboriginal peoples. If a province has no need for the resource that an Aboriginal community may wish to barter, then it may choose not to recognize the Aboriginal authority. Similarly, the present provincial government may be ideologically opposed to the notion of Aboriginal self-government. There will be many instances in which, for one reason or another, a provincial government will simply choose not to negotiate. Worse still, negotiations may be undertaken in bad faith.

71 RCAP, supra note 1 at 269.

72 Charter rights are a special kind of Canadian law, which also accords higher value to certain common law rights as well as human rights laws.

73 Where they do meet all of the requirements for core rights as described in footnote 31.

74 The 1982 Constitution Act required one such meeting, but it was agreed to add three more first ministers' conferences throughout the remainder of the decade.

75 RCAP, supra note 1.

76 Hogg relates that, despite the assertion that federal and provincial governments are to share a coordinate authority, a certain hierarchy does exist in Canada. For an elaboration of this discussion on federalism, see Hogg, supra note 60 at footnote 61.

77 RCAP, supra note 1.

78 Aboriginal governments require the agreement of federal and provincial governments.

79 Would anyone reasonably expect federal and provincial negotiators to overlook these issues when there is nothing to prevent their inclusion as terms of an agreement?

80 RCAP, supra note 1 at 167.

81 Ibid. at 168.

82 Ibid.

83 Constitution Act, 1867, supra note 33, s. 35.

84 Ibid.

85 Although there are other tools for interpreting legislation such as the golden rule (clauses should not be read in isolation from one another but within the context of the whole) and the mischief rule (the court must ascertain what "mischief" the legislation purported to overcome), neither these nor any other rule seems to have obvious value. For an overview of constitutional judicial review, see Barry Strayer, *The Canadian Constitution and the Courts: Function and Scope of Judicial Review* (Toronto: Butterworths, 1988). Although *Schachter* (*Schachter* v. *Canada*, [1992] 2 S.C.R. 679) permits a court to "read in(to)" the Constitution elements that reasonably might be assumed to have been intended, it is doubtful that *Schachter* reasoning could be successfully employed here.

86 Professor Macklem provides a very clear and insightful analysis of the various types of arguments that may give rise to the right of self-government. See Patrick Macklem, "Normative Dimensions of an Aboriginal Right of Self-Government," *Queen's Law Journal* 21 (Fall 1995): 173-219.

87 For example,
    • the limited scope of "vital" matters;
    • not impinging on transcendent federal or provincial concerns;
    • not having a major impact on adjacent jurisdictions;

- applying only to cultural matters;
- the limits of a subsection 91(24) jurisdiction; or
- the dubious practical merits of negotiating with federal and provincial governments.

88 See the opinion of Ian Binnie, "The *Sparrow* Doctrine: Beginning of the End or End of the Beginning?" *Queen's Law Journal* 15 (1990): 217-53.

89 Presumably, the weakness of this form of entrenchment will also hold true for jurisdictional subject areas characterized as "core." Although these few areas do not require agreements before implementation, nothing in the RCAP report suggests that they are somehow more securely entrenched than peripheral subject areas.

90 Although this may be the present position of the federal government, no similar position has been publicly endorsed by the provincial governments. Hence, any one of them is free to argue before the courts that Aboriginal self-government simply does not exist in law.

91 Emphasis added.

92 The Oka and Gustafson Lake conflicts, as well as the shooting of Dudley George at Ipperwash, are clear expressions of such serious animosities.

93 Since realistically the peripheral jurisdictions will constitute more than 90 percent of Aboriginal jurisdiction, and since no such authority may be exercised without prior federal and provincial consent, this jurisdiction is purely hypothetical.

94 Emphasis added.

95 Any exercise of Aboriginal authority could be subject to this challenge and not just a piece of legislation.

96 *Attorney General, Ontario* v. *Canada Temperance Federation* (1946), A.C. 193.

97 Ibid. at 205.

98 Hogg, supra note 60 at 393-4.

99 Such discussions might include an Aboriginal person as a member of the court (perhaps only on cases affecting Aboriginal matters), revision of the appeal process so that the matter is first heard by an Aboriginal appeals court, or any of the matters alluded to in Chapter 6.

100 RCAP, supra note 1 at 230.

101 Section 32 recognizes only the federal and provincial governments.

102 RCAP, supra note 1 at 231.

103 Ibid. at 234.

104 Ibid.

105 Charter, supra note 6 at subsection 11(e) and s. 13.

106 Ibid. at s. 7.

107 The case of Sandra Lovelace, who was discriminated against pursuant to these sections of the Indian Act, was brought to the attention of the United Nations in 1977. This case raised the profile of this issue to an international level. *Lovelace* v. *Canada,* Communication No. R. 6/24, *Report of the Human Rights Committee,* U.N. E.O.A.R., 36th Session, Supp. No. 40, at 166, U.N. Document A/36/40, Annex 18 (1977) (views adopted 29 December 1977); *Lovelace* v. *Canada* (1981), 2 H.R.L.J. 158 (U.N. H.R.C.).

108 Constitution Act, 1982, supra note 4.

109 Charter, supra note 6.

110 Constitution Act, 1982, supra note 4.

111 RCAP, supra note 1 at 232.

112 Infra at note 118.

113 *Canadian Bar Review* 74 (1995): 215.

114 Ibid.

115 McNeil teaches Aboriginal law at Osgoode Hall Law School, York University. His book *Common Law Aboriginal Title* (Toronto: Oxford University Press, 1989) is a leading text in its field.

116 A comment on the results of this study is found in RCAP, supra note 1 at 120. The study may be acquired through the use of federal freedom of information legislation.

117 Ibid. at 214.

118 Surely the laboured reasoning in this analysis resembles a desperate attempt to force a square peg into a round hole.

119 (1986), 2 S.C.R. 573.
120 *Can. Bar Rev.*, at 214; emphasis added.
121 Constitution Act, 1982, supra note 4 at s. 33.
122 RCAP, supra note 1 at 231.
123 Section 33, the notwithstanding clause, only applies regarding Section 2 or Sections 7-15.
124 Since the core areas will amount to less than 10 percent of the total Aboriginal jurisdiction, access to the notwithstanding clause will be of limited value.
125 The notwithstanding clause has only been used once, outside Quebec, in the 1980s. The Saskatchewan government used it in a piece of labour legislation to insulate it from constitutional challenge. The proposed use of this clause in 1998 by the Klein government of Alberta regarding the province's forced sterilization program (1928-72) met with such public outcry that the proposal was withdrawn.
126 The report advises that its recommendations should be voluntarily recognized by federal and provincial governments. See RCAP, supra note 1 at 224-5.
127 Ibid. at 119-20.
128 See W.I.C. Binnie, "The *Sparrow* Doctrine: Beginning of the End or End of the Beginning?" *Queen's Law Journal* 15 (1990): 217.
129 *Delgamuukw* v. *British Columbia* (1997), 3 S.C.R. 1010.
130 Including Aboriginal rights, presumably such as self-government.
131 Although Chapter 4 illustrates that exactly how any amendment is drafted will play a vital role in achieving the desired goals.
132 RCAP, supra note 1 at 120; emphasis added.
133 Ibid. at 126.
134 Ibid. at 119.
135 Ibid. at 125.
136 Ibid. at 126.
137 Ibid. at 121.
138 This would not entirely be the case. As RCAP explains, the Charlottetown agreement may well provide a useful point of departure for future discussions. See RCAP, supra note 1 at 126.
139 Due to the nature and breadth of the issues that would be dealt with in these agreements, it is unrealistic to believe that only one level of government would be involved – hence the need for agreement by both federal and provincial governments.
140 Judging by the amount of money expended by the commission (in excess of $50 million), neither was financing.

Chapter 9: The Future of Self-Government

1 The gender-equality guarantee, though significant, did not introduce any substantive changes to the content of the issues discussed throughout these meetings.
2 The *Maclean's* magazine edition of 28 October 1992 indicated that only 4 percent of voters who rejected the accord did so based on consideration of its Aboriginal elements. In 1993, the Native Council of Canada (now the Congress of Aboriginal Peoples) conducted a survey of six urban Canadian centres, seeking opinions regarding Aboriginal self-government. Between 84 and 95 percent of respondents supported this notion in some form or other. See Native Council of Canada, *Survey by Friendship Centres: Service Based Government* (Ottawa, 1993).
3 For a discussion of the monitoring of this vote undertaken by Elections Canada, see Mary Ellen Turpel, "The Charlottetown Discord and Aboriginal Peoples' Struggle for Fundamental Political Change," in Kenneth McRoberts and Patrick Monahan, eds., *The Charlottetown Accord, the Referendum, and the Future of Canada* (Toronto: University of Toronto Press, 1993), 141-44.
4 Since the Charlottetown Agreement included more than just a recognition of Aboriginal self-government, the next round may be somewhat less confrontational if there is an understanding that these issues will be dealt with later. Even so, generating the full agreement of the provincial parties without their receiving something tangible in exchange remains problematic.

5 For a discussion of this issue, see Derek Ground, "The Legal Basis for Aboriginal Self-Government," in Stephen B. Smart and Michael Coyle, eds., *Aboriginal Issues Today: A Legal and Business Guide* (North Vancouver: Self-Counsel, 1997), 123-5.

6 The Métis, through an annex to the policy, are primarily relegated to the responsibility of the relevant provincial government. For a discussion of this policy, see supra note 5.

7 In fact, there has seldom been a single position shared by all the parties despite attempts to reach such consensus.

8 John Borrows has identified some of the issues confronting Métis communities and the resolution of their constitutional claims. See John Borrows, "Domesticating Doctrines: Aboriginal and Treaty Rights, and the Response to the Royal Commission on Aboriginal Peoples," paper presented at the Conference on Implementing the Recommendations of the Royal Commission on Aboriginal Peoples, Toronto, 22-4 April 1999, 44-7.

9 *Baker Lake* v. *Minister of Indian Affairs and Northern Development* (1979), 17 C.N.L.R. 45.

10 *R.* v. *Van der Peet* (1996), 2 S.C.R. 548.

11 Métis and First Nations communities have disagreed over land claims involving what each has argued is its traditional hunting grounds. This conflict could have important implications for the issue of geographical jurisdiction. Moreover, similar disagreements have occurred between First Nations communities themselves. See Neil Sterritt, "The Nisga'a Treaty: Competing Claims Ignored!" *BC Studies* 120 (1998-9): 73.

12 Reference decision rendered 20 August 1998.

13 The court's advice to negotiate with Quebec should a referendum indicate that a clear majority of Quebeckers wished to secede suggests as much.

14 For a history of these developments, see Patrick J. Monahan, Constitutional Law, *Essentials of Canadian Law Series* (Toronto: Irwin, 1997), Parts 2 and 3. See also Gerald L. Gall, *The Canadian Legal System* (Toronto: Carswell, 1995), Chapters 4 and 5.

15 The first use of the term is generally attributed to the historian Herodotus, who combined the word *demos*, meaning "the people," and *kratein*, meaning "to rule."

16 *Maclean's*, special ed., 28 October 1992.

17 Turpel, supra note 3 at 124, note 25.

18 The subject of territorial jurisdiction received some treatment by the Royal Commission of Aboriginal Peoples, but much more work is required.

19 25 U.S.C. ss. 1901-63 (1978).

20 The issue of full faith and credit or the reciprocal enforcement of judgments by two governments perhaps best reflects the need to canvass this jurisdictional area. For a comment on the issue, see Peter Hogg, *Constitutional Law of Canada*, 2nd ed. (Toronto: Carswell, 1985), 279-81. For a review of this issue in the context of US tribal justice, see "Recognizing and Enforcing State and Tribal Judgements: A Roundtable Discussion of Law, Policy, and Practice," *American Indian Law Review* 18, 1 (1994): 239-83.

21 R. Jackson and D. Jackson, *Politics in Canada*, 2nd ed. (Toronto: Prentice-Hall, 1990), 185.

22 See Gerald L. Gall, *The Canadian Legal System*, 4th ed. (Toronto: Carswell, 1995), 106.

23 See Royal Commission of Aboriginal Peoples, *Interim Report of the Royal Commission on Aboriginal Peoples: Bridging the Cultural Divide* (Ottawa: Supply and Services Canada, 1996), 252, note 399; this is the only recognition of civil law in the analysis.

24 The royal commission was not the first to overlook the importance of civil law in its conception of jurisprudence. John Austin, the father of legal positivism, had a similar oversight in his seminal text *The Province of Jurisprudence Determined* (1832).

25 For those who might presume that Aboriginal communities should already possess clear ideas of what laws they intend and how they intend to implement them, a point is worth clarifying. The wills, commercial agreements, and real estate contracts that all lawyers draft for clients are never actually prepared from scratch. Lawyers use pre-prepared forms, what are commonly known as "precedents," from which to borrow and rewrite individual agreements. They twist and shape these precedents until they achieve the desired goals of their clients. The sample codes and constitutions being proposed here would simply serve the same purpose as these precedents and, thereby, provide a basis from which to generate more culturally specific documents.

26 Brian Maracle, *Back on the Rez: Finding the Way Home* (Toronto: Penguin, 1996), 1.

27 In an article in the *Toronto Star,* 3 March 1999, A6, a reporter describes a presentation made by the First Nations Accountability Coalition of Manitoba to a Senate committee that criticized First Nations mismanagement on reserves. See similar comments by Taiaiake Alfred, *Peace, Power, and Righteousness: An Indigenous Manifesto* (Don Mills, ON: Oxford University Press, 1999).
28 See *Toronto Star,* 29 January 2000, A1.
29 See *Toronto Star,* 13 March 1999, A16.
30 See *Toronto Star,* 17 March 1999, A6.
31 See also Senator Michel Cogger, *Toronto Star,* 18 March 1999, A7.
32 See *Toronto Star,* 4 January 1999, A14.
33 A distinction is drawn between this form and "general pluralism" (discussed by writers such as J.S. Furnivall and L. Kuper) and "English pluralism" (typified by the writings of F.W. Maitland and J.N. Figgis).
34 *Toronto Star,* supra notes 28-32.

Selected Bibliography

Alfred, Taiaiake. *Peace, Power, Righteousness: An Indigenous Manifesto*. Don Mills: Oxford University Press, 1999.

Anaya, S. James. *Indigenous Peoples in International Law*. New York: Oxford University Press, 1996.

Borovoy, Alan. *When Freedoms Collide: The Case for Our Civil Liberties*. Toronto: Lester and Orpen Dennys, 1988.

Bronaugh, Richard N., Michael A. Eizenga, and Stephen B. Sharzer, eds. *Readings in the Philosophy of Constitutional Law*. 4th ed. Dubuque: Kendall-Hunt, 1992.

Canby, William C. *American Indian Law: In a Nutshell*. 2nd ed. St. Paul: West, 1988.

Clarke, Tony, and Maude Barlow. *MAI: The Multilateral Agreement on Investment and the Threat to Canadian Sovereignty*. Toronto: Stoddart, 1997.

Cohen, Felix S. *Handbook of Federal Indian Law*. Washington, DC: US Government Printing, 1942.

Dworkin, Ronald. *Freedom's Law: The Moral Reading of the American Constitution*. Cambridge, MA: Harvard University Press, 1996.

–. *Taking Rights Seriously*. Cambridge, MA: Harvard University Press, 1977.

Esberey, J.E., and L.W. Johnston. *Democracy and the State: An Introduction to Politics*. Peterborough: Broadview, 1994.

Fawcett, J.E.S. *The Law of Nations*. New York: Basic, 1968.

Finnis, John. *Natural Law and Natural Rights*. New York: Oxford University Press, 1980.

Funston, Bernard, and Eugene Meehan. *Canada's Constitutional Law in a Nutshell*. Toronto: Carswell, 1994.

Gall, Gerald L. *The Canadian Legal System*. 4th ed. Toronto: Carswell, 1995.

Green, Ross Gordon. *Justice in Aboriginal Communities: Sentencing Alternatives*. Saskatoon: Purich, 1998.

Hart, H.L.A. *The Concept of Law*. 1961. New York: Oxford University Press, 1990.

Hogg, Peter W. *Constitutional Law of Canada*. 2nd ed. Toronto: Carswell, 1985.

Hylton, John H., ed. *Aboriginal Self-Government in Canada: Current Trends and Issues*. Saskatoon: Purich, 1994.

Imai, Shin, Katherine Logan, and Gary Stein. *Aboriginal Law Handbook*. Toronto: Carswell, 1993.

Locke, John. *The Second Treatise of Government*. 1690. Ed. Thomas Peardon. New York: Liberal Arts Press, 1952.

McRoberts, Kenneth, and Patrick J. Monahan, eds. *The Charlottetown Accord, the Referendum, and the Future of Canada*. Toronto: University of Toronto Press, 1993.

Maracle, Brian. *Back on the Rez: Finding the Way Home*. Toronto: Penguin, 1997.

Mill, John Stuart. *The Subjection of Women*. 1869. New York: Dover, 1997.

Novikov, Igor. *Black Holes and the Universe*. Trans. Vitaly Kisin. 1990. Cambridge: Cambridge University Press, 1995.

Purich, Donald. *The Métis*. Toronto: Lorimer, 1988.

Ross, Rupert. *Returning to the Teachings: Exploring Aboriginal Justice*. Toronto: Penguin, 1996.

Segal, Jeffrey A., and Harold J. Spaeth. *The Supreme Court and the Attitudinal Model*. New York: Cambridge University Press, 1993.

Smart, Stephen B., and Michael Coyle, eds. *Aboriginal Issues Today: A Legal and Business Guide*. North Vancouver: Self-Counsel, 1997.

Sullivan, Ruth. *Essentials of Canadian Law: Statutory Interpretation*. Concord, ON: Irwin Law, 1997.

Tarnopolsky, Walter Surma. *The Canadian Bill of Rights*. 2nd rev. ed. Toronto: McClelland and Stewart, 1975.

Venne, Sharon Helen. *Our Elders Understand Our Rights: Evolving International Law Regarding Indigenous Rights*. Penticton, BC: Theytus, 1998.

von Glahn, Gerhard. *Law among Nations*. 6th rev. ed. New York: Macmillan, 1992.

Woll, Peter. *Constitutional Democracy: Policies and Politics*. Boston: Little, 1982.

Woodward, Jack. *Native Law*. Toronto: Carswell, 1990.

Index

Set in Stone by Darlene Remus
Printed and bound in Canada by Friesens
Copy editor: Dallas Harrison
Proofreader: Joanne Richardson